T0311660

SAGE was founded in 1965 by Sara Miller McCune to support the dissemination of usable knowledge by publishing innovative and high-quality research and teaching content. Today, we publish over 900 journals, including those of more than 400 learned societies, more than 800 new books per year, and a growing range of library products including archives, data, case studies, reports, and video. SAGE remains majority-owned by our founder, and after Sara's lifetime will become owned by a charitable trust that secures our continued independence.

Los Angeles | London | New Delhi | Singapore | Washington DC | Melbourne

Praise for the Book

"I think anyone with a soul or a heart will feel that this is a very special book...your diaries to your dear wife. We are fortunate that you and she have decided to share these with the world."

Dominic Jermey,
Current Ambassador of UK to Afghanistan

"*Whispers of War* has captured Afghanistan's heart. Masood Khalili's voice is at once soothing and disturbing as he tells of the tragedy that has befallen his nation. His words melt your heart, bring tears to your eyes and then inspire you with stories of courage, of resolve and of love for Afghanistan, and for its people, whose strength reminds us of what life has to give, especially when all seems lost."

Kathy Gannon,
Head of Associated Press

"Masood Khalili is the wisest man I know. His blend of courage, conviction, morality, and humility has inspired all those who know him. With his essential humanity untouched, indeed strengthened, by the massive challenges thrown at him throughout a remarkable life, this book will ensure he captures the hearts and imaginations of thousands more who may never have the privilege of meeting him. A very rare man whose story I cannot recommend too highly."

General Sir David Richards,
Former Head of NATO Forces in Afghanistan and
Former Commander-in-chief of British Army (Land Forces)

WHISPERS
OF WAR

WHISPERS
OF WAR

AN AFGHAN FREEDOM
FIGHTER'S ACCOUNT
OF THE
SOVIET INVASION

MASOOD KHALILI

Translated by
Mahmud Khalili

Los Angeles | London | New Delhi
Singapore | Washington DC | Melbourne

First published in 2017 by

 SAGE Publications India Pvt Ltd
B1/I-1 Mohan Cooperative Industrial Area
Mathura Road, New Delhi 110 044, India
www.sagepub.in

SAGE Publications Inc
2455 Teller Road
Thousand Oaks, California 91320, USA

SAGE Publications Ltd
1 Oliver's Yard, 55 City Road
London EC1Y 1SP, United Kingdom

SAGE Publications Asia-Pacific Pte Ltd
3 Church Street
#10-04 Samsung Hub
Singapore 049483

Published by Vivek Mehra for SAGE Publications India Pvt Ltd, typeset in 10/12pt Palatino by Diligent Typesetter India Pvt Ltd, Delhi.

Library of Congress Cataloging-in-Publication Data

Names: Khalili, Masood,
Title: Whispers of war : an Afghan freedom fighter's account of the Soviet invasion / Masood Khalili ; translated by Mahmud Khalili.
Description: New Delhi, India : SAGE Publications India, 2017. | Includes index. | Unpublished original work written in Dari. Translated into English for current publication.
Identifiers: LCCN 2017004713 | ISBN 9789386062772 (pbk.) | ISBN 9789386062796 (e pub 2.0) | ISBN 9789386062789 (e book)
Subjects: LCSH: Afghanistan–History–Soviet occupation, 1979-1989–Personal narratives, Afghan. | Khalili, Masood, 1950—Diaries.
Classification: LCC DS371.2 .K477 2017 | DDC 958.104/5--dc23 LC record available at https://lccn.loc.gov/2017004713

ISBN: 978-93-860-6277-2 (PB)

SAGE Team: Rajesh Dey, Guneet Kaur Gulati, Suhag Dave, and Ritu Chopra

To all the women whose whispers have not yet been heard.

Thank you for choosing a SAGE product!
If you have any comment, observation or feedback,
I would like to personally hear from you.
Please write to me at **contactceo@sagepub.in**

Vivek Mehra, Managing Director and CEO, SAGE India.

Bulk Sales

SAGE India offers special discounts
for purchase of books in bulk.
We also make available special imprints
and excerpts from our books on demand.

For orders and enquiries, write to us at

Marketing Department
SAGE Publications India Pvt Ltd
B1/I-1, Mohan Cooperative Industrial Area
Mathura Road, Post Bag 7
New Delhi 110044, India

E-mail us at **marketing@sagepub.in**

Get to know more about SAGE

Be invited to SAGE events, get on our mailing list.
Write today to **marketing@sagepub.in**

This book is also available as an e-book.

Contents

Masood Khalili's Journey

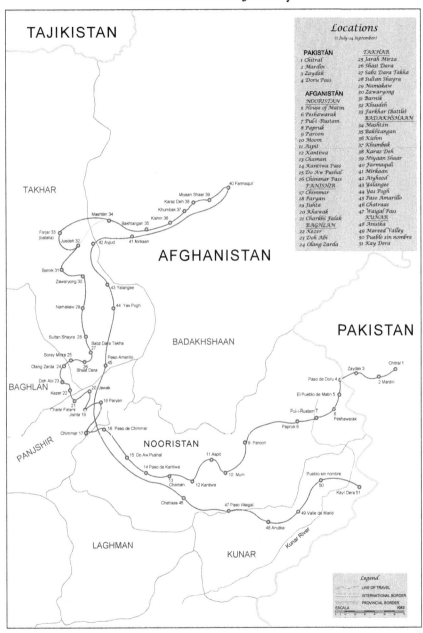

Locations
(1 July–14 September)

PAKISTÁN
1 Chitral
2 Mardin
3 Zaydak
4 Doru Pass

AFGANISTÁN
NOORISTAN
5 House of Matin
6 Peshawarak
7 Pul-i-Rustam
8 Papruk
9 Paroon
10 Moom
11 Aspit
12 Kantiwa
13 Chaman
14 Kantiwa Pass
15 Do Aw Pushal
16 Chimmar Pass
PANJSHIR
17 Chimmar
18 Paryan
19 Jishta
20 Khawak
21 Charkhi Falak
BAGHLAN
22 Kezer
23 Doh Abi
24 Olang Zarda

TAKHAR
25 Jarah Mirza
26 Shast Dara
27 Sabz Dara Takha
28 Sultan Shayra
29 Namakaw
30 Zawaryong
31 Barnik
32 Khusdeh
33 Farkhar (Battle)
BADAKHSHAAN
34 Mashtán
35 Bakhtangan
36 Kishm
37 Khumbak
38 Karaz Deh
39 Miyaan Shaar
40 Farmaquli
41 Mirkaan
42 Aiyhood
43 Yalangee
44 Yas Pogh
45 Paso Amarillo
46 Chatraas
47 Waigal Pass
KUNAR
48 Anuika
49 Marred Valley
50 Pueblo sin nombre
51 Kay Dera

Source: Andrea Maestri and Rebeca De Diego.
Note: This figure is not to scale. It does not represent any authentic national or international boundaries and is used for illustrative purposes only.

Foreword

Dear Reader,

You, yet have no idea how fortunate you are to have discovered *Whispers of War: An Afghan Freedom Fighter's Account of the Soviet Invasion*. In its pages, the period is the summer of 1986, and you are about to embark on a two-and-a-half-month journey across the roof of Afghanistan. Your guide will be Masood Khalili, then a young Mujahideen political officer, who has dedicated his life to the struggle to free Afghanistan from the yoke of Soviet oppression. Khalili is making the journey to gather information on the war, to mobilize people in the fight against the communists in the northern areas, and to meet his friend, Commander Ahmad Shah Massoud, a Tajik leader of the Northern Alliance, the most powerful of the freedom fighter groups opposing the Russians.

Khalili will take you to the tops of 17,000-foot-high mountains, in freezing cold in deep snow by foot, on donkey, and on horseback. Behind him, you will tread along narrow, rough, rocky pathways hacked into the mountainsides often in torrential, freezing sleet, and rain. You will face aching hunger and experience fatigue and numbing, brutal cold. At the end of a long, grueling day, you will seek shelter in a small, dark, dirty cave, and be grateful for a little warm tea from a dirty, cracked cup. You will witness the incredible hardships and suffering of the Afghan people, will stand helpless with Khalili as you try to help wounded fathers, mothers, and children, sometimes with nothing more than a single pill of aspirin left to give to someone suffering great pain. You will feel Khalili's despair as he must turn away and push on, unable to do more than pray for those suffering such agony.

You will experience conversations with Afghans of all types, from all stations of life, and will marvel at the resilience and strength of these simple people in the face of what most of us would consider a hopeless situation. You will see that this book is not about Khalili but about his poor, war-torn people who he sees on his travels.

Throughout this journey, which begins on July 1, and ends on September 13, with Khalili and a group of refugees under fire from Russian helicopter gunships, struggling to cross the raging Kunar River, Khalili's words grab and hold you. They paint a glowing picture of hope and courage, and of the indomitable spirit of the Afghan people. There will be times Khalili's words will move you to tears with their beauty and feeling. And he always paints this story with the colors of his love for his wife, Sohaillah, and his children, Mahmud and Majdood. Writing it day-by-day, often hour-by-hour, he has infused his love and dedication to the cause of freedom for his country into an uplifting, exciting tale with a unique viewpoint. He finds beauty in all he sees around him, even in the most difficult and harsh of times.

I have known Masood Khalili since 1988 and I can testify that he is all that he appears to be in this story and more. His father, whose story appears in these pages, was clearly a nationally beloved figure—poet laureate of the nation, whose poems are part of the lives of so many Afghans his son encounters, an advisor to the king and an ambassador—whose personal traits and values are reflected in his son. Masood has dedicated the past 40 years of his life to working for the freedom of Afghanistan. His body bears the scars of a vicious bomb attack that badly wounded him and killed his good friend Commander Ahmad Shah Massoud on September 9, 2001. Khalili's survival is nothing short of a miracle—over 300 pieces of shrapnel are still lodged in his body—and he is respected as a national figure now.

He is what Afghanistan should become. God willing, he will live long enough to see his beloved homeland at peace and on the road to stability.

Read this book, enjoy, and marvel...

Gary C. Schroen
Former CIA Field Officer,
Author of *First In: How Seven CIA Officers Opened the War on Terror in Afghanistan*

Note from the Translator

Ever since I was a teenager and knew about the box of over 40 war diaries my father wrote to my mother while fighting in the war against the Red army, I wanted to translate a few of them. In 2012, I was in Madrid, the capital of Spain, where my father was the ambassador of Afghanistan and with my mother's help, I decided to secretly start translating one of those diaries. My mother randomly picked up one and we started to translate little by little. I thought it was fitting for her to help because those diaries were written for her.

About a month later, my father found out that we had started this project and decided to take over from my mother in helping me. While reading his own words, some details that he had not written in his diary came back to him and even a few more stories that he did not have time to jot down in those cold, rough, and high mountains popped into his mind. It took eight months for the first translation of his diary and another three years of editing by ourselves and many friends from around the world until we had it ready for publishing.

In the end, from among many publishing houses who were interested, we were lucky to be introduced to SAGE publishing, India, who decided to take up our book and publish it as soon as possible. I would like to thank the Vice President (Commissioning) Sharmila Abraham, for her continued support. We are happy to have the SAGE team on our side in bringing *Whispers of War* to the world.

I would also like to thank my close friend, Johnathan Korowicz, in always sparing time to help edit and polish up *Whispers*; Gary Schroen, for sparing some time from his busy schedule to give *Whispers* an expert edit of his own; Generals David Richards and Steve Coll for their advice and encouragement; also Sandy Gall, Kathy Gannon, Dominic Jermey, Jules Stewart, and many others, who gave us the moral support we needed to keep working at finishing *Whispers*.

Introduction

During the summer of 1986, Masood Khalili kept a diary as he traveled through northern Afghanistan. That record has yielded this elegiac book on the Afghan people in the midst of their war of resistance against the Soviet Union. *Whispers of War* is a memoir but not a diary of self. It is a group portrait of the Afghan nation and its diverse, resilient culture in a season of extreme pressure.

Khalili's journey unfolds with conversations and eyewitness encounters with farmers, refugees, horsemen, villagers, and commanders. We encounter through these extraordinary voices the intimate pain of wartime—children lost to random gunfire, volunteer fighters suffering from wounds that cannot be treated properly so far from modern medical care. And yet, day after day, we also encounter the unbroken warmth, humor, and imagination of a people who rise to cope with hardship collectively.

Hospitality and generosity lift the author around every dark corner. Tea and local dishes shared by people who have little of their own are spread out wherever Khalili stops to rest. And it is hard to imagine another wartime landscape where so much is communicated by poetic stanzas. Khalili's father was a famous poet. On the road to Badakhshan, entering a valley, a young man named Ahmad Amini greets him by spontaneously reciting one of his father's quatrains:

O sweet spring, you are flowing so gently!
Whose message do you bring, where from do you come?
You are like tears streaming from my eyes,
Quietly, softly, slowly and calmly

The author offers up his own favorite lines from Rumi. The exchanges remind us how much this resistance was a popular war for culture, amidst culture—that the uprising against foreign occupation was much more than just violence and battlefield tactics, and that for all their poverty and diversity, the Afghan people fought to preserve a nation they carried with them as remembrance, partly as lines of shared poetry.

It was a war, however. We follow the author step by step down narrow rocky paths, in the darkness after midnight, scurrying off ridges before the sun exposes the travelers to Soviet planes or helicopters. Every leg of the travel—on a mule, on a horse, and by foot—is shaped by challenges, demanding stamina, and conviction.

In a village called Namakaw, the author meets his mentor and friend, Ahmed Shah Massoud, a legendary commander. Their encounter and conversation offers a rich, humanizing portrait of a man now shrouded in a national myth. The pair sleep on a roof, listening to the sounds of a distant river. "Khalili Sahib," Massoud remarks, "let us not talk of war tonight but of other more interesting things." They talk of vineyards and orange orchards, holidays, and sports.

All of the book's portraits are informed by such humanity. When a Nooristani woman, outraged that the group's horse is unleashed and devouring her pasture, curses and throws stones their way, Khalili sympathizes with her, to the bemusement of his companions. Every stop on this road seems an opportunity for empathy and understanding.

There is a sly beneficence in the author's encounters with the world, and it even extends to the beasts of burden that carry him. "Today, I had a chance to ride my new donkey," Khalili records one Saturday in August. "While I was comfortable riding it, I was thinking of two famous donkeys in our history. One was the donkey of Jesus Christ and the other was the donkey of Mullah Nasruddin. .... In our culture, amongst all other animals, these two are celebrities. While my donkey was behaving very well, I said, 'If you are not as good as the donkey of Jesus, at least you are like the donkey of Mullah Nasruddin.' I hope he has understood."

Above all, this a journey dedicated to family. The diary entries are written as letters to the author's wife, Sohaillah, with occasional supplements to his two young boys. The devotion and longing Khalili expresses for his own family informs of the pain he feels when he encounters other Afghan families ripped apart by the war's violence and tragedy.

At varying degrees of intensity, Afghanistan has been at war for more than three decades now. American and European soldiers and their families have lately come to share some of that sacrifice in the recent campaigns against Al Qaeda and the Taliban. Yet too many in the West continue to think of Afghanistan by reference to hoary clichés about tribalism and perpetual fighting. These clichés elide the fact that modern Afghanistan was at peace with itself and its neighbors through the great majority of the 20th century, until a foreign army invaded the country and tried to upend its way of life with a radical ideology. *Whispers of War* offers an additional corrective. Step by step, day by day, the book's journey carries the humane heart of Afghanistan, to its suffering, beauty, poetry, and aspirations for peace.

Steve Coll
Dean of Colombia University
Graduate School of Journalism
Author of *Ghost Wars*

1

First Steps, Long Journey Ahead

Tuesday, July 1, 1986

O God, open the bud of hope.
Show me the flower of paradise.
Fill my soul with its fragrance.
O God, take my hand till the end of my journey,
Step by step, until you are happy, and I am free.

My dear wife Sohaillah, I am in a small airplane, which is carrying not more than 40 people. It does not have a stewardess or perhaps it does, but she is not bothering to show herself. No problem though. It is just an hour-long flight to Chitral in Pakistan and a good time to start writing to you about the journey I am on.

Among other passengers, there are three wounded Afghans, a girl with her mother and a boy with his old gray-haired father. They seem to be suffering a lot. The mother, despite having an amputated leg, helps her 12-year-old wounded daughter with medicine and water. The little girl, who has a hand amputated, is trying hard to hide her tears and soften her cries. Perhaps, she does not want to show her pain to her wounded mother.

On the backseat, a young Pakistani mother gives a piece of candy to her daughter, who is happily playing with her blue-eyed doll. The tears of the wounded girl and the smiles of the happy one make pain and peace mingle in my heart. The stewardess finally shows up, brings us some juice and gives a smile to both girls.

The little boy, while helping his old wounded father, is nervously holding a white pigeon in his lap. He might have brought it secretly onto the plane. His pigeon seems more nervous than he does. They were wounded by a Russian bombardment some months ago and were being exceptionally helped by International Committee of the Red Cross to go back to the refugee camp in Chitral in Pakistan.

Oh my goodness, what a tragedy! What a miserable life it must be for the legless mother and handless daughter, living in a poor, cold refugee camp with almost no food or medicine. I tried to talk to the wounded girl but she did not want to talk and covered her face with her one little hand. The mother saw my tearful eyes saddened by the innocent glances of the little girl and tried to console my heart.

"I lost my two sons and my husband in a bombardment. Thank God, at least I still have my daughter with me. We should be grateful and happy with what we have, not sad with what we do not or what we have lost. Do not worry, brother. We will be okay, but to tell you the truth, I miss my martyred sons and poor home. I hope the war gets over soon so we can go back to our own village in Afghanistan."

The old wounded man sighed and quietly murmured, "What a strong woman! What great patience for such a miserable condition! God is great."

I looked into the red eyes of the white pigeon, almost suffocated in the hands of the refugee boy and the blue eyes of the little doll but had nothing to say.

The plane is flying quietly over the beautiful snow-clad mountains, deep valleys, and blue rivers. I am now on my way to the same war that has ravaged our whole country and led to the daily pain and suffering of thousands of poor people like this mother and daughter. Even the pigeon.

My dear, be patient. It is just the first day of a long journey with many weeks and months to go. There will be ugly and beautiful scenes to watch, difficult and easy problems to tackle, fatal and deadly dangers to face, happy and tearful eyes to see, and various sweet and sour stories to hear.

After all, it is a liberation war against the occupying Soviets. I am Afghan and a part of the war. Thinking of going to war, I hate my long journey ahead, but when I think that I am a part of a liberation war, I appreciate it because I had learnt from my father that mercy to the wolf is cruelty to the lamb. Leaving the wolf free deprives the lamb of its freedom. For me, fighting in a war for freedom is a way of rejecting the war itself. Tell me: Is there any other way to gain freedom from the clutches of a powerful and cruel enemy but war? I wish there was.

The plane is about to land. Let me write to you later.

* * *

It took us 45 minutes to get from Peshawar to Chitral. Rest assured that Shuhaib, my young staff member, has packed my notebook that you bought for me, a few pens, my sleeping bag and some painkillers. Hopefully, after a few days of travel, we will be in Afghanistan.

Commander Ateeq, one of Commander Massoud's men, had come to the airport to receive me and brought me directly to his home in the suburbs of Chitral. I know him very well. In Ateeq's home, I found northern refugee leaders who wanted to see me and had many things to discuss. As a political officer of my party, I had to listen to them carefully and write down whatever I thought was noteworthy. There were also two foreigners, whom I luckily knew. One was Gayle, the director of Freedom Medicine, which is one of the American NGOs working in Peshawar. The other foreigner I met there was Colette Kriplani. She is an American businesswoman from San Francisco. She spent two years of her youth in Kabul as her father worked there from 1957 to 1959 as a diplomat. She is now probably in her forties.

After having tea with Collette and Gayle, I met some leaders from one of the refugee camps and promised I would visit them as soon as I could. Afterward, I told Ateeq to take me to the center of Chitral to refresh the memories of my previous visits.

Chitral is mountainous, dusty, and crowded, with small shops and narrow lanes. It has its share of good and bad people. They are staunch supporters of ours in the war against the Soviets and this is why they have allowed thousands of Afghan refugees to live here. The people of Chitral speak their own dialect, which we Afghans do not understand the least bit.

God has blessed this city with fine weather. The aroma of spicy food, charcoal smoke, and roasted lamb *kebab* billowing out from old restaurants and small teahouses would tease a hungry beggar to distraction. Stray dogs run around a dirty butcher's shop, sniffing out and scavenging a discarded shard of bull-bone to fill their empty stomachs. Swarms of flies and yellow hornets give chase, beseeching the poor dogs to share their bloody feast. The waves of the gray, muddy Chitral River add to the beauty of the city, although its unruly rapids steal from its serenity. The mountains are so high and the boulders so large that as I walk, either my shivering shadow is stretched forth upon the mountainsides or the boulders cast their own upon my small body.

From previous visits, I know only two or three *Mirs*, or land-lords, whose ancestors were once part of the oldest and most powerful local families. Sadly, for them, their own people no longer recognize the status their ancestors once enjoyed. All they now possess are names and positions impoverished by time. Whenever I see them, they show me their old muskets, ancient silver coins, black and white photos of their grandfathers posing with British lords long ago, and family seals embossed on ancient silver rings. They are proud of them. They should be, for what else do they have?

I came upon a barefoot boy, no more than eight years old, with three tiny fish hanging from a decrepit old fishing rod. A hand-made slingshot hung from his neck. A woman, perhaps his mother, accompanied him in a black Afghan *Kochi,* or nomad dress, carrying on her back a great bundle of firewood. Bent by the burden of the wood, she looked herself like a thin branch of an apple tree, pushed downward by its ripe fruit. The boy was holding a rope attached to a slim goat in one hand.

His slingshot brought back memories of almost 30 years before, when I was much the same age as he is now. However, the dif-ference between this Afghan boy and me was that when I was his age, I used my slingshot for fun. The refugee boy no doubt used both his slingshot and fishing rod to feed his family, out of dire necessity. Both the mother and child were refugees. A small gray dog was running after them. Probably, the dog was a refugee too.

Before he could go too far, I asked the boy where his father was. With shyness, he replied, "Uncle, he died in a bombardment. If he were alive, we might not have become refugees, or at least he would help my mother carry the wood bundle."

His mother called out to him to hurry along and off he ran with those three tiny fish, a poor family's meager feast, dangling from his fishing rod.

From Chitral to your own native land of Nooristan, my dear, is the hardest of all routes for Afghan refugees and freedom fighters. Every year, when I go to the north of Afghanistan, I take this path to see Commander Massoud and other provincial commanders, in order to gather all the latest updates concerning the military side of our war against the Soviets. I do not take the other routes, which lead south, east, and west. They are far easier. They are flatter with lower mountains. We make these trips either by foot or on a horse, mule or donkey. War and Soviet jet fighters do not allow us to use cars or other more convenient modes of transport. As I travel, I will listen to the stories of my beleaguered people. I must take note of their suffering, problems, needs, good and bad feelings, right and wrong actions, and successes and failures in our war against the Afghan communist regime and their backers and puppeteers, the Soviet Red Army. I must record the voices of my people. It is simply a matter of talking to them, listening to them, asking them questions and letting them ask me questions. I will learn a lot from them and, hopefully, they may learn a little from me as well.

You, who always prepares my bag, know that I travel lightly. My pack contains the following: one spare pair of boots, two extra shirts, four or five thick notebooks, one camera with plenty of film, ballpoint pens, pencils, painkillers, and, if possible, a little salt and pepper. I always reserve a special notebook for you, my dear, this fine yellow one in which I now write. Here, I record the subtle things I see or hear, and I shall never forget to fill your notebook with the beauty of our motherland.

Yes, I may be a freedom fighter, a warrior, and a political officer, but I am human after all. I love to watch, to feel, and to touch the warm pulse of beautiful Mother Nature, especially when I can share these moments with you. That is what keeps me happy and lends the unkind parts of this journey kindness and even a certain charm.

I will do my best to take you along with me, base-to-base, village-to-village, pass-to-pass, river-to-river, mountain-to-mountain, and even heart-to-heart. I shall hear many things, unpredictable and unprecedented. After all, listening to the stories of the common people requires a lot of patience.

Stay with me and remember the proverb *sabr talkh ast walayken bare shereen daarad*, or 'patience is sour but has a sweet fruit'. However, do not worry. I shall not write about everything. That would require dozens of notebooks and more days than I have to write. A beautiful rose grows in a simple bush, so I too will try to keep my words to you as simple and beautiful as possible.

It has never been an easy job and it gets harder day by day. Physically, it is difficult to undertake such a long journey, by foot, on a horse, donkey or mule, especially when every hour you run the risk of ambush, bombardment, or kidnap by our enemies, the Soviet or Afghan communists. Close to a million people have already died in this war, many thousands have been maimed or wounded, and millions displaced from their homes have fled as refugees to other countries.

What sort of a man walks hundreds of kilometers and climbs the highest rocky mountain passes, with scant food or medicine? The harder the fight for freedom, the higher the hope of victory. The road to freedom and the path to peace are never easy. One has to have strong faith and an irrational love for both. It requires hard work, patience, commitment, tolerance, bravery, wisdom, and, of course, sacrifice.

I shall not be alone for there shall always be another, ever patient, ever content. That is my poor four-legged means of transport, be it a horse or a humble donkey. He shall learn little from me though I shall try to learn patience from him who is ever tolerant. After all, he is not human. We are selfish. We get angry.

My friend Whitney Azoy is also making this journey with me. I think you have met him before. He is an American anthropologist who has taken a great interest in Afghanistan. He is in his late forties. I like him.

When he was younger, he worked in Afghanistan in the American Embassy and then changed his career path by joining the academic world. He spent three years in the Kunduz province, working as an anthropologist. He wrote a book on Afghanistan called *Buzkashi*. He knows many beautiful English poems and is full of short and long stories. You never get bored with him.

I am expecting some old friends to accompany me on this trip. Sandy Gall, the well-known British journalist and author of *Behind Russian Lines: An Afghan Journal*, will be coming along to see Commander Massoud and interview him. In his team is Andy, also an old friend, who manages everything for Sandy and will act as a photographer and camera operator. Another man or even two, whom I do not yet know, will be accompanying them as well.

If they arrive in time to join me, it will be very good. Otherwise, I will go on ahead and they will follow afterward.

*   *   *

Now, my dear, I am again on my way to the north, via Nooristan, that sweet cradle of mountains in our beloved land. Food and medicines are luxuries there, but I trust that the people would not allow us to starve.

The hardest part of this journey for me is leaving you, my little sons, Mahmud and Majdood, and my old parents in Pakistan, and knowing I will not see you all for months. No telephone, no radio, not even a fast messenger. I am totally cut off from you. It is as if I am traveling to another planet.

I envy the olden times, when our people used homing pigeons to communicate. Separated lovers once tied love-filled messages to the legs or necks of those innocent birds. One watches them fly away, another anxiously waits, looking toward the blue sky to glimpse those flapping wings of hope or heartbreak flying toward them. Like we have postmen today, they had post-birds yesterday.

The pigeons never knew if they conveyed the messages of a broken heart; otherwise, they would have wept blood all the way to a waiting lover. Do you remember these beautiful lines of a verse?

Oh pigeon,
I know why your eyes are red.
Carrying my letter to my beloved,
You wept blood for my bleeding heart.
Oh pigeon,
I know why your eyes are red.
You must be a broken hearted pigeon,
To have taken my letter to my beloved.

Stars on the Roof

Chitral, Pakistan
Wednesday, July 2
6:00 AM

Last night, my dear, at Commander Ateeq's invitation, we came to sleep in the open area behind his house. It was funny that all of us, women and men, slept together on a small 10 meter by 10 meter patch of ground. There, under the starry roof of God, equality between men and women worked very well. No one complained. I could not sleep and lay watching the hanging stars, wishing little Mahmud were here beside me searching for familiar stars and constellations. I remember the summers in Kabul when we used to sleep on the roof and one of the elders would tell us the names of the stars and the unforgettable stories of their origins. My favorites were the tales of the Shepherd Star and the Poet Star. We had good luck and bad luck stars as well.

The scattered stars of the Chitral sky provided me with a wonderful opportunity to remember some of the precious stories of our peaceful past. They also brought back to me enduringly pleasant memories of my sisters, brothers, and friends who are now scattered, like little stars themselves, to every corner of the world because of this ugly war.

When I awoke, Gayle was already sitting in her bed like a white monk, waiting for the sunrise to murmur prayers for its first golden rays. I asked her what she was doing. She said that she was writing a letter to Commander Massoud. I was struck with wonder that this woman, a lawyer from America, should be here in Chitral as the head of an NGO, assisting the beleaguered Afghan people, and writing a letter to Commander Massoud, the leader of the resistance in the Panjshir Valley of Afghanistan.

Whitney was awake too, sitting in his bed, like a tall, bearded Kandahari *mullah*. He was writing something too. He had a smile on his face every time I saw him write. I hoped that I was so enthusiastic about writing in my own diary.

Commander Ateeq arranged a nice breakfast for all of us, which we thoroughly enjoyed. So far this year, no horse has come from the north of Afghanistan nor has any horse gone north from here. You have to be patient. I was reassured in our endeavor when I received a word by a messenger from Ahmad Zia, brother of Commander Massoud, that he will be coming shortly from Peshawar. I am confident that he will take care of everything. "But he cannot melt the snow," I heard Mohammad Dean say quietly.

My back and legs are doing well. I am in no pain, thank God. I am taking it easy, remembering the injuries I suffered last year on my way to the north.

Shuhaib, my staff member, has sent an urgent message from Peshawar, with a request from Ustad Rabbani, the leader of the

Jamiat Party: "Please make your trip as short as you can. If possible, come back before September, because we would like to launch a political move against the Soviets, in the United Nations in New York."

Choosing a Horse

Chitral, Pakistan
2:00 PM

Ahmad Zia, Commander Massoud's younger brother, arrived about an hour ago. What happy news! He came to see me directly. I am sure Commander Massoud has instructed him to take care of everything for us. The security of my journey depends on the bodyguards that Ahmad Zia chooses. He told me that he has selected brave and trusted freedom fighters to accompany us, since the security situation on the roads have become worse this year.

Let me not forget to tell you about a wonderful event that happened this morning. One of the Chitrali *Mir* spotted me on the street and invited me to accompany him to watch a game of *chowgaan baazi*, or polo. It was Peshawar versus Chitral, and Peshawar won. We do not play polo in Afghanistan anymore, though it was very much part of our history. In fact, it was once the game of kings and royalty.

A thousand years ago, the Afghan king Mahmud was a polo player himself. They play it with horses and chowgaan, or a long stick. It differs greatly from the Afghan national sport of Buzkashi, which is rough and tough and requires a great deal of courage. A rider in Buzkashi should be like a wrestler or a stubborn fighter, but polo requires more smartness and deftness. Polo horses are generally very handsome, well groomed, trim, with tall and slender bodies. Buzkashi horses are invariably very strong, sturdy, rough, ungroomed, and wild. They could be stronger than the horses of Alexander the Great and sturdier than the horses of the mythic hero Rustam.

In polo, you have a limited number of male or female riders, but in Buzkashi, the players are hundreds of stubborn exclusively male riders playing on an open field. In polo, the players are nice to each other. They even say sorry if any foul is committed. In Buzkashi, the players must be strong. The rule is always that might is right. Only the powerful win, because whipping, beating, pushing, pulling, injuring, drawing of blood, shouting, and screaming are all an essential part of the game.

In polo, they use a ball, but in Buzkashi, the 'ball' is a large and heavy dead calf. The speed of a polo player is limited, but there is no limit to the speed of a Buzkashi rider. The clothes of a polo rider are clean and proper, but the Buzkashi rider has to wear rough, padded garments in order to soften the blows of the whips and fists of other riders. Polo is a team sport, while Buzkashi is anarchistically individual and reflects the character of Afghans themselves. What I liked most was that polo even has a referee with a whistle.

To be honest, while watching the game, I was thinking of that poor Afghan refugee boy with his slingshot, fishing rod, and oversized hat. I wished he were there with me to watch the game as well, but it was just a wish.

* * *

After the game, I talked with Whitney about his experiences in Afghanistan. It was around 4:30 PM when I decided to go and select a horse for my journey. Commander Ateeq, a small group of his fighters, and I went together to choose my horse.

We walked up the side of a fairly steep hill for about fifteen minutes and as we crossed the top, a wide grassy meadow of sorts opened up in front of us. A bit further down from us, you could see hundreds and hundreds of donkeys, horses, and mules. It was as if we had entered another, equine, world. The sounds of these animals filled the skies.

Instantly, images from history started to flood my mind. I saw Alexander the Great's men loading their supplies and weapons in a wide, open Macedonian meadow similar to this one, as his immense army prepared for the march that would conquer lands from Europe to the edge of China, passing through Afghanistan along the Silk Road.

I could see our own king, Sultan Mahmud of Ghazni, readying thousands of his soldiers to head toward Iran and India. I imagined Temur the Lame (Tamerlane), gathering his forces from Bukhara and Samarkand, and marching out to conquer everything in his path. From the east, images of Genghis Khan appeared with his vast hordes, riding westward to destroy and rule from Mongolia to Eastern Europe. My thoughts then went to Babur the Great, who marched southward from Afghanistan to India where he would rule until his death. I envisioned, in the not too distant past, the soldiers of the British Empire amassing here, awaiting orders to enter Afghanistan, in order to check the advance of Czarist Russia. Finally, I could clearly hear the orders of Russian Czars and their communist usurpers dispatching their vast armies from the Red Square to try to take control of Central Asian lands to clear a path all the way to the warm waters of the Indian Ocean.

All those armies of the past, readying themselves in similar places to this, in their own kingdoms, were preparing to go out to conquer other lands, but the poor men and horses before me had exactly the opposite goal of delivering essential war supplies for their own land's liberation. They did not want to conquer others; they wanted to free themselves.

I snapped out of my reverie and told Commander Ateeq that we should go where the horses and men were. As we approached, I could see that the horsemen, who were waiting in the meadow, had noticed our group. They all recognized me. Commander Ateeq told me that these brave men deliver supplies to thirteen provinces, north and south of the Hindu Kush.

I told Ateeq to gather the men so that I could talk to them. When they came, we did the traditional greetings and finally settled down on a cluster of small boulders.

One of the horsemen reported: "The closest distance we walk, with our supply-laden horses, through these inhospitable, snow-wrapped mountains is a fifteen days' journey. The furthest distance requires up to 75 days' hard walking. The supplies we transport are bullets, mortars, rockets, rocket launchers, assault rifles, especially AK-47s, .50 caliber machine guns, Zikoyak machine guns, sniper rifles, anti-tank mines, long-range rockets, RPG-7s, communication equipment, and various other military supplies required in war. The transport of each horse load costs about US$350 for a one-way delivery and then the same for return."

A man named only Nabee said that he takes his supplies all the way to the far end of the Badakhshan province to a district called

Darwaaz, which borders China, and it normally takes him 45 days to reach.

I asked Ateeq, "In the midst of the Cold War, can this little meadow, one of the distribution centers for weapons and ammunitions, really be enough for our fighters?"

He replied, "Khalili Sahib, compared to the numbers of fighters we have to supply, this is only a drop in the ocean. If it were not for the weapons captured from the Soviets, we would not even come close to arming a small percentage of our fighters." I asked Mohammad Naqeeb, who was going all the way to the Faryab province, "You say your journey will take 60 days. Do you have any medicine?"

"I have a few Bayer Aspirin tablets and I have God."

I asked Nabee, who was going to Badakhshan, "Why does it take so long to walk there? Is it because of the heavy loads your horses carry or because of the difficult paths?"

They all started talking among themselves and shaking their heads.

Nabee responded very nicely and to the point by saying, "Khalili Sahib, God is with us. We can cross difficult paths quickly with our horses and supplies, but because of the Soviet bombardments and ambushes, we cannot travel during the day. At night, our pace is slow because of the dangerous cliffs. We do not want to die, but even more so, we do not want to lose the supplies. People are depending on us."

I looked around at the men and said, "May God bless you all. You are brave, dedicated freedom fighters. Do not allow anyone to tell you otherwise. Only men with the hearts of lions can go such long distances and endure such hardships to do their part in our fight for freedom." I wished the men well, and we all prayed for our safety and for the freedom of our beloved country.

While saying goodbye to these men, I thought to myself, "The most difficult and hardest road is the road to freedom."

All of a sudden, we could see Ahmad Zia, the younger brother of Commander Massoud, and Agha Gul, Commander's logistics chief, coming toward us. They told me that they had come to see what kind of a horse I would select.

We walked over to Qudus, one of the horse-handlers. I could see that his horse looked strong, healthy, and had a beautiful light brown coat. Qudus brought over a few more horses, which also seemed fine to me. I looked at Agha Gul and said to him, "I trust your judgment."

I am happy I was able to meet the poor horsemen and I am happier still that I am able to write about it in my notebook.

Waiting is a Plus

Chitral, Pakistan
Thursday, July 3

While waiting for the snow to melt and the passes to open, I once again spoke to my friend Whitney about poetry and literature. He recited an English poem for me. I could see its beautiful images but did not really feel the beauty of the words. For me, sometimes form is more important than content. In our language, the form of the poetry is so beautiful that I mostly do not care about the meaning. In the English language, while the beauty of the content attracts my heart, its form cannot satisfy my eyes. After all, it is not my own language, but despite these shortcomings of mine, I still liked Whitney's poem. As he was reading, I was translating it in my mind for you.

Last night, Ahmad Zia and Agha Gul came to go over the supplies the resistance would need this year. Agha Gul had brought along some almonds and raisins for me to take on my trip. I was surprised to see that he had also brought a few cans of sardines. I asked him whether it was his idea to bring the sardines or someone else's. He said that Peter Juvenal, my British journalist friend, had sent it for me from Peshawar.

Agha Gul has been working for Commander Massoud for about seven years now. I thanked him. He touched his dark, curly hair and thanked me. He is in his late twenties. He is very humble and always wears a great smile.

Yakubi, the head of the Panjshir office in Chitral, came and asked me to pay a visit. I accepted and went. Besides being the head of the Panjshir office here, he is a lively, energetic young man and a poet too. He shaves his beard and always wears a black turban.

He is himself from Panjshir. He was once with the Hezb-i-Islami Party, a rival group, but now has changed to my party, Jamiat. Some people around here do not like him, but to me, he seemed like an industrious, active young man. I talked to him for an hour and encouraged him to stay on board because we need hardworking people like him.

In the Panjshir office, I met an interesting old man, from the Balkh province. His name was Kareem Baay. He possesses a Sufi-like character. He claimed that he was able to treat all types of skin problems by only touching them. Surprisingly, some Afghan refugees who were there confirmed his spiritual power of healing. He charges no money.

He told me that Prophet Kizzir transferred to him this healing power in a dream and instructed him to go to Pakistan to treat Afghan refugees. We believe that Prophet Kizzir is immortal because he discovered the life spring, or the fountain of youth.

It is also believed that whenever a needy person remembers Prophet Kizzir, he instantly appears to offer help. If in a moment of dire necessity, a desperate person calls to him, "Oh Prophet Kizzir, please come and help me!", he immediately appears. I think he is the son or the grandson of Prophet Noah.

According to our Holy Book, besides being immortal, he is also the epitome of wisdom. I simply asked the healer what he would ask for if Prophet Kizzir were to appear in his dream again. He looked at his old silver ring, checked his ancient Russian watch, and replied, "I would ask him to end the greed of the enemy and reduce the poverty of our people so that I can go back home to spend my last living days among my beloved grandchildren and be buried in our family graveyard."

Later, Ahmad Zia, Agha Gul, and a few others joined us too. Meatballs, chicken kebab, and *palow*, or baked rice, were served. We left at about 2 PM for a walk in the city and to have a cup of tea at Terajmeer hotel. The stores and streets of Chitral are small and narrow. Here you can find limited Pakistan-made products, including spices, herbs, and rice. Other than these, you can find foreign goods and products as well. There are a few small hotels here but the best ones are Terajmeer and Mountain Inn.

Everywhere you go in this city, either you follow the Chitral River or you are followed by it. It is muddy, dark, gray, wrathful, and rushes southward. This noisy river originates from the ever snow-capped Mount Terajmeer.

Every sunset, the golden fingers of the sun's vibrant rays play with the silver-white strands of the snow blanket on the mountain pass below. In the mornings, the mountain has a different beauty and looks exactly as if God has placed a silver crown upon its peaceful peak. This high mountain can also be clearly seen from Afghanistan.

My health, thank God, is good. I wear a special belt every day so that my back remains secure. My slipped disc, which has bothered me for the past fifteen years, does not bother me.

Mosquitoes, whirling fans, meetings, countless meals and cups of tea, poetry, sleepless nights, and the hustle and bustle are all for one end—to fill in time waiting for the snowy passes of Nooristan to melt so that our horses can travel more easily through the mountains.

Engineer Ateeq has found a room for us inside his humble house tonight. Once a rich man, he now lives as a poor refugee. The room has no windows but has a large sunroof, about one and a half meters across, through which flies easily enter. He has hung a multicolored fabric from the ceiling. There is a large double-paneled door, far too low for someone of Whitney's height. Thin, narrow foam mattresses are spread out against the four walls for people to sit on and sleep.

Much of the time we spend in the room, we are lying on the mattresses, looking upward. Despite it being a small, humble room, the large sunroof and old pillars provide the best of shelters when we wish to think or write something. We are grateful to the mason who built it. I think this room suits Whitney, because when he writes, his eyes are often fixed on the cracks in the ceiling or the pillars. He might be writing poetry or perhaps his own description of our journey. He first twists his head and neck, scratches his head, holds his breath, and repeatedly sighs while he writes, especially when he uses his larger notebook. Strange!

I hope I do not do the same while I am writing. While Whitney looks great, I would probably look silly if my writing were accompanied by such actions.

Oh my goodness, just now a white, thin cat jumped out in front of me. Perhaps, this adorable little animal is also a refugee.

Hurry

Chitral, Pakistan
Friday, July 4

Dearest wife, early in the morning, Ahmad Zia came to my room to deliver a note to me from Commander Massoud. "Khalili Sahib," it read, "if possible, reach us faster, and on the way, talk to Haji Ghafoor, commander of Kantiwa, Nooristan. I have information that Hekmatyar and his Hezb-i-Islami party want to establish a base in the Kantiwa area with Ghafoor's help. If Haji Ghafoor allows such a base, the problem of our military supplies shall be greatly escalated."

Ahmad Zia was adamant that I leave now, even though the passes have not opened yet. I looked at him and said, "I know I must go and that it is very important, but I have already promised Andy that I would wait for him and Sandy's team. I cannot go back on my promise."

He shook his head and said, "Khalili Sahib, you move on and I promise that I will make sure they reach you safely. Do not worry."

I suggested that he send word to my guests and tell them that they should arrive as soon as possible. Ahmad Zia agreed and mentioned that he would like to join me to visit the refugees.

Around sunset, we headed toward the refugee camp, which was a mixture of old and new tents. At sunset, the Chitral River was dark and angry. The waves were screaming aloud and banging their heads against the stones. They resembled the khaki-clad holy warriors rushing headlong with all their strength, running from rock to rock in pursuit of their enemies.

Little children with light complexions, dressed in their colorful, threadbare clothes, looked upon us from next to their dusty tents, like little goats. Some poor, old, white-bearded Panjshiri refugees from the village of Aanaba, in the Paryaan province, received us. Their war-ridden, wrinkled faces and tearful eyes shot arrows of pain right into my heart.

They knew me first of all as the son of Ustad Khalili, or the grandson of Mustufi-Mamalik. We ate dinner together, prayed together, read poetry together, wept together, and even laughed together. They asked me more about my father's health than my own. They miss their homes and had only painful stories of separation from their beloved lands to tell.

One of them said, "We can accept and tolerate all kinds of separations but not from home. Take everything from us but give us back our homes." I could feel the bitter pangs of exile among these refugees, especially the older ones.

A younger refugee told me that his grandmother hid herself in a closet when they were fleeing Afghanistan, and when her sons pleaded with her to come with them, she cried out loudly from inside, "Let me die here in my own home and in my own closet. I would rather lose my life than leave my home. I prefer to die in my dusty, old closet and not in the country or land of others. I can hide myself here from the eyes of the enemy. Do not worry about me."

Among all the refugees, an old man of about 80 years of age professed a more stoic point of view for when I asked him if he needed something, he said, "Pray to God to give us nothing but patience. Everywhere is the land of God. I was happy in my home and I am happy in this refugee camp, because God has filled my heart with patience."

2

No Journey Goes as Planned—
On the Way at Last

Saturday, July 5
4:00 PM

Ahmad Zia came to me at about 8:30 AM and told me that everything was ready and that we would depart at 11 AM. He gave me the good news that Andy, Sandy Gall, and his team had arrived. My friend Whitney, our two Afghan cameramen, our horses, and horsemen were ready too. The weather was crisp and clear. It was a good day to start our journey.

However, this first day we did not get far. We moved by jeep to Garm Chishma. We rested an hour and left for a small valley even closer to the border. While the horses were ready, they were not here. Unfortunately, there were no trucks available to bring them to us, so they had to travel on hooves to join us.

Tonight, next to the river and under the shade of the mountains, we will stay here. Tomorrow morning, when the horses arrive, we will, God willing, leave for the first mountain that we have to cross. We will spend the night at its base and if all works out well, hopefully, we will be in Afghanistan on Monday.

We are now sitting in a valley on the borderland. Our expedition consists of about a dozen freedom fighters who serve as our bodyguards; eight men to care of the horses; Whiney Azoy, our anthropologist; Sandy Gall; Andy Skrzypkowiac, the freelance photographer; Noel Smart, the cameraman; Basit and Naeem, two Afghan cameramen; and myself, our group's political officer. All have different reasons for being here. It is sure we will not get bored on this trip with such a diverse group.

The sun is shining. There is a slight breeze. The corn has just reached maturity, and all around me there are willow trees with small chicks running underneath. In the distance, little children can be seen playing with their goats and sheep. You really have to strain your eyes to differentiate between the children and the goats.

After we ate some food, the men started to wash their clothes in the river. Sandy Gall brought out the British leather saddles he bought on his way here. He had paid 12,000 Afghanis for each and wanted to show them off to the men. I think that perhaps he paid too much for them. I said nothing, my dear, and just smiled admiringly.

The one thing I have done differently on this trip is that I have brought a few cassettes with me so that I may listen to some music on the way. I was surprised to find a cassette of Mozart among them. I may not like the music, but it will refresh the fond memories I have of my 1977 visit to Vienna, where classical music could be heard around the big cathedral.

At this point, a man came to me and introduced himself. "Salaam, Khalili Sahib, Ahmad Zia has selected me as head of your convoy. My name is Dost Mohammad." I shook his hand. "Yes, Ahmad Zia has already told me that you are an experienced and careful horseman who will take care of everything and everybody, especially our foreign friends. Just concentrate on keeping their things in order and helping them. If you have any problems, let me know; consult with the security men and be a good convoy leader."

He was very happy to hear what I said. "Sir, I am no leader. God save me from that responsibility. I am just a poor horseman. You can just call me Keftan or Captain."

I laughed. "I did not mean the leader of a country. I meant the leader of our convoy, a job which may be, on such a difficult journey, more difficult than even leading an empire."

He thanked me and walked away to take on his duties. Dost Mohammad is a strong, well-built man, with Panjshiri manners. He talks in a voice that is louder than necessary, looks authoritative, is of medium height, and has broad shoulders, very black eyes, and dark brown hair. He seems to be a happy man and, as we say, 'he does not have pickles on his forehead.' He is about 35 years old.

Tonight we are here and tomorrow we will start walking toward the first mountain of Nooristan and into the Afghan territory. It is late now and we cannot move forward. Tomorrow, we will have to travel for many hours to reach the base of the mountain. Now I need some rest. I am going to try to find a flat place to lay out my sleeping bag and try to sleep for as long as I can.

My dearest, my thoughts fly to you like a small pigeon. I will write again tomorrow.

Sunday, July 6
5:30 AM

Last night, we were awake until 11 PM. The men made two large fires. The light and heat made us feel better. The men bought a sheep costing 2,000 Afghani (14 US dollars), cooked it, and shared it with everybody. The light of the stars, the silence of the night, the sounds of the water, and the crackling flames of the fire made us feel superb. My men had forgotten to bring a lantern, which was very necessary, especially last night when the wind was blowing very strongly.

I called Dost, the captain, and told him to find some way to get a lantern for the rest of the journey. He made it clear that if it were not impossible, it would be extremely difficult to go back and buy a lantern.

Around 11 PM, I tried to find a flat place to sleep. I found a spot amongst the boulders, which was flat and relatively dry. I slept a little and then woke up again. The weather had become very windy and freezing cold, and I settled back down to sleep. Luckily, I had the sleeping bag given to me by my brother-in-law, Omar Rasuli.

I slept well until morning prayer time. I got up a little bit late and found that the men were making their breakfast. I hoped they had brought some homemade cookies and shared a few with us too.

We are now waiting for breakfast; thereafter, we will go toward the first mountain pass, which is called Doru. Although the pass we are going to take is more rocky and steep, it is not as snow-covered at this time as other passes. A few minutes ago, Andy gave me a wonderful surprise by showing me a picture of our little son Majdood. It was a real surprise. In the meantime, he showed me a picture of his cute little daughter, Shah Noor, with her beautiful blue eyes.

Sandy, Whitney, and the others are doing well. That is to be expected, as we have not yet started the real journey yet.

Whatever the rumors are, no one cares for now. Everybody is in a good mood. This is more or less the nature of the first day of any long walk, as per my experience. The mood is good. Andy just showed me his daughter's photo, Whitney has started to recite poetry, and the horsemen are preparing to move forward toward the Zaydak Valley.

Zaydak Valley

Chitral, Pakistan
11:00 AM

Now it is 11 AM. We are at the Zaydak Valley, the most remote north-western part of Pakistan. We left this morning at 8 AM and arrived here half an hour ago. Today, we still have to move on for a few more hours in order to reach the last base, where we will stay for the night and next day we will cross the first mountain into Afghanistan.

The weather is colder here. There is no one around except a few Pakistani militiamen who man the border post. Their commander is a young man named Wazeer. A messenger named Rahman Shah arrived with a message for Wazeer from Garm Chishma, giving us permission to cross their border.

Wazeer wears a black Pakistani militia uniform and has one Silver Star on his shoulder. He knows a little Pashto. They are men of good temperament, but they have no idea what to do with us. One thing was sure that they would not create any problems for us.

Today, I called the horsemen and Dost Mohammad and told them, "You already know the hardship of the journey to Nooristan and Panjshir. The dangers that we may face on our journey will be much more than in the years before. You have to be (a) punctual, (b) ready with all the necessary preparations, (c) as vigilant as possible, and (d) ever attentive to the instructions of Dost Mohammad, who is, for the time being, your leader and is to be obeyed as much as possible."

How much they actually listened to what I told them is a matter of my luck and their mood. One horseman sarcastically asked another, "What was the instruction number three?"

The other one commented, "How should I know? He counted a hundred numbers or something. Let him count, we do our job with the help of God, not with the help of his numbers."

A number of them laughed among themselves. I did too.

A man stepped forward and said, "I am Azimullah, your horse handler. Qudus could not make it, so they selected me."

I saw that he had a skinny little boy with him. He said that the boy was his ten-year-old son and he intended to bring him with us to train him in horse care. I was worried that the boy was too young for such a journey and asked him why he was taking his son.

He simply said, "I have no one else to look after him and a boy needs to be trained. Do not worry; he is very strong and he can do it." Poverty is such a heavy burden. No father wants to take his son on such a difficult journey. But the burden of poverty must be carried by the whole family, whether a boy of seven or a father of seventy. I looked into the innocent eyes of the poor boy and murmured to my heart, "No matter if the pass is high or low, the load is heavy or light, the size and strength of the poor boy remains the same." The boy would come along.

My dear, read this and be patient. A typical Nooristani man with a high and hawk-like nose came to see me. From foot to knee, his legs were wrapped in white woolen cloth. His Nooristani boots were made of goatskin, as is the custom. His clothes were of a deep-blue color. He had a long walking stick, a black beard, a shaved moustache, a big mouth, brown skin, and an unclean, white Chitrali hat.

I asked him, "What is your name?"

He said, "I am a border guard."

I said, "I asked for your name, not your designation."

He laughed, "Everybody has a name, but not everyone has an official designation. This is why the designation given by a power is more important than the name given by a father."

He had a small, short, black donkey. He spoke to me in Dari, but with a Nooristani accent. I asked him again what his name was.

"I will tell you my name on one condition, that you never call me by that name but always use my designation, because in this case, people will respect me more." I agreed. And, by the way, his name is Deen Mohammad.

He is in his mid-forties. He spent 24 years in Kabul when your father was the mayor. He worked in the Kabul Municipality and became a policeman. He knew your family very well. Remembering your family, tears swelled up in his eyes.

While looking at me with sorrowful glances and deeper sighs, he said, "God, what can be done? War has ruined everything. So many families have been killed, so many homes ruined, and so many cows and goats have died. Poor Afghanistan, poor Nooristan!"

I asked, "Did you know the mayor?"

"If you mean the martyred Kabir Khan, yes. Actually, he was the one who took me from my village when I was very young and gave me the job of a policeman for the municipality. In those days, there were just four or five people from Nooristan working in the municipality and I was one of them."

I introduced myself and told him that I was the son-in-law of that mayor. The minute he heard this, he became a totally different person.

My dear, then he narrated the tragic story of how the communists killed your father. I could not understand his words well because he became so emotional that he repeatedly mixed both languages, Dari and Nooristani.

From his patched side-pocket, he pulled out a colorful blue and red handkerchief, wiped his tears, and said, "The day the mayor was killed by the communists was the most tragic day of my life. I will never forget it. The communists killed him mercilessly. He was a God-fearing and faithful person. He was helpful and kind to everyone, rich or poor. Although I loved my job as a policeman, on that sinister day, I took off my uniform and left Kabul for Nooristan."

With tears flowing from his eyes, he continued, "After all, he had personally given me that uniform with his own holy hands. I will never forget his big fatherly smile, the day he put the gray police hat on my head. How could I forget it? He was my mayor. He was my mentor. He was my supporter. After that, I swore to God and to the Prophet that I shall fight till death to revenge my mayor. It is almost eight years since that unholy day."

He gave me some raisins and asked me two or three times if I needed any sugar or tea. These were the only things he could generously offer to the son-in-law of his mayor. What else did he have? I thanked him. I was in tears as well, thinking that this painful story is not only the story of a broken-hearted man but also of a broken-hearted nation.

My dear, I am sorry if I have made you sad.

The weather has become a little warmer. Soon, we will leave for the base of the mountain.

You Plan, God Decides

We are now at the base of the mountain, on the Pakistani side. Around 2 PM, we started from the Zaydak village. It took us about three hours to reach here. This place is like an open, flat field. It is now around 5 PM.

The gray mountains with their snow-capped peaks and long shadows make for a beautiful panorama. High mountains and daunting rock formations indicate that the real journey starts soon. The path so far has not been so bad. Sharp, slippery shale packed the trail, but we arrived safely. The donkeys and horses had some difficulty, but my horse, Kahaar, did well. The horse handler's little son did well too.

On the way, I asked the boy several times how he was feeling. Thank God, he was fine and actually was doing even better than his father. I did not ride for much of the trip due to the slippery shale nor did the boy. He was happy walking along throwing stones to the left and right, as if he were hunting small birds.

Now, Dearest, listen to what happened! Everybody was happy, the horsemen had seen to the horses, the bodyguards had cleaned their guns, the young boy was in a cheerful mood, the weather was perfect, the sun caressed our skin, the wind was blowing nicely, the streams of water were running calmly, tea had been freshly brewed, and Sandy and Andy had opened the first cans of sardines, when all of a sudden, four Pakistani border guards showed up. The same messenger, Rahman Shah, whom we had met yesterday was with them. They all wore border patrol uniforms and held old five-shot rifles.

The men started guessing that they might have brought bread and chicken for our foreign guests or they may have even brought us an urgent but good message. Rahman Shah had a written message for me from the border post below that stated: "Respected Khalili Sahib, as quickly as you can, you and your guests must return because the District Commissioner has sent an urgent message from Chitral that you cannot cross the border without further authorization."

You plan. God decides.

Back to Foot of Zaydak Pass

Tuesday, July 8

I won't go into the frustration and disappointment we experienced over the last two days. In short, due to bureaucracy and obstinacy, we were forced to return halfway to Chitral, to the border post at

Mardeen, and seek further permissions for our journey. We had permission from the military but the ISI wanted their say too. After sending out messengers this way and that, we were finally given permission to move again.

It is now 1:45 PM. My dear, thank God, with all the difficulties we have faced till now, we are once again at the spot where the Pakistani border guards forced us to turn back. Now I can joyfully see Afghanistan just behind the mountain in front of me. Once again, everyone is happy, the horses are neighing, the horsemen are laughing loudly, Dost is humming some song, the horse-handler's boy is happily sliding on the smooth stones, our foreign friends are full of smiles, and I can clearly see the beauty of the scenery around me.

I see two or three small birds with their vibrant wings, flying around and touching the vivid flowers with their tiny claws and beaks. I wish I were a poet like my father, or a painter like Michelangelo, to compose poems for this beautiful scene on a piece of paper, or paint a masterpiece of it on a canvas.

Perhaps, it is a beautiful scene for the horses too and must be like a grand adventure for them, especially the new ones, climbing on the snow clad peaks, crossing the blue rivers, and grazing on the wonderfully scented wild herbs and beautiful flowers caressed by the morning dew.

Dost, the convoy leader, told me, "We pray that we can find a deer somewhere around here to hunt."

I instantly said, "Even if you see a deer, do not kill it. Let it graze on the riverside, play with the flowers, watch the beauty of the horses, run with its tiny beautiful legs on the newly grown grass, and smell the sweet fragrance of nature."

Dost looked at me with a surprised look on his face and smiled in a special way. Maybe, he thought that I was not of sound mind and because of the lack of oxygen, I could not think straight; otherwise, why would I stop him from killing a deer. I read his mind quickly and without paying any attention to him, I tried to finish telling him about the images freely flowing through my mind, "Dost, we are all fighting for freedom. As long as we cannot appreciate the freedom of that deer, we may not be able to enjoy ours too." He laughed very loudly and maybe rightly.

The snow reminds me a lot of our little son Mahmud. Family, friends, and home are the sources that vibrate the soul when one feels happy, smells a flower, sees something beautiful, reads a piece of poetry, or hears an old song. It is natural that in happy and sad moments one remembers his or her loved ones.

The night has fully covered the mountains with a thick, black, featherless quilt. It looks like a black, pregnant queen waiting to give birth to her golden prince, the sun. I moved a little further away in order not to be disturbed by the sounds of the noisy horsemen and the guards who were hovering around. I just wanted to have a deep sleep wearing my combat jacket, my sweaters, and even my New Balance shoes.

Wish for me a good sleep tonight. For the time being, goodnight, my dear. God willing, I will write to you again tomorrow, hopefully from Afghanistan.

3

Home is Home—Nooristan Awaits

Wednesday, July 9
9:30 AM

My dear, after almost nine days of ups and downs, forward and backward, of good and bad, and sweet and sour experiences, after having been forced to return to where we started, I am now finally in the place where I always wish to be: Afghanistan. I am in my own land, with my own sun, my own stars, my own sky, my own mountains, my own valleys, my own villages, and, above all, with my own, poor people. We are in this tiny village for maybe an hour or so to relax our muscles.

I am writing to you from under bright rays of the sun and the blue skies. It seems the sun, the wind, tree, birds, the wild flowers, and all nature's things have joined to comfort my spirit and my body.

Last night, at 14,000 feet, I slept among the boulders and sharp rocks of a snow-clad mountain. I do not know why but a kind of repeated shortness of breath robbed me of sleep. It was maybe because of the lack of oxygen that I felt like a heavy rock lying on my chest.

I woke up at 3:30 AM. I felt some strange wind was reaching me from far away, carrying the sound of a howling wolf or the cry of a wounded animal, bringing a strange message from an unknown remote mountain to the mountain I was sleeping on. It sounded as though the mountains were talking to each other, or maybe it was the cry of a wounded tiger asking for help or perhaps the distant shouts a shepherd staving off a leopard's attack on his poor sheep.

I forced my eyes fully open, shaking my head, trying to listen carefully. I saw a rush of stars, maybe hundreds of them raining down toward me. I instantly closed my eyes and then heard noises all around me as if someone was pulling a sack of hay across a rough wooden surface. I jumped up thinking maybe there were snakes. I stood there for a moment and things went still, except for the sound of the wind moaning. I thought, "In this cold weather and at this elevation, snakes cannot move around." I decided to go back to sleep.

Anyway, I think I probably slept for two hours but, thank God, it was a deep sleep, which I needed very badly. When I opened my eyes, I heard Dost shouting at the men to wake up.

His calls broke the silence of the night and enveloped the cold and windy valley, "Azimullah, where are you? Put the saddle of Khalili Sahib on his horse. Naqeebulla, prepare the clothes. Jamal, hurry up! Mubarak, prepare our breakfast. Abdullah, fasten the belts of the horses. Meerza, be quick! Meraj, make the weapons ready. *Hala, hala, hala!*" (Quick, quick, quick!)

The first to reply was Azimullah: "I am awake, I am awake. We are already doing what you have just ordered."

I asked Dost, "By the way, is it your ten minutes or a real ten minutes?"

He could not answer and instead asked, "What is the difference?"

I laughed to myself and told him, "A real ten minutes is ten minutes but your ten minutes is one hour."

He replied, "I do not know what you mean by this? You confuse me, say it again."

I did not reply but just said that we were waiting for breakfast. My dear, do you know what they mean by breakfast? It means a loaf of dried bread and a glass of tea, with or without sugar.

A quick breakfast was served. The tea tasted smoky. By the way, I like that smoky smell, especially early in the morning. I called Azimullah's ten-year-old son, who told me his name was Naqeebulla, and asked him how he was feeling. He was not so lively this morning and did not even want to talk. It was too early for him to wake up. I told his father to put more sugar in his tea and said that his son could use my horse if he wanted to.

Hearing this, the boy looked at me and a beautiful smile spread across his face. His father did not pay attention to my words as he was busy saddling my horse.

Our convoy was finally ready and at 4:30 AM we departed. The pass proved easy. Thank God, I was feeling better than at any other time since we started on the trail, and was strong enough to climb the mountain pass in three hours. At 7:30 AM, I put my right foot on the top of the pass. I thought of Whitney who was not feeling well, whose foot was still sore, and who had vomited twice yesterday. I could see him coming up behind me and he was clearly feeling better, and he smiled and waved at me. Poor Sandy Gall, however, was suffering from high blood pressure and was moving very slowly.

My Dear, you know that walking at such altitude is much more difficult than at normal elevation. The horses were doing well, though, and little Naqeebulla had also perked up. Let me stop here and talk to you later while I reach the village ahead. We have to move on.

Village of Mateen, Nooristan

12:30 PM

We arrived here an hour ago. Climbing down was harder for me than climbing up. It took about three and half hours from the top of the pass to reach here. For the first half an hour we had to run down. The upper part was very steep and slippery. My knees hurt terribly. It was just as if someone was pushing me down. Luckily, the ground was dry, but it was very cold.

Since Dost had rushed ahead to reach here earlier than us, Mateen, the headman of the village and generous to a fault, had given him a big, clean white teakettle to prepare tea for us. Thank god, by the time we arrived, Dost had already made some tasty tea with less of a smoky smell than usual. We ate some nuts with it as well.

Well, now we are in a place that looks like a village from paradise. It is the first village of Afghanistan and also the first village on Nooristan's eastern border. It is indeed beautiful. The sky is a crystal-clear blue.

This small village looks like a deep green piece of emerald touching the very base of the silver, snow-clad mountain. The shadows of the willow trees are extremely beautiful. The fingers of the gentle winds gently move the yellow, purple, and white wild flowers. A kind of sweet scent of mixed spring and autumn comes from far away. Tiny, colorful birds with their small gleaming wings and long tails are flying around.

In our villages, in the north of Kabul, we call them *suttala, din-din-gak, saayera, qaf-khorak, gaw-qarcha, and gulsarak*. Ah, I can even see around me some walnut and apple trees too. They do not look so old. Maybe they were planted in the past six or seven years by people traveling through this village. Or perhaps by a kind of bird that we call *aka*, a beautiful black and white bird with a long tail. People say that these birds collect wild walnuts in the neighboring mountains, bring them to their own territory, and hide them under the earth. Maybe they hide them in order to eat during the winter. So, what seems to happen is that they forget the location of these hidden walnuts and next year you can find beautiful tiny walnut saplings involuntarily planted by these aka birds. Whenever I see a walnut tree in Nooristan, I remember this lovely story of the aka, or the walnut planters.

I see children playing around here. Not many animals can be seen. This village has no more than thirty small houses. The people are very poor and have very limited food to eat. They live off the few animals they possess. Since it is very mountainous, the villagers have only small pockets of land. They get essential goods such as tea, sugar, and matches from Pakistan.

Besides lacking the basic necessities, they have no shop, no school, no doctor, no medicine, no hospital, no clinic, no bakery, no grocery store, no barber shop, and nothing else. Despite all the nos and nothings, I love it.

The village is named after the headman, Mateen. He has lived here for many years and has always been helpful to the many fighters who pass through here. He always has a big smile on his toothless face. He is about six feet tall, very thin, with a black and white beard, and, when he smiles, you see he is toothless. He wears black Nooristani pants and a long shirt. He has a beautiful black *buzi*, a goatskin cloak, upon his shoulder. In his left pocket, he has a big handkerchief. Ah, it is very colorful. His moustache is carefully trimmed. He wears an old lapis ring on a finger of his left hand. He has on *moza*, or black Russian winter boots on his feet, which look older than his ring. I think he probably dyes his hair with the natural dyes of walnut leaves or other natural herbs. He has a wife, but I do not know how many children he has.

I talked to old, kind Mateen for a little while and he is still in front me with a jug of streamwater in his hand, serving the guests. It seems to me as if I am watching a film about Ancient Greece or Rome, where a tall old man serves white wine to hungry, exhausted warriors. I asked him about the name of the mountain close to me. He said that it is called *Kafir Kotal*, or Infidel Pass.

Mohammad told me: "Hundreds and hundreds of resistance fighters have taken shelter in this village for a night or two, going either to the north of Afghanistan or to Chitral, in Pakistan. Five years ago, when the Freedom Fighters started to use this route, he used to help by giving them food and shelter. After that, people started calling this village the village of Mateen."

Mateen came to me and requested that we stay for lunch.

I humbly said to him, "If you allow us, we will move on. We do not want to impose on your hospitality; there are so many of us."

"Please stay," he replied. "You have foreign friends with you and when they are in our country they should be taken good care of. We consider our guests to be sinless friends of God. The Almighty has sent for me his friends. It is good that you all have come through my poor village."

I agreed that we would stay and eat with Mateen and some villagers.

This is the kindness of the common people of Afghanistan toward the freedom fighters and their guests. For now, goodbye. I will write soon.

Village of Peshawrak

Eastern Nooristan
Thursday, July 10
7:00 AM

My dear, yesterday we left the village of Mateen at 3 PM and after three hours of easy walking, we reached this village, called Peshawrak. It is my fourth visit to this place.

The path was long, very wide, flat, and endowed with beautiful streams of water. The long valley was wide enough and I could see the breast of the blue sky with a patchwork of small, thin, white clouds moving from north to south.

The people of these villages look the same as in other parts of Nooristan. The elders are poor but cooperative, the children are unclean but adorable, and the men are jobless but content. The women wear long black dresses and carry baskets made of goat or sheep felt, tied neatly to their backs. Sometimes they carry their children in those baskets but mostly they carry wood or other necessities.

The streams of water flowing under the cold shadows of mulberry, poplar, cedar, pine and other trees look as beautiful as ever.

But let me tell you something that happened on the way, something I had experienced never before. Haji Aziz, who is a commander of eastern Nooristan, our so-called State of Nooristan, and his deputy, Zikria, welcomed me and summoned me to their office. The furniture was typical of Nooristani style and had seven chairs and a table.

They were nice people, but they did not know what to do with us and did not know anything about border protection. They wanted the foreign guests to have Nooristani identification cards or a visa for their State of Nooristan. They were gullible and innocent people who did not understand what to do with foreigners. Both men were illiterate.

These two believed that they were part of a real government, the State of Nooristan, and a foreigner needed a visa. I told them I would talk to their bosses. The problem here is that, due to security reasons, I could not disclose my true identity. I asked for a meeting with their superior officer.

Therefore, we went to the head office, which was the only real office in all of Nooristan. There were some small Nooristani chairs and two old tables in the room. The head officer was alone at his desk. He checked the papers we had obtained from their representative office in Chitral. Despite recognizing me, the officer told my guards that the foreigners should carry Nooristani ID cards. But he did not cause trouble for us, and we were allowed to move on.

I was happy and thanked God as we left the area. We stopped in a field next to the river after an hour or so to rest a little and have some tea. It was a beautiful, small field with a network of streams flowing all around. Although I was not feeling ill, I did not eat anything or drink any tea of water. And surprising for me, I did not even feel like talking. I lit a pipe filled with tobacco that belonged to Andy. After one or two puffs I gave up on that also.

As I am writing to you now, I once again see the black lines of women, carrying their small children in old woolen baskets. They go up to the beautiful mountain nearby to collect wood or tend their goats. At this moment, I am thinking of our little son, Majdood. If he were here, every morning you would put him in your basket and take him along with the goats, horses, rams, and chickens up to the mountains. How happy would he be in the basket? Naughty little Majdood, as we both know, would definitely jump out of the basket and throw himself right into the river.

Bargi Mataal Valley of Shapo

Friday, July 11

It is now early morning. Listen to what happened yesterday.

From Peshawrak village, we arrived at Bargi Mataal, which is the center of the so-called State of Nooristan. This village is the headquarters of Maulavi Afzal, the Head of the State. He is a follower of sorts of a new Islamic trend called *Panj Peeree*, or *Salafi*, which is a religious commodity imported recently from Pakistan. His second-in-command is called Akbar.

Neither of them looked to me like well-mannered Afghans. Both tried to show off, especially when they recognized we had foreigners with us. Their insistence that their government was the real government of Afghanistan made me understand they are very naïve. They stated that eastern Nooristan is a kind of de facto capital of the whole of Afghanistan. They both treated me with respect, but they were both trying to ask me something that I could not agree to. They wanted me to recognize their small town as the official seat of power of the government of Afghanistan. This was absolute rubbish but I had to deal with them nonetheless. Whatever the case, even that was not as bad as what I must tell you now.

After leaving the office of commander, and rejoining my convoy, Nooristani men surrounded us, with Akbar, the deputy commander with them. Strange enough, there were also three young Arabs amongst them. One of the Arabs approached me and in broken English asked my name, where I was going, and pointed to my foreign friends, asking who they were. Without offering any reply I asked them to accompany me to the office of Afzal, their leader. The group of men, including the three Arabs followed.

I spoke in a loud, booming voice because it was too much for me to listen to these Arab foreigners asking me questions in my own country, questions that were not theirs to ask.

I angrily told Afzal, "A Nooristani can ask me any question they want, they can stop me, even shout at me. But I will not countenance an Arab asking me questions such as who I am, where I am going, and who my friends are."

I pointed to the three Arabs and furiously asked Afzal, "Who are these three Arabs to question me?"

The Arabs did not understand what I was saying to Maulavi Afzal, and surprisingly, in front of him and his deputy, they started once again to ask me impertinent questions. "Why have you allowed these non-believers to enter Afghanistan? Why are they meeting Commander Massoud? Why does Commander Massoud have contact with non-believers? Where are your papers? Which political party do you belong to?"

"Who are you?" I demanded of the Arabs.

They said that they were friends of Afzal. Immediately, it came to my mind that they must be Salafi Muslims, who have come here to be with Maulavi Afzal, who follows more or less the same kind of Islamic trend.

I could not believe these Arabs were interrogating me about my papers—in front of Afzal and Akbar.

I angrily repeated their questions to Afzal. "Who are these Arabs? Where are their papers? Who has allowed them to come here? What country are they from?" Afzal said nothing.

Oh, you can imagine what feelings were boiling up inside of me as I listened to these young foreigners asking me those insulting questions. I have never been against Arabs and never had any good or bad feelings about them. This was the first time I had been confronted by foreigners in my own country. I could not hold my temper.

I turned back to Maulavi Afzal and began to use very undiplomatic language with the poor man and his deputy in front of the Arabs. I used words like "slaves," "liars," and "traitors" for them. "You are insulting the good name of Nooristan and the Nooristani people. I cannot say you should not have friends, but they should just be your friends and nothing more."

Afzal and his deputy, Akbar, quietly held their tempers in check, but at last the old leader looked into my angry eyes and quietly said, "Young man, be careful of the words you use with me. I hope you understand what I mean, because I understood what you meant. Am I clear?"

I could see the strength and dignity of this man, and I knew he was being very serious. I had been more angry and aggressive than

I should have been. Despite the fact that we were in his area, and he was clearly more powerful than us, he held his anger in check, and did not make the situation more difficult.

At that moment, my men called us to come outside.

I looked at Afzal and said, "Yes, Commander, I understand you very well," nodded at him and turned and left the room.

Sandy and the others stayed with Afzal. I gathered the men and instructed them to be alert and as ready as possible in case some trouble started. I told our security chief to have all our weapons ready, and not to allow anyone to touch any of our possessions. The situation was tense, and I knew if Afzal wanted to stop us, we could do nothing.

At this point, I fortunately discovered that the local people surrounding us had recognized me. They interjected in kind tones, apologizing for not recognizing me. They said that the Arabs were just guests, nothing else, and added that the things the Arabs asked from me were wrong. They admitted that it was not their business to ask the questions they had asked.

In the meantime, my men advised me that now was not the time to start a useless battle, and it was better for us to move on without creating any problems for Afzal and his Arabs and not give them a pretext to create any problems for us. They also told me that some of the villagers were not at all happy to see Arabs in their valleys acting like their bosses, but that they were helpless.

I talked to the people for a few minutes and made them understand that it is not good for the people of Nooristan to endure such a situation. I thanked them all for their kind words. Then Sandy and the others came out of the office. Sandy assured me the matter was solved. Maulavi Afzal also came to me and we talked in a nice manner, which helped me calm down and made my mood brighter. He also mentioned my father and your father. We shook hands and hugged each other.

I thought I should say a few words to the Arabs before we left this area. I called them over and said, "Be careful. Afghanistan is a different and difficult country. We are all Muslims but when the questions of land, liberty, and pride are at stake, we are Afghans. If I used harsh words against you, it was because, all of a sudden, you asked questions of me that were not yours to ask. Talk to Afghans as if you are their respected guests, and never talk to them as if you are their disrespected bosses."

Oh, my dear, do not worry, these things happen in wartime, especially when you are fighting against a Godless enemy. I am sorry for talking about this incident with the Arabs instead of telling you about the beauty of Nooristan, your father's land. I laughed when I thought that if you were here, you would have stopped me from using bad words with those foreigners. I hope you and the boys are well.

By the way, I am writing down these adventures from the roadside tea-tent of Abdul Jabar. He is a good man. He told me he would get married soon. He is around 22 years old. He did not know his age, I just guessed. The girl with whom he will marry is one of his cousins. I asked him what he really wants to buy for her if he could.

He scratched his neck and said, "A radio."

I laughed loudly and asked him, "Why a radio?"

He responded, "*Laa laa* [big brother], it is very difficult for you to understand. If she had a radio, she would sit on a big rock and listen to Hindi songs without any worry or problem. The freedom fighters only know boom boom and that is it."

I laughed to myself at his description of gunfire but I knew that he was not totally right because this is a war and with war, you will always have boom boom. Hopefully we can end it sooner than later.

Deeper Valleys, Higher Mountains

Tea Tent. Papruk Valley
11:45 AM

We are now in a beautiful village called Pul-i-Rustam, which is located in the more beautiful valley of Papruk.

It took us a good five hours of easy walking to reach here. The path was not difficult. In fact, it was easy for us, easier for little Naqeebulla boy, and maybe, easiest for the horses. We are now having a cup of tea in a so-called teahouse.

There were two so-called teahouses near each other on the way here and we stopped in one to have a cup of tea. The word "teahouse" should not deceive you. Sometimes local people call it a restaurant, or even a hotel, but in reality, it is a very large rock or boulder with some sort of old fabric hanging from it. Underneath that, you usually find a small cave, with hardly enough room for four or five people.

This one has several teapots, a large stone cooker, and a tall, self-trained Nooristani cook, who makes tea and prepares only one kind of meal. No spices, no salt, no pepper, no cooking oil, or any kind of vegetables can be found. What a lucky cook, what an unlucky customer! He has only meat and water to cook boiled goat or beef. The cook has absolute power in his makeshift cave. The unwritten rule is that the customer can never criticize the quality or quantity of the food, because the man does not have any other choice.

Thank God, they are kind by nature and hospitable by tradition, otherwise, the poor hungry customer would starve. Do not even think of any kind of drink except water. And never think about waiting for a waiter to provide with you a menu, dessert, or tea because the cook himself shows you what he has in his crude, handmade stone cooker and that is your menu for the day. This is what they call a hotel, a teahouse, or a restaurant. It is the same all over Nooristan.

In order to get a reaction from the Nooristani cook, I explained to him how many dishes they serve in restaurants in other countries and even told him about their large menus.

He simply said, "They are greedy. Our stomach is not like a *gow-khana* [stable] to be filled to capacity. God does not like the one who eats too much. If you want to be healthy, never try to shovel in more food and never be a stomach worshiper. If you eat more, you waste your time every hour by running to the toilet."

Whatever the case, we love such cooks very much because, in a war situation and on the roughest mountaineous roads of Nooristan, there is nobody except God and these poor teahouses or caves to offer us a cup of tea, a piece of bread, or a slice of boiled meat. This is why, the minute we see a cave-type teahouse, we rush like children running to a toyshop.

Anyway, after an hour or less of traveling on an old, deserted, and bombed government road, we reached here. There are two small, unclean cave-type rooms, which serves as a military office. Luckily, the officer in charge has allowed his office to be used as a teahouse too. It was oddly called Bahrain. I thought that maybe one of Maulavi Afzal's Arab guests, could have come from Bahrain and helped to make this room.

When I entered the room, a skinny young man, with a full beard and shaved mustache, stood up from behind his old Nooristani desk to greet me. He had a .303 sniper rifle leaning on his old, broken Nooristani table. He was a good man with a pleasant demeanor.

Once his eyes had discerned my foreign friends standing behind the door, he said, "Call them in here."

While I told our men to call Andy, the officer took out from his pocket a small, old, round silver box of *naswaar*, or chewing tobacco, which had a palm size mirror on one side of it. He proudly checked his blond hair, blue eyes, Nooristani hat, thick yellowish beard and shaved mustache. Standing next to Andy, the Polish-Briton, this blond-haired, blue-eyed, and clean-clothed Nooristani seemed more foreign than any of my foreign guests did.

The young Nooristani showed very good hospitality and manners. I think he did not know how to read but, as he diligently checked our papers, he pretended as proudly as he could. I loved this pretense very much. Then he shook hands with others too and started to give a kind of lecture on the great State of Nooristan, as well as on the power of their leader and other things besides.

After giving another shorter speech about his own talents, the best thing he did was to offer us some tea.

By chance, my dear, I found that he had worked in your home in Kabul and in the house of your uncle, Malik Khan, in the Kunduz Province. The minute he found that I am your husband, he stood up instantly and, in order to show his pleasure, he put more sugar in my cup and shouted, "Why did you not introduce yourself earlier? Why did I ask for your papers? Your wife is a Nooristani and you do not need any papers in Nooristan. You are our son-in-law. You shamed me in front of your friends."

I thanked him and he started to reveal the hidden words of his heart. "We cannot go to Kabul to work now. The communists hate us. The poor Nooristani has no place there. We had some generals from Nooristan in the past working in Kabul. The mayor of Kabul was a Nooristani and the Nooristanis were even close to the king.

The communists killed so many good Nooristanis. Our world has become so dark and our dreams have grown even darker. No longer do good Nooristanis live in Kabul; there are only those Nooristanis who have sold their names, dignity, and faith to the godless communists."

I quoted a saying of the Holy Prophet, "'*Have hope in your heart and light in your dreams.*' God willing, the time will come that you will once again go to Kabul to work there."

* * *

After almost an hour, we left there and traveled three hours to reach this spot. As we traveled the climate grew warmer and warmer, and soon it felt like full summer. I remembered that back in October 1983, almost three years now, when I was traveling through this area, I fell from my horse and injured my back. By a strange coincidence, this time, when passing through this same area, we came upon a fresh water spring. I was hasty to taste the cold water and bent quickly to drink. At that moment, I hit my head on a branch, and, instantly, blood began to pour from the cut into the water. Everyone was worried and gathered around. But I knelt and put my head into the spring deep enough to cover the cut. The water was so cold that in less than two minutes the bleeding has stopped. Thank God, this time I was not badly hurt.

This valley has a deep river of blue water. It gives off a cool breeze, which clears our lungs. Otherwise, it would be worse than the blistering heat of Jalalabad. The mulberries are ripe. Like goats, we stretched up, and one by one, and picked the mulberries from the branches.

The horses were tired. The horsemen, wherever they found water, they would throw some on their horses' testicles so that they would not scab from the heat. The only horse that did not need water thrown on its testicles was Whitney's mare.

Right now, I am next to the Papruk River. I have written about this river before in my notes to you from last year. We will be here until 3 PM, before departing and traveling for however long we can. Then we will stop and stay there for the night.

Andy had instant noodles with him and he went off to get some boiling water. Without the addition of meatballs and *quroot* (dried strained yoghurt balls), how could it be that tasty? He returned and seemed to enjoy eating the noodles.

Mullah Dost, the leader of my convoy, is lively and whatever comes to his mouth, he uses against the Nooristani people. I told him, "Be careful. Show some respect. My wife is from Nooristan."

He stopped and looked at me. "Your wife is a different sort of Nooristani."

"No, no, you are wrong. She is the same as the others."

My horsemen chimed in, "She is different because she must have learned a lot from Khalili Sahib by now."

Here, I thought all of them wanted to hear something new, and I instantly said, "In fact I have learned from her how to be kind at home and patient outside the home."

Mohammad Dost nodded and said, "I do not think so. If a man would ever learn anything from a woman the world would collapse."

I took a tablet of aspirin last night and another one right now. Every three hours, I am probably going to have one tablet. The boys are good; the horses seem strong; and Sandy looks great, Whitney is tired; Noel does not have an appetite; Andy is well and the Afghan cameramen are looking good. I cannot eat meat and when I hear the name of sardines, I become nauseous.

Anyway, my Dear, we go on. I miss you and the boys.

Papruk Village Ends

6:30 PM

Papruk is dotted with quaint old homes with small wooden doors and windows. The walls are made of mud, river-rounded stones, and a kind of hard blackish wood. Most of the doors and windows have some beautiful artwork painted and carved in pre-Islamic Nooristani style. The paintings are mostly of flowers and the heads of animals, or maybe of their ancient gods. The Nooristanis were converted to Islam 97 years ago by the Afghan king, Abdur Rahman. Before their conversion to Islam, they had their own beliefs and their own ways of worship.

The architectural style here is not found in other parts of Afghanistan. The walls are built strongly to resist the extremely cold and windy mountaineous weather. Although the village itself is very beautiful, inside, the houses are very unclean because the people are poor. Climbing up and down to the village is extremely hard. You have to go up and down many times before you reach the top of the top.

The people make their living through limited agriculture and animal husbandry. They cultivate corn and some other simple beans. They cannot grow wheat here. They have several types of fruit tree, but their number is limited to only two or three kinds. They make their own clothes out of goats' wool and goatskin, like the ancient Greek and Macedonian soldiers who invaded this part of the world, over two thousand years ago.

They have many kinds of goats, sheep, cattle, and a small number of horses. For the Nooristani, the King Goat is the best breed of goat. They make their own Nooristani-style cheese and their own variety of quroot.

Women work in the fields and men take care of the animals and children. They wear Nooristani clothes, which they make themselves. There are no shops. Here, people have no school, no hospital, no clinics, no roads, no grocery stores, no postman, no bakery, no barber, no butcher, no electricity, no proper water channels, no transportation, no telephones, and no administration. People also do not expect much.

Anyway, we had to climb to reach the village and pass through it. It was easier to go up but the downward parts of the track were very difficult since our path was flooded due to heavy rain. The horses were moving with great difficulty. We used them on the way up but, on the way down, they actually used us in order to steady themselves. It was indeed a difficult job.

Since we could not stay in the village, we descended in order to find shelter at the bottom of the mountain, but there we found nothing but boulders, large rocks, and sharp stones. The first thing we did was to accommodate our exhausted horses in between the rocks, next to the river. Then we had to find better places amongst the boulders for ourselves to stay the night. For that purpose, we had to first move the rocks and boulders to make small, flat spots to lay out our sleeping bags and rucksacks. The horsemen and guards helped us too.

After doing all these necessary things, we all craved for nothing but tea. Our men believe that tea is a divine herb, which is essential fuel for a human being on a hard journey. One mistake they made was misplacing the sugar. I jokingly told them that if tea is the divine herb, then sugar is the divine sweet, and misplacing it must be a divine sin. Although our tea was infused with a smoky smell and was without sugar, it tasted divine.

We are now sitting next to the boulders and enjoying the last cups of our deliciously divine tea. The weather is getting darker. Hope to God that it does not rain because there is no place to take shelter here. Among us, only Whitney has a small tent. It is a tent for two but if it rains, all eight of us may go into his tent. We Afghans can do that but can the foreigners?

One of the horses had slipped free from his rope. A Nooristani woman wearing a long black dress and red pants, took great offence at our runaway steed and, with two of her neighbors, began throwing stones at the frightened animal, all the while screaming in Nooristani. She was screaming in the Nooristani language, hitting the horse repeatedly and asking why this horse was free. Everybody was alerted. While the horsemen were trying to help, two more Nooristani women entered the battleground by throwing bigger sized stones at the poor horse and at the poorer horsemen. One of the horsemen was badly hit by a rock thrown by one of the women. What a scene it was!

In the end, thank God the horsemen caught the escaped horse and stopped the women from throwing more stones. Except for the one horseman hit on the head, no one else, including the horse, was hurt. Dost and the other horsemen were sweating profusely and cursing the women.

I entered the discussion and took the women's side, by saying, "The Nooristani women had every possible reason to stone your runaway horse because it was eating their grass and other vegetation. This poor woman had the right to stone you, even to death, instead of stoning the poor horse. This time, a Nooristani woman attacked your horse with stones; next time a Nooristani man will kill you with a gun."

Later, they told me that the horsemen were jokingly saying that, thank God, they do not have a Nooristani wife as Khalili *Sahib* does, otherwise they would already have been stoned to death. I liked their joke, by the way.

A better tea, without the smoky taste, was served. Thanks to Andy, this time we also fortunately had tinned-cheese and travel biscuits.

My dear, just a minute ago, I saw a mirror. Do not ask me to write how I look. I look more than horrible. The skin on my cheeks and on my nose has come off and looks awful. My head is injured. My beard is dirty and full of everything, even dead flies. My hair is indescribable. My eyebrows have become at least four times heavier than before with dirty mud. My lips are swollen. My eyes look like black eggs. My eyelashes are sticking to each other like spiderwebs and my ears seem like two frozen mice.

God knows what you would say if you could see me. Tomorrow we climb the second highest mountain pass in Nooristan.

Anger Appears, Wisdom Disappears

Saturday, July 12
11:30 AM

Yellow, red, violet, blue, purple, white, green, brown, crimson, orange, pink, jasmine, matt gold, and dark silver are the colors of the flowers that my horse was walking through from early morning until now. Charming scents and sweet fragrances are emitted by these wild herbs and beautiful flowers.

We started out early this morning. The first hour was extremely difficult, the path was rocky, icy, and slippery. It was very hard on the horses too. The sharper rocks and boulders and some unpredictable cliffs forced us to walk very slowly and carefully but after an hour or so, the path became easier and I was even able to ride my horse from time to time.

Each horseman tried to be soft on his horse. Donkeys were doing better mainly because they went the same speed from the beginning to the end except when they were passing the man-made snow bridges. These snow-bridges were not easy to cross for the horses either. At this time of the year, the weather becomes slightly warmer and blocks the snowfall down from the top of the mountain to the bottom and into the rivers. These snow bridges are made by locals or by passing travelers.

On the way, we encountered the sad scene of refugee families, along with their small children, on foot, on donkeys, and on mules, leaving Afghanistan for Pakistan. They were all from the north. I did not have anything to share with these destitute war-scarred children but the two remaining sweets Andy had given me. The pure crystal-clear water of this area seems like it has come directly from paradise. The weather was tolerably cold.

* * *

It is early in the morning. The teahouse we are in now consists of two relatively large tents but it has only boiled soup with camel meat on offer. I have started to read a book called *Lord of Khyber*, written by Andrew Singer, and if there is any time left, I will read more but I do not think I will.

The weather is gorgeous. It is like a generous perfume seller who offers his perfumes for free. The only thing you should do is to tell the wind what kind of flower you like the most and it delivers the fragrance right to your heart. The water streams whisper nature's sweetest melody. The light of the sun feels so good as if it is blending every element of beauty at its disposal, in order to make this valley into a fantastic theater, for the pleasure of the whole universe.

The men have laid out all around in different places. On three sides, there are high mountains. The horses are grazing and from the far-off *baanda* (shepherd's hut in a summer pasture), smoke can be seen dancing upward in beautiful circles. I hear the twittering songs of two very colorful small birds, which I have never seen before in my life. Their beaks and claws are crimson and their wings have dozens of flower-like colors. They both look the same, sitting very close to one another on the branch of a wild bush, but I cannot tell which one is singing.

The sky is so very blue. It has the deep blue color of Lapis lazuli. Over the mountains on the left, some thin, silver-colored clouds are slowly descending lower and lower, touching the rocks and kissing the upper branches of the pine trees. Beautiful multicolored goats and their young have come nearer and are now grazing next to the horses. They look like Majdood, Mahmud, and Ghezal, my little niece. Beautiful!

Ah yes, besides the horses, we also have five donkeys. They have rusted bells dangling from their gray necks.

In cultures around the world, the horse is more important than the donkey. We even discriminate among animals. We think that donkeys are stupid and dirty but horses are smart and holy. If you say to someone that you are like a donkey, he might kill you, but if you call someone a horse, he may thank you. I am reminded of this little verse by Sa'di, the great Persian poet:

However rude the poor donkey is,
Since he carries my load, he is the dearest.

I like it because it is only Sa'di, the great poet of the 14th century, who praises the poor donkey. The mountain pass that we will climb tomorrow has the elevation of about 4,600 meters.

I called Dost and asked him what he had prepared for lunch. He said that he had acquired a goat to slaughter. I instantly shouted back to ask whether it was a King Goat or a regular goat. He answered that it was a regular goat. I smiled thinking that a poor goat is going to be slaughtered, whether it be a King Goat or a regular one.

2:30 PM

Our lunch is not ready yet. It is bad because we are starving and it is good because I have time to talk to the travelers going back and forth, to the horsemen, tea-tent owners, our foreign friends and, more importantly, my beloved, to write to you.

To satisfy our hunger pangs a little, we ate some almonds and raisins. The wind has become stronger, and drop by drop, it has started to rain. Still we are waiting for lunch.

Little Naqeebulla is sitting far away from us, leaning his slim back against a large rock. Maybe he is dreaming of one day becoming a king or a rich man and returning to the same place with hundreds of horses and hunting dogs, sitting on the same boulder, and instructing his soldiers, bodyguards, and butlers to prepare food. In his dreams, he is also probably ordering his cooks to take care of his father first, and only then serving the other exhausted horsemen and his friends.

Who knows, maybe his dreams will come true one day and why not? God has created dreaming free for the rich or poor, king or cobbler, man or woman, you or me. God is just and generous.

Let me stop writing here and dream that one day you and I shall be able to witness freedom in our land and the prosperity of our people. Dreaming is free.

6:10 PM

Raaz, the owner of the tea-tent, called me, "Laa laa [big brother], have you had your tea? Without waiting for my answer, he poured a cup of jet black tea and gave it to me. He is very kind and helpful.

Two hours ago, it hailed very intensely. None of us had seen anything like it before. Even the tough Nooristani farmers and shepherds were running to find shelter. The hail fell hard and fast, with the white stones flying down in blinding streaks as fast a lightening.

The horse owners began to get very worried. Except for the donkeys, everybody else, even the horses, ran to find some sort of shelter. While I was trying to find my own nook, I almost fell into the river. Thankfully, Dost he grabbed me just as I was about to fall.

A bitter chill descended and the wind began to rage. Shivering, I whipped out my sleeping bag and got into it up to my neck.

I asked a Nooristani, "What do you think about the pass? Will it be blocked by this hail or do you think we can climb it tomorrow?"

While trying to see into the distance, he put his hand in a straight line over his eyebrows almost as if he was trying to shelter his eyes from the hail and looked toward the pass without saying anything for a minute or so. I laughed a little because in that weather the pass was too far away for a person with the best eyesight or even with the best binoculars to see.

Still, he kept saying that I should allow him a moment to try to see the pass. "Yes, now I can see the thin clouds over it."

While he looked like an untrained soldier saluting with his left hand, he proudly added, "Yes, yes, you can go. The pass is not blocked and will not be blocked."

I cannot say for sure, but it seemed impossible for him to see that far.

The tea-tent owner quipped, "With or without binoculars, for a non-Nooristani, it will take a long time to reach the top of the pass whether he goes fast or slow."

Obey Nature

Sunday, July 13
7:30 AM

We are in the same place at the foot of the same mountains in Papruk. We could not move forward as it rained intensely the whole night and it is still raining. Last night the neighing of the horses did not allow me to sleep for more than an hour. The wind was slapping the rain on my face so hard that it made me jump. The river became noisy, muddy, wavy, and angry, pushing the big rocks one over another. The cracking sounds of rocks in the hands of powerful waves added to the disruption of my sleep. The forceful rainfall sounded like hundreds of wolves howling with hunger, or dozens of tigers delivering their babies simultaneously.

My Dear, I hope that the rain finally leaves us alone but most likely, it will remain only a hope.

5 PM

The rain continues unabated. There are no weather forecasts here. Once or twice, I called some Nooristanis and asked them how they predict and forecast the weather. They look into the sky, measure the thickness of the clouds in their own way and say whatever comes to their mind.

After asking a relatively old refugee from the north to predict the weather for me, he pointed to the thick clouds and said, "If the cloud is black, rising from the direction of Mecca, expect a really heavy storm, but if it is from the other directions, expect a softer rain."

To prove his theory of forecasting he recited a poem from somebody:

If the dark cloud rises from Mecca,
Wait for the storm and flood
If the King is not just,
Wait for killing and blood.

Although I had heard this verse before, I loved the way he recited the poem and the passionate way in which he believed in it. Forecasting the weather fortunately brought to mind some poetry dedicated to the subject of clouds and rain. He asked me to recite something but requested that I should not recite anything against the beauty of the rain.

I asked him why.

He answered, "Because rain is the mercy of God. It is like the tears of Jacob for the love of his son, Joseph. It is our friend from the cradle to the grave."

Despite the rain giving me much grief over the past few days, I composed a short poem to make him happy.

O, the Rain,
O, the tears of Jacob,
Come gently, drop by drop.
Bring to my heart,
Fragrance of the lillies,

Aroma of the wild mint,
Smell of the wings of cranes.
O, the mercy of God,
Touch my chest,
Wet my breast
Feel my heart,
Caress my soul.

I wish poetry could stop the rain. Instead, it continues heavier than before. As my horseman said, "It is just like a strong whip on the weaker hip."

Anyway, I took advantage of being stuck under the heavy rain and had the chance to speak to a group of fighters from Yaftal, in Badakhshan Province, who were on their way to Pakistan. They had come a long way, at least 15 days' walk.

All these freedom fighters wore ancient, patched clothes. Their shoes had more repairs than their hats and shirts. Their complexions were yellowish, or they looked yellowish to me. They had very slim bodies, long beards, and cracked lips. Their stomachs must have been half-empty, no doubt deprived of proper nourishment for days.

Most of them knew me. We talked for about an hour about Afghan politics, religion, and even the economic situation of the different resistance groups of the North. I thanked them for talking to me and wished them good luck.

4

Eagles Soar Higher

It is now about 5:45 in the evening but thank God, the rain is not as heavy as it was. I did not tell you that we had our lunch very late. We boiled a certain amount of rice and ate it. It had the worst possible taste but at least it filled my stomach.

Sandy Gall shared his *Seven Oceans* biscuits. He said they are packed with energy and power. God knows. But Sandy is in his sixties and has energy and power enough to take this journey with us. It is these small things, like the way they have stocked tiffin or snack foods for the journey, which remind me how the foreigners add their flavor to our journey.

After lunch, I met some Pashtoon fighters traveling from Pakistan to their home province of Kunduz. The Chief Commander in their area is named Arif Khan. They were equipped with a kind of Chinese Kalashnikov. They were in a hurry and said they would proceed as fast as possible to reach their home. I asked why such haste?

"This is a Holy War, the sooner we beat the enemy of God, the better," one of them replied.

In the north, there are mainly Tajiks, Uzbeks, Hazaras, and Turkmen ethnic groups. Thank God, so far in the war against the Soviets, we are ethnically united. I hope it remains so. When discussing the subject of Afghan unity a few days ago, Whitney said, "In the war against foreigners, you have always been united, but in peace time you have lacked unity."

Another fighter, about 20 years old, sitting there, said he believed that irrespective of the West or the world staying to help us, the resistance would continue to fight until the enemy has left Afghanistan.

I said that there was no doubt we need help from the West, but first we need the support of our own people and the determination and strong will of our fighters. The West is not our cousin. Everyone is the cousin of his own interest. If they give us something which will empower us to destroy the enemy on the ground and in the air, it is good. After all, we share a common enemy.

I asked them if they knew some *landi*, or Pashto war poetry, to recite for me. The youngest one, who was 20 years old or younger, recited a really beautiful one.

O, my beloved,
May the time come
That you and I take the gun
Go to the front, hand in hand
To free our land.

They call this type of four-lined, Pashto love poems landi. They are composed mostly by unknown girls, separated from their beloved ones, or poor mothers bewailing the loss of their children, in war or in peacetime. What else do they have to fill their hearts but their soothing poems?

Whitney's condition has worsened. He is nauseated, suffers from cough and cold, but he is still, thank God, strong-willed. He is not complaining much until he is asked about how he feels. His coughing is really loud. Maybe this is because he is tall and the long journey from his chest to his throat amplifies his cough. If a tall American like Whitney suffers so much on this trip, pray for a short Afghan like me.

Valley of Paroon

Monday, July 14
4:20 PM

We are in the first village of the Paroon Valley and finally out of the reach of the rain. It took us eleven hours of difficult walking from the time we left behind the 14,000-foot high mountain pass of Papruk and reached the small village of *Neetee*. As usual, we started at 5:00 AM on our long and difficult journey. I took a tablet of vitamin B-1 before we started out. The weather was cold but, thank God, the rain had finally stopped. Even though I was wearing my field jacket, I also wore my overcoat. For the first half an hour I rode my horse, but then the trail became very steep, with slippery, narrow tracks and dangerous cliffs. I had to walk, leading the horse. I was scared.

The horses were frightened also. The donkeys were not doing well either. For them it was harder to come down than go up the trails. Two donkeys and three horses fell off the trail and wounded themselves badly.

The horsemen were trying their best to help their horses with whatever travel tactics they knew, but the pass is so steep and the tracks so slippery that they could not do much. Once I tried to hold the tail of my horse while climbing the pass but that did not work. At another point, some of the horsemen tried unloading cargo from their horses and donkeys to help their animals progress, but even that did not work. Their legs trembled from the fear of steep cliffs and extreme exhaustion.

I watched one of the horses fall like a child's toy, tumbling down three hundred meters of rocky cliff. The poor horseman, like a wounded cat, raced downhill after the poor beast. He was injured before he reached the animal.

The steady flow of refugees, coming down from the pass made it more difficult for those climbing up. We had to tuck ourselves tight against the corners of these dangerous cliffs in order to give way to the downward passage of assorted refugees, fighters, and animals. With the slightest wrong movement, they could easily lose their balance and fall to their death.

One of the horsemen told me that sometimes the woebegone, exhausted horse would rather commit suicide than continue. They willingly throw themselves over the edge to die and be released from the hardships of the pass. This may not be true but when you are there yourself and see with your own eyes the horrible condition of the animals with heavy loads climbing up or down on dangerously narrow, rocky tracks, you accept this theory of suicidal horses and donkeys. Let us call them the victims of the mountains.

In contrast, I saw children of six or seven walking on this mountain in such high spirits that I could not believe my eyes. Two of them held their mother's hands, supporting her with each step. I thought she was blind but, in fact, their mother was so frightened of heights, she could not bear to open her eyes.

Even more jubilant than her two children was another boy of eight or nine, who was helping his own mother. They were coming down from the pass, the mother sitting on a gray donkey and the boy helping both along the path.

His name was Kabir. He was from the north. His father was 100 yards further up the trail, holding the slim hand of his daughter and walking behind a donkey on which a sick boy of about 16 years, covered with a thick, colorful woolen blanket sat trying to prevent himself from falling.

Kabir told me that his older brother had a bad fever, and without him, he was feeling lonely. The minute I gave him a few sweets, he stopped moving and when I asked the reason for his pause, he said he wanted to give one to his younger sister who was holding his father's hand.

I assured him that I would give one to his sister too. He said it was harder for his mother climbing up than climbing down.

I guess since I gave him sweets, he wanted to please me when he said, "Do not worry about the height of the pass, *kaka*, [uncle] the pass is not too high."

Oh, God is so great. You never know how and when and to whom he gives a strong spirit. The spirit of that little boy flew higher than mine today, thank God.

The only animals who enjoy climbing the pass were the goats. For them, the high cliffs were like wide stages to be danced or performed on. They did not require an audience. They were both the dancers and the spectators.

Today, close to the top of the pass, a wounded old woman on a small donkey was moaning like a child with high fever. I asked the reason. The donkey handler told me that she had fallen three days ago on a previous pass called Moom, and was injured. She had broken an arm and a leg. I gave some painkillers to her. She looked half-dead. She was on the way to Pakistan.

Moom Pass, where she fell, is famous for its high flying cliffs. Watching, talking, and listening to the painful stories of my people sapped my will to climb. Maybe, this is why I fell at least two times today and my horseman could do nothing. Thank God, it was not serious and my fellow-climbers were quick enough to help me.

It was exactly a quarter to nine in the morning when we cleared Papruk Pass. It took us three hours to reach the top. After hearing those sad stories, my soul gripped with pain, I forced myself to enjoy the beauty of the sky for a few minutes and the proud feeling of conquering another high pass.

Sitting on the top and listening to the silent whispers of nature, my lungs felt wider than the skies, my spirit flew higher than the mountains, and my thoughts were deeper than the valleys. There was a little snow around. I filled my lungs with clean, clear, cedar-scented air. No water flowed there so I ate some snow to quench my thirst.

In the higher parts of the mountains in Nooristan such as this one, you cannot find water, especially in the mornings, because the only water sources are frozen solid. The pass is very long and high, rough and tough, and the second longest and highest pass in Nooristan, the land of light.

Little Naqeebulla was not doing well. His father told me that he was very tired. He rode his donkey until the donkey fell, and then he had to climb up on foot. He had a severe headache while on the pass. Now he is fine and is eating a piece of cornbread with yogurt.

These wretched stories should not stop me from writing to you about the beauty of the pass. Both are created by God, beauty and ugliness, bad and good, high and low, rich and poor, war and peace, and hope and disappointment. The mountain itself was a piece of beauty.

The boulders, the rocks, the cliffs, the tracks, the shallow streams, the thin silver clouds, the river, the wild untouched flowers, the colorful singing birds, the old oak and cedar trees, the sweet fragrances of wild herbs, the sunrise on the corn fields, the cold wind of midnight, the caressing breeze of the early morning, the poor old huts, the donkeys and horses, the black dressed women carrying their children or cats in their goat-skin baskets, and, above all, the hopeful freedom fighters hiking to victory, looked and sounded wonderful.

Despite the problems climbing to the pass, God gave me a lucky moment too. I saw two large, beautiful eagles flying westward, almost above the pass. I wish I had a pair of binoculars to see them properly. My Super-8 camera was not at hand. The birds were already flying far from me. I tried to get Andy, if possible, to take some shots but he was not fast enough either. The birds were swift and majestic, and they glistened radiantly as they soared. They were black and gray with a dash of white. Perhaps they were a pair.

I remember when I was very young, my father told me, "Son, live like an eagle, even if it is for one night. Do not live like a crow, even if it is for 100 years." I spotted other birds, including one I had not seen before. An old man from the north told me that it was a species of *bulbul*, or nightingale.

At the bottom of the pass, a small beautiful mountain flower appeared in patches. Someone said they are wild *yasameen* or jasmine. I do not know whether they are jasmine or not. They looked like tiny yellow cups, rimmed with blue petals. They were extremely pretty, permeating the air with an unknown fragrance. Sandy Gall said that they were called "forget-me-nots." I am sure he is right.

The corn and barley fields stretch out wider now, gifting the eyes a wider space to scan. The other valleys of Nooristan are often very narrow. Here they even grow wheat. Fifty or sixty two storey traditional stone or wood houses also can be seen.

The teahouse where I am writing now is much larger and better equipped than the previous one. It is right in the middle of a cornfield. The owners are all from this area of Paroon. Their names are Rahman, Abdul Qudoos, and Mateeulla. They are very proud to be from this poor place.

Rahman says proudly, "Our dialect, our quroot, our weather, our trees, our king goats, our food, and our people are the best in all of Nooristan, and even the best in all of Afghanistan."

I quickly added that maybe they are the best in all the world.

"Laa laa, it is not a joke. I have not seen the world yet, but when I see it, I will let you know," he replied. I told him not to bother, for it is indeed the best in all the world.

After hearing this, Dost winked at me and laughed. Although Dost was usually the first with a proverb to hand, this time I reminded him of one: The eye of the lover is blind.

Let me finish here, talk to more people, have a cup of tea and eat my dinner. Later, I may write to you more. Andy looks at me and I think he wants me to stop writing.

9 PM

We ate some fried quroot with a few pieces of saltless cornbread for dinner. Not bad, thank God. Sandy kindly offered us some of his cheese and sardines.

Now, everyone feels good. The weather is fine. The horsemen have already started with the Panjsher songs they call *karsak*. They sing beautiful poems in their own unique style. It is all folk poetry, belonging to everyone, for the poets are unknown. It is mostly illiterate women, girls, and boys, who compose these poems.

They also call them *hijran,* or separation songs. Sometime they are composed in the praise of folk heroes or in order to encourage beloved ones to rally to the fight for freedom. They are very simple but very sweet. The one they sang some minutes ago I knew from my childhood. Read it.

My beloved asked me,
Why do you look sad?
Who has broken your heart?
I jumped,
Gave her a mirror,
The one you see.

The men sing these folk songs so passionately, so lively that you do not want to miss a second of it. They have no musical instrument to play on. They sit in a circle, shoulder to shoulder, and sing together as a type of choir. Little Naqeebulla also joined them. The Nooristanis, one by one, joined the Panjshiri singers too. Nooristanis have different singing and dancing styles, which are unique and typically Nooristani.

Now the war has ruined everything. People do not sing or dance here much, except at weddings. That is also very rare. Religious people do not like these things. In pre-Islamic times, Nooristani boys and girls used to dance together at night around a bonfire. These dances had beautiful names such as *dance of eagle, dance of war, dance of peace, dance of love, dance of tiger,* and *dance of the moon.*

I talked to Mullah Jalal, a young man from this village. He looked like a remnant of the army of Alexander the Great. His eyes were as green as shiny emeralds. He told me that in this area there are about 90 houses and a mosque, but no school. In the mosque, the boys do not learn reading, writing, or math. They just memorize some short verses of the Holy Quran in order to perform their ritual prayers and learn some of the basics of religion. In the whole area, there are not more than ten literate people.

Do not even ask me about their medical facilities; otherwise, you will be in tears. A middle-aged man by the name of Ghafoor told me they have no doctor, no paramedic, no pharmacy, no medicine, no one to help their women in childbirth, no pre or postnatal care, and, of course, no hospital. In one word, they have *nothing.* Poverty and war is an awful thing.

The weather is good now. No rain, no blustering wind, and no hail. This is a quiet place. You can hear the sound of the smallest creatures moving. The friendly croaking of frogs makes my soul more comfortable and takes me back to the farthest corners of my childhood. Once the night spreads its dark and black wings, the village becomes pitch-black because there is no electricity and there has never been.

Paroon, Nooristan

Tuesday, July 15
12 noon

I am writing on the bank of the wild, blue Paroon river, surrounded by farms of wheat and barley. We left Rahman's tea-tent at 7 AM and walked for three hours this morning. What a wavy river it is and what a blue color it has! What an unforgettable beauty that I am surrounded by and what a sweet fragrance that is coming from every corner. It is a beautiful place.

Soon we will start out toward the base of Moom Pass. We will sleep at the foot of the pass and, God willing, tomorrow we shall cross over and reach the district of Kantiwa.

Rain is Pain

Base of Moom Mountain Pass
10:00 PM

I am tired. After a difficult walk we finally arrived at the base of Moom Pass two hours ago. Everything has a limit, but my exhaustion seems to have none. I feel like a tiny ant under the foot of a giant elephant. This is what happened.

After 30 minutes of travel, it started to rain very heavily and what a rain it was! Buckets and buckets of cold water were coming down from the sky upon our heads, backs and shoulders, as well as upon our four-legged animals. We could not see a meter ahead of us, and walking on the slippery paths toward the mountain pass was extremely dangerous. Strong winds blew from every direction.

The horsemen were forcefully pushing the poor horses forward. One horse broke his leg. One donkey refused to walk any further, and his owner stayed behind with him, stuck in the middle of nowhere. I insisted on leaving the donkey behind, but he would not agree because the donkey was his life and his only source of income. He could not leave it behind.

Every drop of rain tumbled like a wrathful decree from a cruel king to torture whatever moves on his territory. No longer was it a kind message from the clouds to the earth, or the mercy of God upon his subjects. The pine, cedar, walnut, and oak trees looked like wandering ghosts walking down from another world into ours. I tried calling out to find Azimullah and little Naqeebulla to know how they were, but because of the heavy rain, no one could hear me, and they could not be seen. I slipped badly three times, once right into a strong stream of water. The horsemen helped me to get out.

We arrived like confused, exhausted, hunting dogs at the nearest village, called Pushkee. First, we went under a big tree to find shelter. It did not suffice. Luckily, we found a *baranda*, or roofed veranda, in a summer pasture, under which to take shelter. The horses were neighing and making a lot of noise. The other horsemen and donkey handlers could not be seen, or had missed this hut and gone on. Suddenly, the tall, strong, bearded owner of the hut appeared, along with three Nooristani women. They were soon joined by three or four more black-clad women and girls. Even though it was still raining, we felt compelled to leave the veranda because of the presence of the women. We Afghan men do not sit with unknown women and women do not sit with unknown men.

We walked for another half hour in dreadful conditions until at 6 PM the rain suddenly stopped. After another hour's walk, we reached a beautiful summer pasture, in our weary eyes an earthly paradise. No pain, no gain. Until you feel the heat of hell, you cannot gain the peace of paradise. I asked about Naqeebulla. He was stronger than I was and his father was all the happier because of it.

The large, wooden, shepherd's hut where I sit now is truly beautiful. It has magnificent views of mountain and valley. Food was prepared. The horses and the donkeys became calm. All exhaustion from both the journey and the rain disappeared and the sounds of our laughter filled the room, which added to the beauty of the flames from the fire. In these kinds of situations, one can see why some people worship fire.

Despite the cold weather, the fire made us feel warm enough to see and enjoy the beauty of the valley. Let us hope that the rain stops and weather becomes warmer.

Friendly Punch

Valley of Moom, Nooristan
Wednesday, July 16
10:05 AM. Tea-house of Saydaa Jaan

My dear, we have finally conquered Moom Pass. Let me tell you how.

Yesterday at 5 AM, we started out toward Moom Pass. My head and joints were aching since I woke. Andy walked with me. The track toward the pass had many trees along it. I was not feeling well and had to take a break more often than I usually would. Slowly and cautiously, I picked up the pace.

Half an hour before the pass itself, there was a baanda that belonged to an old Nooristani shepherd. He called himself Haji. He offered me a glass of *dough* (a traditional cucumber yoghurt drink) and a small piece of quroot. I ate a little.

The minute I introduced myself and he realized who I was, he hugged me very tightly and excitedly punched me on the back at least five times. They were friendly punches but very painful in my state. To justify a few moments' rest, I asked the old man which one he loves the most of his flock: the goat, the cow or the sheep.

He replied that he loves his king goat the most, then his cow that gives him milk, and lastly the sheep.

I asked him why he liked them in this order.

He said that he loved his king goat the most because it is strong and it has a lot of meat. Second, it does not move fast, and so does not bother him like the other goats.

I asked him if he was an actual Haji, and had been to Mecca. He replied that he had been on the pilgrimage a long time ago. I asked if it was boring for him to be up here all alone with his goats and cows. He looked at his animals and said, "If it is not boring for them, it is not boring for me too."

After saying goodbye and thanking him for the drink, Andy said, "With the stupid questions you asked him, you deserved even harder punches."

It is good the shepherd did not understand him.

At 8:02 AM, we reached the top of the pass. Climbing down, however, took only about one hour. It was very steep, so much so that we had to run down. In fact, coming down the mountain was harder than going up. Walking down, the pressure on my knees and the ensuing pain were so intense that I felt like they would stop working altogether.

On the descent, I met another shepherd, who gave me a small piece of *moomlayee*. I immediately asked him to tell me more about the other natural herbs found here. He said that on this mountain you could find mountain mint, mushrooms, cumin, and moomlayee.

You know well the qualities of moomlayee. It has a very interesting effect on animals and human beings. It is used as a natural medicine. It was first found when people, thousands of years ago, noticed that injured animals, like deer and tigers, would go to the tops of very high mountains and lick the deep dark crimson, tar-like substance, discharged from within the cracks of rocks and boulders. The people saw that, in a matter of only a few days, these animals were wondrously healed.

Taking that lesson from the animals, they did the same and found that moomlayee had an amazingly positive effect on their broken bones and dying cells. They started using the wonder drug not just for healing their broken bones but also for every impossible, incurable disease. Men trek long and hard up mountains to find this moomlayee and to gather as much as they can. It is not a herb. It looks like a volcanic substance. It seems to promote the regeneration and rejuvenation of cells.

I recall last year, when I was injured on my trip, the doctors of Red Cross diagnosed me with a fractured disk. You gave me moomlayee with milk, mixed with honey, for ten days. I remember very well that after a few days I was actually feeling much better and my post-moomlayee X-ray surprised the Red Cross doctor no end.

After a cup of tea, we will move on the next village.

Near the Village of Aspeet

12:30 PM

We arrived in the village of Aspeet a few minutes ago. It took us an hour to reach here.

Aspeet is a beautiful village with fine cedar and oak trees. Nooristani huts decorate both sides of the valley. Streams of water add to its charm, and the small cornfields, so close to harvest, glisten like pretty green patches on the gray dress of a young shepherd girl. The sun is shining brightly. The horses look tired but they are happily grazing. The owners of the horses are tired too, but sadly, they cannot graze. Naqeebulla does not seem so weary. He is coping as well as the others. I closed my eyes.

I was roused from sleep by a man holding some pieces of cornbread in his hands, and saying that it was *khayraat* (charity) and I should accept it. I gratefully took a piece, which tasted very good. Maybe because it was charity or because it was free. I asked him what has prompted this charity? He said after five daughters, God has at last given his wife a baby boy.

I asked him if God had given his wife another baby girl, would he still have given charity.

"Brother, do not be a *syaah zabaan* [black tongue]. Enjoy your cornbread and thank the God who gave a baby boy to me and a piece of bread to you," he replied in Farsi but with a very harsh Nooristan accent.

He gave a piece of cornbread to Andy too.

I jokingly asked him, "Brother, he is an infidel. Do you still give him charity?"

He angrily said, "Where are you from, *deewana* [crazy man]? You do not know the real meaning of Islam. Charity is good for everyone. Your stomach is not Muslim or infidel, it is either full or empty. In the next world, God shall ask about the charity you have given, not about whom you have given it to."

It impressed me greatly, to the extent that I translated it for Andy too.

Andy looked at him and said, "Can he give this infidel another piece of bread?"

I laughingly said, "Do not even think about it."

My dear, the skin on my hands has cracked. My eyelashes are full of dust and dirt. My beard is wild and unkempt. My clothes stink. My lips and nose are not even worth seeing but, thank God, my spine does not hurt. Soon we will be in the Kantiwa district.

5

Grandfather's Castle—Kantiwa, Heart of Nooristan

Kantiwa, Heart of Nooristan
Thursday, July 17
10:00 AM

My dear, this is the birthplace of your forefathers. Your relatives lived here for centuries. I love this place. It is an ancient settlement, wild and green. A beautiful blue river passes through here. I stayed last night at your grandfather, General Wakeel's old, half-ruined castle on top of a high hill surrounded by higher mountains.

Your distant relatives Haji Ghafoor and Halim received me joyfully. They are always good to me. They like me and I like them. They have lived here all their lives.

Haji is now about forty-five years old. He is a tall and strong-boned Nooristani with black hair and charcoal-colored eyes. His beard is not as long as it should be, in this place where most of the men have long, thin beards. Besides Nooristani, Haji speaks Farsi and Pashto fluently. He started his war against our enemy eight years ago, when the Nooristanis became the first in Afghanistan to start fighting against the communist regime. They are always very proud of this fact that they were the first.

He is kind and humble. People like him and respect him. He was not a member of any party before but now he has joined Hekmatyar's dubious party. Maybe his brother, who is a staunch member of that party, convinced him to do so. As long as he does not pollute our friendly relations with party politics, I will keep good relations with him. War ends, but relatives stay forever. He assured me that Jalal, one of your distant cousins, would be at my service, and my foreign friends would be taken care of.

* * *

This always quiet valley has changed much this year. Throngs of refugees, horses, and donkeys, have broken the peaceful atmosphere. Thousands upon thousands of refugees, escaping the war, break their journey here for a day or two, before proceeding to Pakistan. Hundreds of supply men and fighters do the same.

My dear, I have bad news. My friend Whitney is not doing well. He has pain in his legs and back and he suffers from nausea, fever, and tiredness. Last night he was not at all in a good way, and, unfortunately, he has decided not to go on any further. He will rest here for a while until he feels better and then will return to Pakistan. It is hard for me to see that he is not able to go on.

I spoke with him and said, "Don't worry, my friend. Be strong and tolerant. Whenever you feel the time is right and you can walk better, start your return journey. I am sure all will be well and we shall see each other when I return to Pakistan. You will not be alone. My prayers will accompany you to the end of your journey."

* * *

Last night, I talked with Haji Ghafoor, Kantiwa's fine commander. As we had promised each other, Haji took me to his home. He gave me tasty dark green tea with red raisons and almonds, and started talking in detail about everything in relation to Nooristani politics. He makes lot of sense when he explains things. Common sense is a part of the character of the common people.

He talked about the economic, military, and security situation in his area. In a very simple way, he was trying to tell me clearly about his own stance on Mr Hekmatyar and his party, which he is now a member of.

He asked me to assure Commander Massoud and the other commanders in the north that he would not create any problems for them. Repeatedly, he told me that he is a servant of the people. He talked harshly against Sarwar Nooristani and boasted that he would kill him and anyone with him, if they tried to create any problems in Nooristan. Before I even had a chance to ask him anything, he preemptively accepted and agreed to everything I requested.

In my own turn, I also talked with him about internal and external politics in relation to Afghanistan. Then I went on to give him my views about the Afghanistan's neighbors, their short- and long-term policies and strategies, especially the position of Pakistan and its intelligence services. At last I summed up by saying that we worry about the following: (a) Sarwar Nooristani, (b) Hekmatyar activity, (c) some of the Arabs who have become active in the eastern part of Nooristan, (d) the poverty of the people here, and (e) unnecessary tax on our lapis lazuli.

He paused a little and said, "Worry about nothing. As long as you are here and I am here, things will be okay. The council of the people will deal with Sarwar Nooristani and Hekmatyar will not be allowed to create any problems. The Arabs will be dealt with as guests. The taxes will be discussed with the people but, for the time being, we will stop taxing."

* * *

In the meantime, I visited a granduncle of yours who is not at all crazy but also not entirely of this planet. He is Kaka Malik (Uncle Malik). He is the oldest person in the village. Everyone respects him.

Three years ago, I was here with Humayoon Tandar, our representative in France. Humayoon told Kaka Malik that there will be, God willing, a time when we bring tourists into this tiny beautiful village. Kaka Malik flew into a rage and demanded why he intended bringing tourists to his village.

Humayoon replied that they would take photos of the people, show them to the world, attract others, and so bring in money for the poor. Humayoon, who was a young Afghan, educated in Paris, and married to a Parisian girl, naturally had a great vision to help his nation after the war is over.

Kaka Malik being a very traditional, religious person, did not seek to attract any foreign tourists, and raised the hem of his shirt and showed his private parts to Humayoon, and said, "Oh yea? Why don't you take a picture of this right now and show it to them, instead of waiting so long?"

Humayoon looked at me, shocked and upset. "What should I do?"

I was laughing "If you have a camera, then why not take the photo? Is it not the easiest way to attract tourists, especially the adventurers looking for strange things to see?"

Angrily Humayoon replied, "You should take the photo, since he is your relative."

No photo was taken, and Humayoon said as polite a goodbye as he could and left.

Haji Ghafoor and I had a good laugh about it.

* * *

It was late afternoon. I was sad when I saw Whitney leaving to start the journey back to Pakistan. I wrote you a letter and gave it to him to give to you. Maybe this letter will reach you on the 28th or 29th of July. He had so much enthusiasm and desire to go along with me to the north. I wanted him to visit there and fill his notebooks with beautiful words. No doubt, I will miss a friend on this trip, but even more so, Afghanistan will miss a friendly writer. Whitney would have written about its wonders, pains, and problems. I am sure his travel companion, Jalil, will take good care of him and make him happy.

Tomorrow we set out to cross the highest mountain in Nooristan. Pray for us.

6

King of the Passes—Kantiwa Pass

Friday, July 18
9:00 PM

We walked for 13 hours straight, to reach this place, the foot of Kantiwa Pass. It is also called Pushal Pass.

I woke up at 5 AM today. I was feeling good and Jalal's wife provided me with tea, cornbread, and the obligatory one-year-old piece of Nooristani cheese. I predicted that we would walk for at least fifteen hours. Fifteen hours of rocky mountains with long, high, dangerously narrow, and zigzag tracks.

Haji Ghafoor showed up to say goodbye. He brought a pistol, which he wanted me to carry, but I refused. He told me to assure Commander Massoud of his cooperation.

We traveled well in good weather to the village of Chaman. I was unlucky in that Kaka Musa, the headman of Chaman, was not there. A woman gave us a teakettle to make tea. She was herself a refugee from the Badakhshan province, and now lived here with her family. She was from the Ismaili sect and could not speak Farsi, or at least, I could not understand her distinctive Farsi accent.

From Chaman, the track got worse. Each rock was stained with the blood of our miserable horses' hooves. I could not bear to look into the horses' innocent eyes, and anytime I had a chance, I advised the horsemen to be soft on them. The donkeys too were weeping and moaning non-stop. The rough, rocky, blood-marked track had no mercy on either the four-legged or two-legged creatures.

The further we went, the colder the weather became. The bitter effort of this part of our journey reminded us that we were approaching the pass of Mt Kantiwa, the hardest, highest, driest, coldest, and roughest of all Nooristani passes, and the second highest pass in Afghanistan.

The shepherd's cave we are in now looks like a cave from the time of Prophet Moses. The walls are stained black from smoke. There is barely enough space for the goats, let alone ourselves to pass the night, but what can we do. I am laying in between boulders.

On the way to here, my sleeping bag fell off my horse, down to the valley and into the river. Three men went down and miraculously retrieved it from the other side of the river. It took them four hours to bring it back to me and it was soaked. I have to make do with one *patoo* or shawl. Now, in the dim light of a lantern, I am writing to you. It is indeed very cold.

There is no wood here because of the high elevation. It is at least 15,000 feet high. We have brought a certain amount from below, and now there might be just enough left to boil one last pot of tea. Nothing grows here. Everything is frozen to its core: the rocks, the boulders, the earth, the sky, the moon, and the stars. It seems as though, except God's mercy, everything else is frozen. No water can be found among the millions of tons of ice. The freezing wind blows as fast as possible. There is no vegetation or greenery alive, to be swayed by the wind. It looks like another planet.

The horsemen can be seen covering their horses with bags of hay to keep them warm. Everyone is preparing themselves for the final push to the top of Kantiwa Pass, the *king of passes*. Throughout the world, there might be four or five peaks, which can be described as the roof of the world, and Kantiwa is one of them.

Sandy Gall is well and Andy looks as strong as he was last night. As for Noel, I still do not know how this silent man feels. Whitney is no longer with us. Dost is singing loudly, to increase his own morale and that of the other men.

A few meters away from me, I saw little Naqeebulla sitting close to a big rock, looking very sad. I thought that he must be very tired or might be in poor spirits. I waved at him and he looked at me without waving his hand. I gestured to him in our way to know how he was. He nodded sweetly, showing that he was fine. We did not exchange any words. Then he put his hands to his head and said in a loud voice that his father had a severe headache and fever.

I stood up and started walking toward the little boy but went very carefully as it was extremely rocky. His father was not so bad. It was just a normal headache. I talked to the boy for a little while and gave him some raisins.

Tomorrow we shall pass the area of Sarwar Nooristani. God willing, they will not bother us. My stomach is cramping up today. Perhaps it was the cold, saltless goat-meat soup that I drank last night by mistake, thinking it was water.

Valley of Pushal. Do Aw

Saturday, July 19
2:00 PM

It took us about nine hours walk to reach here which is called Do Aw of Pushal.

The pass which caused us so much anxiety, trepidation, and nightmares from the beginning is behind us. Today, our poor, small convoy, with the help of the soldiers of our spirit, occupied the kingly pass of Kantiwa, which has ruled for millions of years without moving an inch from its kingdom.

We started out at 5 AM. Our difficulties started right from the beginning of the track. We were quite close to the pass from where we started but the path was steep and it was freezing cold. Early-morning sleet gave way to snow. I did not have gloves. I don't think anyone had.

In no time the weather was getting even colder, the tracks narrower, the rocks sharper, the cliffs higher, the spirits lower, the steps slower, and our breath shorter. The more closer to the pass, the harder each step. Everyone kept to himself, doing nothing except walking slowly skyward.

I had a headache and even a slight toothache, which started for no reason. A headache, yes; but why a toothache? There was no one near me whom I could ask for help. The last half an hour was like hell. The pressure was so much that I could not even breathe. My fingers were almost freezing. My ears and eyes were like small pieces of ice, my knees were in pain, my breath was pushing hard in my chest, my tongue felt very heavy, and my heart was racing fast and loud. I was so tired that I could not even bear the weight of my eyelashes. And worse still, the cliff rose higher, the track narrower, and the rocks more treacherously icy.

At 7:45 AM, I reached the top of the highest pass in Nooristan. Despite my weary state, I stopped on the pass, at 16,000 meters, marveling at the breathtaking scenery with real pride and shouted loudly, "YOU ARE NOW UNDER MY FOOT!"

I was relieved and pleased to be at the top of the mountain but also in awe of it. Everything was either white, stone colored, or ice. Dost came to me and showed me a large formation of snow.

He pointed to the different layers and said, "Look at that, sir, each one of those layers symbolizes a year of snow fall."

From what I could tell, there were at least 30 to 35 layers. Height, history, and stark beauty converge on this wonderful spot.

I could have touched the blue soul of the sky hanging over me, my dear. It is hard to conquer a kingdom but when you conquer a kingdom such as this, you enjoy it even more, knowing that you have killed no one and bothered nobody.

My dear, I should also mention that while climbing up, I was living a nightmare, but when on the top, it felt like I was in a sweet dream. I asked my ten-year-old companion how he was. He said that he was fine but his father had a very bad headache. God gives even the smallest of humans, the biggest of hearts.

Dost told me that two horses stayed behind because they were unable to climb any further. A donkey fell and broke his leg. Two horsemen also were not able to climb any further and stayed behind. He was happy that there had been no bombardment by the Soviet jets and happier to tell me that, except for the two already mentioned, no horseman or anyone else got sick due to lack of oxygen.

Why? Why? Let Me Cry

Du-Raahee
5:00 PM

It is five in the evening. We left the previous teahouse around three in the afternoon, and reached here some minutes ago.

The deeper one travels into Afghanistan, the more painful are the stories one either hears or sees. Today, I saw four families from the Taaliqan province, on their way to Pakistan. Little barefoot children, destitute and dirty. The sticks they held in their hands were thinner than their bodies. The smallest children sat in the supply sacks on the backs of donkeys.

The boys reminded me of Mahmud. The girls looked like little Ghezal. They were tired and exhausted. I tried to strengthen the hearts or morale of their little siblings in the donkey sacks, but they did not even want to look at me.

For some minutes, I talked to the head of one of the four families. His name was Khayr Mohammad. He was about forty years old and accompanying his family of six, including his ancient parents. He told me that he has lost two of his bothers, a sister, one of his own sons, and his little daughter when their house in Taaliqan was bombed by the Soviets. His son Nasim was only fourteen when he was killed along with his sister in the same bombardment, while bringing water from a nearby water spring.

Since then his mother has been in shock. Except to call out the name of her dead grandson, she has stopped talking. His father was also severely wounded, and lost his eyesight and left hand. His right leg was injured too and he was still bleeding. He said that the other three families traveling in the same convoy to Chitral have tragedies more painful than his.

He mentioned a nine-year-old girl in the convoy who had lost every member of her family in a bombardment. Since there was no one left to take care of her, the village Mullah asked them to take her to Pakistan, and if possible, to ask someone to look after her as their own.

Khayr Mohammad wondered aloud, "Who would agree to look after a crazy girl like her, who every second shouts and screams like a wounded cat? We even have to force her to eat. She cries day and night. Since that sinister bombardment, over and over again, every five minutes, she repeats the same word: why, why, and why. Even if you approach her donkey, one can still hear her saying this over and over. She has gone crazy."

Here I was no longer able to hold back my tears and wept loudly on her behalf. How could I stop my tears? After all, this is the time for tears to console the heart. I murmured to myself these words:

Oh, tears come,
Help my eyes.
Oh, mother come,
Help my cries.
Oh, sorrows come,
Help my sighs.
Oh, God come,
Answer my whys.

All four families were on their way to find a small tent in the refugee camps of Pakistan to live. Khayr Mohammad had very little hope of being able to return home.

We have hundreds and hundreds of victims like these in refugee camps in Pakistan and Iran. We have around three million refugees in Pakistan and two millions in Iran and many thousands in other parts of the world. Still, the *why*s of the little girl echo through my sorrowful soul. My dear, you are one of these victims too, living as a refugee in Pakistan.

The place where I am writing to you now, and will spend the night, is one of the last summer pasture huts in Nooristan, before I enter the Panjshir valley. It is small with some cave-like rooms made of stone. They have no windows and no doors. The ceilings are full of cracks and holes. They are for the animals and now we use them too.

I talked to Mohammad Zahir, the owner of this summer pasture. He is a young man and very proud of being able to take care of his animals in such a remote corner of the world. He told me that his father is still alive, but his mother died a year ago. He has three children and a Nooristani wife. They got married five years ago.

He is proud of his father who was a tiger hunter when he was young. He is still very proud to have the skins of the tigers in his home. Until he dies, he will not lose them because they show the bravery of his father. I asked if he, or his father, ever hunted deers. He said no. I asked, what about foxes?

He pushed his chest out and said, "Cowards hunt foxes but we hunt tigers and wolves."

I jokingly pointed to Andy and told Zahir that he has hunted foxes, but he is not a coward. He looked at Andy and said, "Infidels are different."

To change the topic, Andy asked him the name of the area we are in now. "You do not know the name?" He asked in astonishment.

Andy quickly replied, "If I knew the name of the place, why should I have asked you?"

Mohamad Zahir responded by saying that he thinks one should be wise enough to ask the name of one's destination before starting on a journey.

I supported Andy by asking the man to tell us the name of this place. Since he could not believe that someone could not know the name of the place where he is, he proudly told me, "If you do not even know the name of the place that you have come to, then what do you know?"

I did not reply. At last, he compromised and mentioned that the name of the place is Qala Tak.

At this very moment, someone entered, interrupted us and asked if I was Masood Khalili. I just waved my hand at him. He gave me a letter from Maulavi Razaaq, the most powerful and influential man in the area, a supporter of General Sarwar.

Here the pasture owner looked at the messenger and asked, "Are you sure that the most influential man in our area has sent a letter to the man who does not even know the name of the area?

The messenger moved his lips and scratched his neck but did not say anything. The pasture owner nodded and said, "If this is true, then the world has changed and doomsday is closer."

In short, the letter said that he was not a puppet of Sarwar Nooristani, and that I could feel at ease when crossing his area of control. I wrote back and thanked him for the letter and suggested that if it were true and he were not a puppet of Sawar Nooristani, then he should send a team to Commander Massoud and others to convince them that they had the wrong perception about him. I am not so sure, he will take my advice, but I told him that I trust his word and believe him.

My dear, I still have one or two of those tiny packets of soup powder that you put in my bag. I wish I could get tonight a plate of tasty Basmati rice, nicely cooked in fresh oil or butter, with a touch of some scented spices. I know it is not possible. It is a cat's dream in his quick nap.

The horse owners along with Dost came to see me some minutes ago. They talked about many things, good and bad, and ultimately I asked them, "How much did you spend so far?"

Dost said, "It is about 43,000 Afghani" (300 dollars).

7

Goodbye Nooristan—Welcome Panjshir

Sunday, July 20
12:10 PM

Last night, we bought some food from the teahouse to keep us going. Each plate cost us over 300 Afghanis (2 dollars). After eating, I slept for three hours or so, until some drops or "seeds of rain" work me up at 4:00 AM in the morning. It was a beautiful dawn.

The horsemen were already up and had a breakfast of saltless cornbread and sugarless tea prepared for us. At 5:20 AM we left Qala Tak. The first river did not have a bridge for the horses to cross and we had to lead them through the waters. Of the six horses we now have, the strong current swept off two of the weaker ones and no one could help them before they were injured. One of them was the same white horse that was transporting Andy's film.

It took us about seven hours to reach here from Qala Tak. The first four hours were bad. There were many boulders and lots of rocks on a long, troublesome, zigzag track. The poor horses and donkeys were in real trouble. I was not feeling good myself. Each tiny rock moving under my feet, causing pain in my legs, even up into my neck.

Thank God, the trail improved and the last three hours of the trek were not so bad.

We are in a Nooristani summer pasture hut, which, I should announce loudly to you, God bless the angels, is the last summer pasture hut in Nooristan. It belongs to someone named Wakeel and he knows your family. I had a chance to talk to him a little. He was a nice man who knew little Persian and had a very rough Nooristani accent. He was tall and wore thick, black Nooristani clothes. He had an old dagger hanging on the left side of his woolen coat. He was in his forties, maybe a bit older than me.

Civilized Caves

Beginning of Paryan
6:15 PM

We are finally in the first village of Paryan in the Panjshir Valley. Here one can see large caves, where travelers stop to eat a little and gather their strength. They are called 'Kurahaay Chimmar' or the Chimmar Caves.

The first part of our long walk is over. The rest of our journey, though filled with its own challenges, cannot beat Nooristan for the height, toughness, and roughness of its mountains. The mountains ahead also form a part of the Hindu Kush range but are not as tough or high.

Now I will tell you how we traveled the last stretch to here. It started to snow when we were close to the top and then freezing cold and fast winds followed. My arms and legs had almost stopped working. I was feeling very tired and weak. First, my jaws started chattering, and then a severe jaw pain followed. After some minutes, my jaw became so heavy that I could not open my mouth for at least 20 minutes. Even Andy, who has always been our strong man, was not feeling well.

Although the Chimmar Pass is not as high as others are, it was highly tiresome. I could not breathe properly. I vomited twice. My horseman helped me by holding my hand, and even in some places pulling or pushing me upward. At the top of the pass, when Meerza, a young man from Panjshir, saw that I was not feeling well, he kindly gave me some dry mulberries, which made me feel amazingly better and warmed up my frozen jaw.

My dear, the pass was not just pain, but was full of beauty too. Tiny scattered flowers could be seen on the patches of ground that did not have snow. They had short, thin stems, and were of a purple color with three or four petals.

They were so small and beautiful that, even though I was not feeling well, I picked up some. To me they looked like the pupils of the eyes of the deer. The special, unknown, wild fragrance of the flowers penetrated my whole body and soul. Although the cold wind had muffled somewhat my power of smell, I could savor the sweet and soft scent of the tiny wild flowers.

From the top of the Chimmar Pass, we could see the high, white, and silvery snow-clad peaks of Mir Sameer Mountain. Many mountaineers once came to climb this mountain but could not conquer it. Mirza told me that a Japanese mountaineer died in his attempt to climb it years before because, as Mirza said, the highest part of this pass is just one piece of ice. God knows.

All our horses have now reached safely, except the white horse, which was carrying the films for Sandy's team. Andy was worried about the condition of the horse and told me that the horse's owner was staying behind until the horse gets better. When I asked him why he did not stay behind as well, he told me that he needed to keep moving because he was not feeling well.

I called Dost and instructed him to do something about the film left behind on the white horse. He suggested that Ghiyaas the donkey man should take a fresh donkey and go back to help the white horse and his owner and bring them here. I hope he will be able to find them amongst millions of rocks. Otherwise, all of the running and struggling and efforts of Sandy and Andy will be wasted.

I found a *kur* (cave) to relax in, write notes to you, and pass the night. It is very cold. Each kur feels like a dark, empty refrigerator. We are in the middle of summer and I am still shivering from the cold. Andy is lively.

People have used these caves for centuries. Some carvings on their walls indicate that they are extremely old. People made use of the caves in ways fit for their own purposes. Travelers, merchants, shepherds, mystics, and even thieves have used and are still using them in their times of need. The resistance uses them too. Amongst these kurs, there is one, which serves as a shop selling cookies and homemade bread. Who ever heard of a cookie-cave?

Let me tell you about little Naqeebulla. The poor boy was not feeling well at all. Earlier I looked for him in all directions. I finally saw him lying next to a boulder almost totally frozen, and with his father trying to help him. I rushed to him. His teeth were grinding together, his face was dark blue, and his hands were stiff from the freezing cold. He could not talk. He was close to death. His eyes had become small and his thin nose was getting thinner. I called out to everyone to help this boy. It was probably a mix of extreme cold and a lack of oxygen.

He began to howl like a cat. I took off my combat jacket and put it under him, over his coat. His father and I started rubbing his hands. I told the boy to move about, to get up and try to run. We managed to get him to his feet and, with me supporting him, we two began to walk as quickly as I could move him. His father helped and we pushed him along, and I rubbed his neck, his face, and his hands as hard as possible. Then we started running, moving faster. I took off my sweater and wrapped it around his neck as well.

He started to shiver like a goat under the butcher's knife and then he began to show signs of recovery. Thank God, he felt better. We gave him some dry mulberries too. In the process of helping him, I somehow heard our little Mahmud calling me, "Father, help the boy. Do not allow him to die." To my relief, the boy started smiling and asked his father for more mulberries.

Little Naqeebulla's pain, suffering, moaning, and crying, brought my own childhood to mind. I have told you many times the story of my wet nurse and how much I loved her. May God bless her soul! What a kind woman she was. She loved me more than her own children. She breast-fed me for six months when my mother was extremely sick. She kindly agreed to do so. She had five children, all older than me. Until I was twenty-three, I used to go and visit her every week or she would come and see me.

When I was a child, the best day of the week for me was Friday when I would stay the night in her poor home. Every Friday she would be waiting at the threshold of her home to receive me. She had always some dried mulberries and walnuts to pour into my dirty side pockets. Sometimes, if she had money, she used to buy for me a kite or some colorful balloons.

The last time I visited her was when I was on the way to India in 1971 for my studies. She hugged me, kissed me a hundred times, wept for me, and gave me a handful of sweets and the same kind of dry mulberries she used to give me when I was a child.

Now she must be in Kabul and I cannot go there. Hope one day that we see each other again in this world or the next.

* * *

In another one of the caves, there is an old cobbler too. I went to his small cobbler kur. His name was Maad Hakeem. He was from Paryan. He was an interesting man, of about fifty, who worked with very simple tools. He did not have shoe polish, which I thought was essential for a cobbler. As soon as he recognized me, he addressed me in an affected eloquent and lofty language.

"I can fix the shoes of men or women, rich or poor, fighter or writer, Muslim or non-Muslim, in a second. I mend them in such a way that they look better and newer than new. A comfortable shoe is a guarantee for good health. I also make shoes which feel better than Bata shoes."

He fixed the soles of my shoes in a minute and even did not want to charge me but I gave him a few Afghanis anyway.

I met another shop-cave owner named Aadeen Mohammad. Despite it being a small cave, barely a meter squared, I was surprised to see the amount of products it contained. There were cakes, cookies, socks, combs, flash lights, needles, nails, ropes, tea, sugar, salt, red chili powder, raisins, chick peas, rice, pain killers, including expired Aspirin Bayer, and palm-sized round mirrors. They also have a radio-cassette player. A song by Mohammad Agha Panjshiri is belting out of it.

Arriving here, I knew that the rest of the journey shall be taken care of by Commander Massoud's men. I thought now is the time to thank the people who have helped us so far.

I called Dost, the horsemen, and the others, including Naqeebulla and his father, and told them, "You have done a great job until now for us. Such a difficult journey would not have been possible without you, your horses, and your donkeys. I will never forget it. If I have shouted at you, wrongly or rightly, I am very sorry. You were all stronger than your horses.

"The most difficult part of the journey is, thank God, over now. Therefore, you can go to your homes. If we need you for the return trip, we will surely call you. For the time being, may God bless you and keep you safe. Nooristan and its difficulties are over."

Dost, the convoy captain was almost in tears. I especially thanked my own horseman Azimullah and asked him to take good care of his son. Little Naqeebulla looked at me, and with a meaningful glance and a smile, thanked me for being friendly toward him, and especially toward his father.

In this moment, I wished I knew the language of the horses and donkeys as well, in order to thank them from the depth of my heart. Actually, without those innocent animals, we would have not been able to do much. Anyway, I looked at them and thanked them too.

Gun Gate

First Freedom Fighter Base
Monday, July 21

It is 9:20 in the morning. This is the first base of Commander Massoud's warriors, located in the upper part of the Northeastern corner of the Panjshir valley.

Let me tell you first of what happened last night, which was indeed unique and strange. I do not know if it was a dream, reality, or both. I went into my sleeping bag under a brilliant clear black sky filled with shiny twinkling stars. There was complete silence. In the left corner of the sky, I saw a group of stars that looked like a cluster of grapes, hanging down from a vine. I was neither asleep nor awake, but hanging in between. I also saw a group of starry women with sacks slung around their shoulders, making toward this grape vine to collect the silver colored grapes.

A few steps behind these lady-stars, a hunter-giant began to shoot steely arrows from a great bow, protecting, in my mind, the grape-gatherers from some malign spirit. The lady-stars gathered impervious to all else. With a bow in his hand and larger steel arrows on his shoulder, all of a sudden, the man started to shoot his arrows, which looked exactly like shooting stars. I instantly closed my eyes for some seconds and opened them again.

Whether a vision or a sweet dream, it inspired me to pray and wish that a time will come when the baskets of all women, wherever they are in the world or in a free Afghanistan, would be full of stars, living freely under the arrow of justice and the bow of peace.

In the morning, we left at 7 AM and now we are in the first of Commander Massoud's bases, in the northeastern corner of the Panjshir Valley. It took us almost two hours to reach here. It is my fourth time in this base. There are about twenty-five to thirty fighters, armed with Kalashnikovs. The weather is good.

On our arrival, the base commander came to greet us. He had been expecting me. His named is Abdul Rasheed. He welcomed us with the usual words of 'may you not be tired!'

I thanked him and asked him if he has radio communication with Commander Massoud. He said he does not, but that he could send word from a nearby base. He went on to say that Commander Massoud is not in the valley and he thinks that we might have to go to the Takhaar province to see him.

Anyway, I gave him a little message to dispatch to Commander Massoud, wherever he is in Takhaar. Almost immediately, he returned with Massoud's reply telling me to hurry up and come to see him in Takhaar.

My dear, the bad news is that the white horse, which had been carrying the film before he was injured crossing the river, lost his life in Nooristan. Luckily, the men were able to save the film for Andy. Baba Jaan, the poor horse's owner, who is skinnier than his horse was, has now also become sick. I hope he survives. A horse like his has a net worth of 40,000 Afghanis or $278. I promised him that in Peshawar I would give him a certain amount of money. He lamented that his horse has died and his household has been ruined by its death.

Rose of Love

Tuesday, July 22
7:00 AM

Yesterday, during dawn prayer, in the old village mosque, with Maulavi Raaz's soothing voice to the fore, I glanced through the right side window of the mosque and saw a beautiful rose bush. It attracted me like a magnet does iron. It was so beautiful that it made my eyes blurry. Its fragrance was so strong that I felt as if the rose bush was right on my lap.

After the prayer completed, I asked Maulavi Raaz about that wonderful rose bush. He said this bush was planted years before by Sahib Mubarak, a great Sufi or mystic of his time. A blue tombstone can be found there too, which has the name and sign of that *ruhaani* (spiritual man). The strange thing is that that blue stone has spiritual powers. Any problem you have, just go there and that is it.

Every Friday night, people say they can see hundreds of candles illuminated around that blue stone, without anybody having lit them. Moreover, strangers still come from the remotest areas to pay tribute to the blue tombstone to watch the red roses in bloom. Some women call the holy Sahib Mubarak Gullab Shah or King of the Roses. It is now a shrine, especially for those who are desperately in need of help, in particular young girls who are depressed, pain-ridden, and deprived of their loved ones.

On the wall of the mosque, there were paintings of roses and a variety of different fruits. For carpeting, the mosque had a *namad* (a traditional woolen rug) made, perhaps, by the shepherd wives in the summer pastures. They had placed a white cloth over it.

The story of the rose bush, the magic of the blue stone, the murmur of the prayers, the whispers of the worshipers and the recitation of Rumi's poetry created a unique vibration in my soul and peace in my heart.

Commander Torah Meer's family prepared for us a dinner of rice and northern-style *korma*. He and his brother, Commander Mirza, are well-known local commanders. Torah Meer had his own particular style of talking and laughing. He likes to appear clever saying he even knows where the KGB chief sleeps at night.

After tea, we went to sleep on the roof, under a canopy of falling stars. Remembering you and our children, I searched the bright lanes of the dark sky and heard the musical sound of a wild river.

Today, I woke up early. The sky was like a blue wine glass with no star but the sun. I went to a nearby wheat field, which was heavy with dew. I washed my face in the freezing water of a nearby pond. Commander Torah Meer had tea and warm bread sent to us.

In this resistance base, lapis lazuli brought from the north is taxed from 5 to 10 percent. Caravans of blue lapis come from Badakhshan; the traders pay their tax and proceed toward Pakistan. The tax goes toward the war expenditure. Last year, the freedom fighters of this area collected 12 million Afghani, or around 83,916 US dollars, in tax from the lapis lazuli trade.

It is now early afternoon. Battles in the southern part of the Panjshir valley continue. Fighting against the Russians has increased all over the country.

Waiting for Massoud

Chimmar Village, Panjshir
7:00 PM

I am still not sure whether I should go to the north or wait here for Commander Massoud. To take advantage of my time, I called some local commanders to talk to me. They were interesting sub-commanders from the Baghlan province. They knew much about the war and the nature of weapons, but not much about how, in the long run, to deal with their own people.

I explained to them how we should mobilize our people and said, "A political officer has to go from village-to-village, mosque to mosque, school to school, and front to front to mobilize his people for war and peace. War is war. We have to take it seriously. People's lives are in danger."

Raziq, who was political officer in his area, took a keen interest in our discussion. Commander Mohammad Issa joined us too and gave us useful information about the enemy's air attacks. He explained the difference between the various Soviet jet fighters, such as SU-25 and SU-27. He said that when the Soviets use their jets and helicopters in tandem, they create hell. He also talked about the real danger posed by MI-24 Russian military helicopters.

I told him if America were to provide us with Stingers, things would change for our benefit. Since Mohammad Issa is the commander concerned with heavy weaponry, he assured me that it is very difficult and impossible for the enemy to reach the area where we are now.

Commander Issa is the one who lost his eye in the war two years ago and whom I helped go to the States to receive treatment. He was treated at the Walter Reed National Military Medical Center, in Washington, DC. Last year, during Ramadan, after he had come back from America, he brought down three Russian army helicopters. I joked with him that it is better to be one-eyed, since he destroyed more helicopters than when he had two eyes.

Since I was the one who sent him to America, he shows a lot of kindness and wants to keep me happy. He was still so appreciative and grateful toward the staff of Walter Reed, where everybody was very kind and helpful to him.

On a lighter note, the horsemen have either forgotten or deliberately not taken the small bag, in which I had the garlic and onion powder that you gave me. Therefore, the taste of my food is not as good as it should be.

As I mentioned, the place where I am was once part of the historical Silk Road, but now, I could easily call it the Story Road, for rich or poor, fighter or civilian, old or young, male or female, all have a happy or sad story to tell. The war touches every person and makes thousands of stories.

Here on this particular story road, I met a woman with her old lame father who had come from Kabul to find her lost son. She was a teacher in her forties. She looked miserable and was crying, moaning, and lamenting like a child. Her husband had been killed and the Intelligence Agency of the communist regime in Kabul forcefully took two of her young sons and her daughter from her.

Since then, she has been going daily to the regime authorities to find out where her children are. At last, she found that her seventeen-year-old daughter had been forced to marry someone and her 14- and 16-year-old sons had forcefully been sent to the battlefield to fight against the resistance fighters. Later, she was informed that her daughter's cruel husband had taken her to another remote province. Then she found out that one son had disappeared or was killed and the other son might have defected to the resistance movement of the north. Unfortunately, she had given up on her other children. Now, it was only the youngest son she sought.

She grabbed my collar, started crying, and asked me for help.

"Please help me find my son. Why won't you help me?"

Her name was Khadija, her sons' names were Qasem and Raheem. Qasem was the disappeared or killed one and Raheem was the would-be defector.

"Whatever my husband has done, wrong or right, the communists killed him, but why has Dr Najib (the Chief of Intelligence) arrested and taken my other young children? They were totally innocent."

As she took a fistful of dust from the earth and forcefully rubbed it on her head and face as a sign of anger and sadness, she shouted at me, "I have nothing in my life but pain, misery, and suffering. My destiny is like black dust. My days are dark. My nights are full of pain. My home is like a funeral home. The communists have buried me alive."

I told her, "Sister, it is not us who have committed this sin, it is the communists."

"You are all like wolves, like wild animals. You are all godless butchers. You are the enemies of God. May God and the Prophet shower you all with shame. It doesn't make a difference who has killed my children, freedom fighters, or communists. You are all sinners. Oh, people help me to find my sweet children."

I patiently listened and tried to calm her. Understandably, it did not work. In a fit, she picked up some stones and started beating her face and head, and then began throwing them at me. I stopped her. In order to show her deepest feelings, she again grabbed a handful of dust from the ground and forcefully rubbed it to her hair, face, and chest.

Again, I stopped her. Then she started weeping like the rain from an angry cloud. I let her weep, while I was myself in tears. When she saw tears in my eyes, she stopped crying.

At that very moment, my dear, I remembered you, my mom, and my own sons, and I thought if this would happen to you or my mom, you would do the same. She was right, but what could be done? It was the communist leaders, who had taken her children by force, not we, but as she rightly said, it makes no difference to a mother who has done it. I promised her that I would send messages to our commanders in the north, to see if anyone has seen her young son who had defected.

Oh, it is a long process, with little means of communication, no system of transportation, and no time nor the will to follow it up. I consoled her to the extent possible and asked the commander to take care of her. At this moment, she showed me a photo of her two boys. I asked if I could keep the photo in order to be able to better pursue her case.

She immediately pulled the picture to her chest and held onto it tightly.

With the most sorrowful and tearful voice she said, "Brother, I only have one copy. If I give this to you, I will have nothing left in this world to remind me of my sweet children."

She turned and walked away. I thought that the photo was the only tiny remedy for her heart's great pain, so she can look at the photo of her lost children and cry louder.

Still Waiting

Village of Chimmar
Wednesday
7:30 AM

I am still in Chimmar Village, waiting to receive a message from Commander Massoud about which direction I should take down to Panjshir or up to Takhaar. I am 100 percent sure that I will go toward Takhaar.

Commander Torah Meer came early in the morning, greeted us in his own way and said that tea was ready. Commander Issa keeps coming, offering whatever he can to make me happy. The best thing he does for me is, from time to time, he brings me dried mulberries and almonds. Thank you, Walter Reed!

Maulavi Raaz visits me often. He reminds me of one of my uncles. He has a flat nose, big eyes, dark eyebrows, long eyelashes, a well-trimmed beard, dark skin, and a special way of looking at the ceiling while talking.

Andy, Sandy Gall, and Noel are doing well. God willing, the weather will clear today so that they may shoot a few minutes of film. Andy is getting restless. Today, I may send Abdul Basit and Abdul Raheem, the cameramen, toward Kishm, in Badakhshan, with no camera.

My dear, last night, I dreamt of you and little Mahmud. I hugged him repeatedly. My brother Nejatullah and Jafaayee, my friend, also appeared in my dream. The fighting continues at the end of the Panjshir Valley. Soviet fighter jets fly over daily like loan sharks, kicking in our doors, in the hope of collecting money. Their currency is blood.

8

A King's Wrath, Tears in Herat, and a Royal Wedding

Jishta Village
6:00 PM

I received a letter two hours ago from Najmuddin requesting, if possible, to come to Jishta as his guest. Under pouring rain, we traveled for an hour to reach there.

When we arrived, Commander Najmuddin received us with great kindness. Tea and cold bread was brought and we were informed that they would cook dried meat and *palow* in the evening. Every five minutes he asked me if I was feeling well or not.

He introduced me to his six-year-old son, Abdul Nabee. He was very sweet and smart. The names of the ten friends of the Prophet came quick to his tongue as he pronounced them aloud. He could sing some war songs too. Najmuddin himself is an interesting man, who knows many stories of the war in the valley. He has a tall body, thick beard, and high nose. When he talks, he closes his eyes and wrinkles his forehead. Sitting with us was an old relative of Najmuddin. He had a long beard with white hair under his Afghan hat or pakol. He wore an old brown vest over his very worn Afghan clothes which were dark blue.

There is another very interesting young man here called Saleh. He is deaf and mute. He is around 19 years old. He works for Najmuddin. When the old man recognized who I was, tears filled his eyes and he started to tell me a story which was very close to my heart.

"In 1919, Mustofi-ul-Mamalik, your grandfather, was in charge of everything. He was the second most powerful man in Afghanistan. While the king was asleep, five or more people entered his tent and killed him. The killers escaped. The rumor was that the prince had ordered it done.

"In Kabul the next day, the prince declared himself king. His first order was that an investigation should be conducted to determine who had murdered his father. He soon ordered that your grandfather come immediately to Kabul. It seems that a day or two before the murder, your grandfather told the king that informants had told him the prince was planning to kill the king. Your grandfather had even given the king a letter outlining the evil plot hatched by his son, Amanullah. The king had put the letter into his pocket and ignored it. He did not want to believe your grandfather.

"Now this same son, this plotter, was the king. What could one expect from the new king, that he would hug your grandfather or that he would hang him? The new king had your grandfather's letter in his hands. He could not let your grandfather live. So when your grandfather arrived in Kabul, the king had him placed in chains, accusing him of the murder. He had your grandfather brought before him in the royal court and in front of at least 20 dignitaries and addressed him. 'You have mentioned my name in the report you gave to my father. Is this your letter and your seal? Tell me, who is the killer?'

"Your grandfather replied, 'Yes, your Majesty, yes, that is my letter I wrote and gave to your martyred father. My informants reported the information to me, and I wrote the letter to your father before he was murdered. Unfortunately, right or wrong, your name is the one mentioned in my report. I had to report it. I could not hide the information, could I?'

"The king now angrily shouted, 'I was in Kabul far away from him. You were there in the same area when he was killed. Tell me, how could I have killed my father? Why did you not write any other names but just my name in your report?'

"Your grandfather replied, 'Amir Sahib, [Your Majesty] because my informants did not mention any other name except yours. I could not write otherwise.'

"The king wrathfully responded, 'I am sure you yourself plotted to kill my father and mentioned my name to implicate me in this horrible act.'

"Your grandfather calmly replied, 'You may be right, your Majesty. It is a matter that must be investigated until we find who is guilty and who is not. Justice should be done.'

"The king's voice rose even more. 'You killed my father and made up the entire story to put his blood on my innocent hands.'

"Here your grandfather stood like a mountain in front of the king and said in a more humble way than before, 'Your Majesty, now I am accused by you and you are accused by me. Hence, we must find who is guilty and who is not. Justice should be done. I swear that I was the servant of your martyred father and your late grandfather, not their killer.'"

"While the other court members were listening motionless, suddenly, the king picks up a stone paperweight from a table and throws it at your grandfather. The heavy stone hits him in the forehead and he starts to bleed. Your grandfather straightens up and stood tall once again in front of the king while cleaning blood from his face. He said, 'The same forehead that your father, the slain king, used to kiss, you hit with a stone.'"

"The royal court instantly became as silent as the silence after an earthquake. The king broke the silence in what sounded like a thunderous voice, sat on his golden throne and shouted, 'Now I am the king of Afghanistan, Mustofi. You must obey me. I am the power and you are nothing. I am the shadow of God and my judgment is His. I can imprison or kill anyone I want.'"

"Your grandfather bowed his head toward the ground and replies, 'Please go on, Majesty. Do whatever you want. You are the power.'"

"The king in an even louder voice called the guards. 'Take him and hang him instantly. Mustofi must be hanged. He is a traitor. He is an ungrateful liar. He is the killer of my beloved father.'"

"At his moment your grandfather called King Amanullah by his name without any formalities and said, 'Amanullah, without any proceedings, you are going to hang me.'"

"The king shouted, 'This is justice for a killer like you. This is justice for a traitor like you. A killer must be killed.'"

"Your grandfather might have murmured his prayers, but he loudly addressed the king, 'Amanullah, I am a faithful person. I believe that no one is more powerful than God. We will be seeing each other in the next world, where you and I will be standing before the Absolute Judge. I am sure your father will bear witness that I am innocent. I pray that you will not be found guilty by your own father.'"

"They hung the great man. Thank God, his kin have held up his honorable name."

The 85-year-old man wiped the tears rolling from his eyes, sighed deeply, and asked me to tell the version of the story to my father. I promised him I would.

I hope you have not been saddened reading about my grandfather. I do not know if it was the rain or his story that caused my joints to hurt more. I pray the pain does not increase. I have Cosprine and Advil painkillers with me, so do not worry.

More Rain

8:00 PM

Rain, rain, rain, and more rain. The once pleasant rain has become an unmerciful whip that strikes our hips, backs, heads, and shoulders with intensity. No longer is this rain a beautiful message of life from the silver clouds to the colorful friendly fields.

It is like the edge of a dagger. It is no longer a rainbow creator, no longer does it gently fill the tulip-cups with its divine wine, no longer does it play with the leaves of the trees and petals of the roses, and no longer does it invite the birds to happily fly about the fields.

I went outside and addressed the dark sky, "What blight has befallen you?" I received no reply; only more rain.

Now, I will make you smile a bit. On such a wet day, just an hour ago, Andy naively wanted to wash himself. He took Saleh, the young mute, to help him. A few minutes later Andy returned, and, in between yelling angrily at the mute or *gunga* boy, told me that the young lad had taken him to a muddy ditch and wanted to push him into it and kill him.

The poor boy, obviously, could not speak. All he could do was to wave and shake his hands and head. I immediately blamed Andy, and said, "You are responsible. Why do you shout at him?"

"No, I am not responsible. He wanted to push me into that dirty ditch. We should talk to him, seriously."

Noel started laughing at Andy, and there was a lapis lazuli seller who could not control himself and burst out laughing as well. Andy really lost his temper then, not just because of what had happened, but because all the people around him were laughing at him. Even the boy, without knowing what was going on, started to laugh.

Andy looked at me and said, "Look Masood, why is the gunga boy laughing at me?"

"Never go with someone who cannot talk or hear to a place you do not know. Whether there would be a dangerous ditch or a cunning witch there, you never know the intention of someone like him. Maybe he was trying to help you. Maybe he wanted to stop you going into that ditch and you thought he was pushing you. Maybe at that moment he wanted to pull you out."

Andy looked at me and said, "Again philosophy?"

I laughed and told him, "When I have such naïve friends like you with almost no wisdom, I can easily play Plato and Aristotle."

We both laughed loudly together and moved on.

9:30 PM

My dear, earlier I heard on BBC radio, in its English broadcast, that one of the Princes of England has married in the wedding of the century. I listened to the ceremony from beginning to end. Wow, what a ceremony it was! The whole of the United Kingdom seemed to have stopped for the day.

The splendor of the ceremony brought to mind our own most humble wedding on May 10, 1979. Do you remember you and I, along with my mother, my father, my brother Nejat, your brother Ehsan, and our uncles, Ibrahim and Esaaq, went to the mosque in Manhattan to get married?

Do you remember we were so poor that Uncle Ibrahim brought a simple bouquet of roses and a roll of film for us? Do you remember we had no reception, no music, no wedding gown, and even no smiles? What a painful happiness it was, for the communists had only recently, mercilessly, killed your father and uncles. We could not delay because we had to rush back to join the struggle for freedom in our own Afghanistan.

Though the wedding was small and unostentatious, we had the richest hearts, filled with a great challenge to fight for the freedom of our beloved land. We rushed from the mosque to our apartment at number 33, 275 Beach Street, Hackensack, New Jersey. Next day, leaving our poor wedding bed, I went to lead demonstrations against the Soviet invasion in front of United Nations Headquarters.

However great the marriage of the Prince of England or however small yours and mine, God has given us a happy life until now and I am happy that I have you and you are my significant other. Time passes so quickly. It is not important how fast or slow, it is important how we live it. In addition, I always pray and I am still praying, "May God keep us happy in whatever conditions we are, whether in a $244 rented Hackensack apartment, in a prison, or in the paradise."

10:30 PM

In the past, the Shamaali plain where I am was famous for its vineyards and sweet mulberries, but today they are being burnt down by bombs and smashed by rockets. The beautiful gardens of Istalif, Gul Bahar, Rukha, Charikar, and Sayed Khayl have been ground to dust and the crowded villages of Kodaman, Kohistan, and Panjshir have been deserted by most of their inhabitants.

No longer do people enjoy going to their gardens. No longer are the sounds of people reading poetry and songs in praise of Alexander the Great and Mahmud of Ghazni heard. No longer do soothing recitations from the Holy Book, the spiritual songs of Rumi, Sa'di, and Hafiz emerge through the windows of mud houses. No longer do the echoes of school bells reverberate. No longer the partridge fighting, the kite flying, the horse riding, and the Qarsak dancing which once formed such an essential part of the lives of the poor people.

They all have gone with the wind and been replaced by the sounds of helicopters and jet fighters. The common people, who have left their once sweet homes, now live in holes or caves in the mountains, with no warm clothes, lacking food, and with no fixed abode

This misery of one part of Afghanistan brings to mind the tragic stories of other parts. Two years ago, I went to Herat in the western part of the country on foot to visit the people and the freedom fighters. I walked all over for two months. I saw hundreds of villages completely and totally destroyed by Russian bombs or by long-range artillery; most of their inhabitants were killed, wounded, or forced to flee to Iran. Eight years ago, in 1978, the communist regime had killed about twenty thousand in just three days. One night, I was passing through the deserted villages of Rabat, Qulook, Howz Karbaas, and Maladaan, where we reached a place in which I saw a small half-destroyed house, with a light flickering in the distance. I was surprised how there could be a house with an inhabitant. The door was half-broken. I entered.

I found a dirty room, half-ruined, with no windows. A piece of old cloth with small holes was blocking a part of the broken window. There a woman sat alone on a filthy old mattress. Perhaps she was fifty years old. She could not be seen clearly in the flickering candle-light. I turned on my flashlight.

She instantly covered her face.

I said, "*Salaam*. Please do not be scared. I am a freedom fighter. I am your brother. *Ishtawnin?* [How are you?]" Instantly, I added, "Why are you living in such a dangerous place alone? Why did you not leave your home and go to Iran or Herat?"

She kept silent. I repeated my question.

She quietly answered, "I have lost my husband and my two young sons on this part of the earth six months ago. They were the bravest boys in the world. This home is full of their sweet memories, their voices, and their stories. That is why I stay here. Where else in the world should I take shelter? Do you understand?"

I said, "What are you waiting for? Are you a crazy old lady?"

She straightened up, looked at me in the eyes, and said very confidently, "I am waiting for one last bombardment to take my life as well."

I said, "This will be suicide and it is a sin."

She angrily said, "Take the light off of my face, brother. I do not care if it is a sin or not. Who are you to advise me? Just leave me alone."

I told my men that they have to help her and that we must take her with us. The men said that we should do this in the morning.

With anger she asked, "Why do you wish to take me from here?"

I responded, "Because you are alone."

She instantly replied, "No brother, you do not know. I am not alone. In the sky, God is with me, and on the ground, the memories of my beloved ones surround me. Just leave me alone. To me, you are all sinners. Just go and leave me alone."

While I was leaving, a white cat jumped onto her lap and I thought maybe it is a family cat, which keeps her from solitude. I left the area and did not stay there that night. What a miserable condition some of our poor people live in.

Barber, the Story Teller

Thursday, July 24
3:30 PM

I met some young scholars from the north, going to Pakistan. They were in their early twenties. They were bright students and I even met two poets among them. I told them they must help the common people as much as possible.

After talking to these boys, I went to have lunch with them. After the lunch, I slept more today, that is, at least four hours. This was when Commander Najmuddin kindly brought for me an old barber. His name was Khayrullah, the son of Hafeezullah. He looked in his late 50s and had a white beard like Ho Chi Minh, the leader of Vietnam. Khayrullah's father and grandfather were barbers as well.

He is from Shawa, in Panjshir. He does a great many things in the community: trimming beards, cutting hair, taking care of broken bones, fixing displaced joints, performing circumcisions, and extracting teeth.

Ah, what a man with so many interesting stories from past and present of the people whose hair and beards he has trimmed! He talked slowly and precisely. If a barber were to write, he could tell hundreds of stories about hundreds of people.

He did not know how beautifully his tales beguiled me. I wish I had time and another notebook to sit and write his 'trimmed stories'. He was also very proud of the fact that his grandfather trimmed my grandfather's beard and hair. This barber also knew of the story of how my grandfather was hanged.

Khayrullah's 35-year-old son was arrested and put in prison a year ago by the communist regime in Kabul.

As a father and a barber, with a deep sigh he told me, "Sir, I don't know who is cutting the hair of my son in the prison now. I wish I were there to do that for him."

When he left, I prayed that God may help him to see his son soon and cut his hair, before, God forbid, his head is cut off by the communists."

4:30 PM

My Dear, the weather is clear today. Though it rained this morning, now the sky is blue once again. The following poem came to mind. If I cannot send you a flower, at least let me share this flower poem with you.

Oh, the autumn wind
Do not come, do not come.
Do not make the flowers dry,
Do not let them die.
My beloved is coming.
Let her dance,
Let her enjoy.

O, the autumn wind,
Do not blow, do not blow.
Let my beloved dance.

The Deaf Boy

Jishta Village
Friday, July 25

Thank God, today since morning, the sky is blue and the *bodana* birds (woodpecker) were chirping their songs. From among the fields of wheat, the *tak tak tak* sounds of those birds beat a beautiful rhythm.

An hour ago, Saleh the gunga or deaf boy appeared, took his front-loading rifle or musket, and left the room. After five minutes, he returned with a small woodpecker in hand. The bird's wings were broken. The innocent glances of its tiny eyes broke my heart.

Here is Saleh's own life story. At nine years of age, he was playing football with some other poor boys around an old graveyard, in one of the poorest areas of Kabul, called Naw Abad. He was the best of all of them, fast and strong. He was a jolly boy. He was in second or third grade. He read well and sang the school songs beautifully. He was considered the nightingale of the class.

While playing football, the ball rolled in the direction of the graves and disappeared. Each boy searched here and there to find the ball. After more than an hour of searching, the ball was still not found. The ball was not cheap and they were all poor boys.

The day was getting dark and, finally, little Saleh saw an old grave in a corner at a lower part of the graveyard. He went toward it and saw that there was a hole on one side of the grave. He thought that the ball might have rolled into that very hole. He was scared and did not go forward.

He called his friends. Most of them did not agree that the ball might have rolled into the grave. They avoided crawling into it to look for the ball. Saleh insisted that he would go and look in the grave. The other boys left. Saleh was scared. He went to the hole and, all of a sudden, saw that his ball was resting in the hands of a skeleton. He first hesitated and did not know if he should take it or not. The beauty and value of the ball compelled him to take it from those dry old bony hands. As he grasped the ball, his hand slipped and the hand of the skeleton snapped.

When he reached home he told the story to his mother and then he went to sleep. When he woke up in the morning, he told his mother that he had had a nightmare, in which the skeleton appeared and remonstrated him for breaking his hand.

After recounting the nightmare to his mother, Saleh fell asleep on her bosom. When he woke up, he could not talk. His family blamed the nightmare for his ailment. Maybe they were right. I don't know.

1:30 PM

The little mosque of Jishta where we prayed has a carpet made of hay or straw. Maulavi Fatah led the prayer. With his white beard, short stature, wheat-like complexion, and a Mongolian face, he is the head of the religious scholars of Panjshir.

Today the weather is warmer and the sky is a deeper blue. The jets have not showed up this morning to bomb the area, maybe because it is Friday. At least everybody has a day off, the invaders and the invaded. I am not feeling that good. I have absolutely no appetite.

4:30 PM

My dear, a Soviet defector came to see me. Two years ago, he joined the resistance. He is a young man of 21 or 22. He has a thin, yellow beard, date-colored hair, and brown, almond-shaped eyes. He is of medium height, with a skinny body.

The first thing he told me was "I am not Russian, I am Romanian." He was wearing an anti-soviet fighter's *pakol* (soft, round-topped hat).

At first, he was a little bit reserved, naturally. Then slowly and gradually, he became open and friendly. I asked him, "Are you really a Romanian or a Russian?"

He confidently replied, "No, I am not a Russian, I am Romanian. I escaped during an operation and hid for two days in a small garden until an old lady helped me to reach the freedom fighters. Those were two of the most horrible days of my life: scared, hungry, thirsty, and lonely. It was a nightmare until I was sure that the fighters were not going to kill me. The minute I saw Commander

Massoud's friendly smile, I felt safer and even happy. He shared the little food he had with me and told me that I could stay with him. I will never forget that moment."

The Romanian also said that people in his country do not even know where Afghanistan is. "The Russians lied to us that there are thousands of Americans here and we were told that the people of Afghanistan hate America, but when we came here, we saw no Americans. That was when we found out that we were wrongly informed and had been cheated by the communist regime. Even the Russians themselves do not want to fight in Afghanistan, but they are sent by force or by deception. I have promised Commander Massoud that I will stay with him to the end. He is like my elder brother.

"It was still a difficult choice to defect. One of my friends defected in the east of Afghanistan but some resistance fighters killed him. Anyway, I am happy here and can do whatever I like. Fighters share their meager rations with me and even sometimes give me more than they should. People are generally good to me, especially the older women and men, they show me a lot of sympathy. I do not feel good when the Soviets attack the villages and kill the poor people but I am glad I am no longer one of the killers."

I shared with him some Russian sweets. He said we should avoid eating Russian sweets because the Russians may mix poison in them. I told him if he ever needed me he should let me know through Commander Najmuddin. I took a photo of him and we parted ways. Whether in good or bad hands, it is the worst thing to be a captive or a defector in another country. Home is home.

I might write to you later in the night or if I'm too tired, I will write to you tomorrow. I hope you and my boys are doing well.

Getting Impatient

Jishta Village
Saturday, July 26
12:00 noon

Last night I went to sleep early. My sleep was not so bad. It was on and off. Despite the fine weather, my mood was not good. When I woke today, I was not feeling well. I called Commander Najmuddin and asked what was going on and requested a briefing concerning Commander Massoud's situation. I said whatever the situation may be, I would be leaving soon.

The commander explained, "Russian attacks have started on Khost and Firring, in the areas where you have to go. Their commando troops have been dropped in the areas of Shayra and Mondara, which are located right in the areas where Commander Massoud is busy now."

Anyway, I started taking the antibiotic Flagil. Here we take antibiotics with no advice from a doctor and it works.

I decided to take a wash. Commander Najmuddin brought warm water and I took a good bath and felt much better which reduced my tiredness. If Commander Massoud has become stuck in the north, maybe tomorrow I myself will depart for there. It is better that I see him sooner. Today, the jets are flying overhead in sorties. They have bombarded Dasht-Raywat with no casualties on our side. I thought that they might start an attack and bomb the area that we are now in but it did not happen.

I sent someone to bring my rucksack from Chimmar. The sole of one of my New Balance boots, which in general have fared well, required repair so I gave the damaged shoe to the only cobbler in the area. He put some strong nails on the sole, which saved it from being totally ruined. The cobbler, like the barber was also a very interesting.

The cobbler said, "When I am repairing someone's shoes, I can read the character of that person. My grandfather taught my father and my father taught me how to be a good cobbler. My grandfather could even predict the future of a man by looking at his shoes."

I did not believe it and I frankly told him it was a smart way to catch more poor customers. He laughed and swore on his father that it was not a trick.

I asked Commander Najmuddin to find me a book of any sort to read.

He told me, "You are busy writing for hours, why do you also need to busy yourself with reading for hours?" I laughed and asked him to try and find one anyway.

By chance, he had an old book at home by Hafiz, the Sufi Poet, but immediately he said that someone in the lower village had a book on the life of Hitler, if I was interested. I laughed loudly and said, "Please bring both, Hafiz the farmer of love and Hitler, the planter of hatred; one plants love in your heart and the other provokes war in your mind."

When Commander Najmuddin went to get the book, his generous wife kindly sent us sweet delicious parathas, or Indian bread mixed with cheese. I would dearly like to thank her but here tradition offers me no other place to thank her, except here in my notes to you. She is a most generous and hardworking housewife. She makes us different kinds of delicious food.

She works from morning to night to feed the many guests who visit her husband. Most fighters' womenfolk do the same. They also believe in freedom and the victory of their husbands, sons, brothers, and fathers against the enemy.

These women are our unknown soldiers. They are not in uniform but they are braver than uniformed men. In such harsh circumstances, when they still rally and encourage their beloved ones to sacrifice their lives for the freedom of the land, they are our real heroes.

They suffer so much. They do not have pain merely in their hearts but live in the heart of pain. I wish I could go personally to every woman and thank them wholeheartedly. May God bless them.

9

Crossing the Hindu Kush Range—
Wheel of the Sky

Sunday, July 27
12:30 PM

My Dear, now I am on my way to the Khawaak Pass. At this
moment, I am sitting and writing in a nomad tent. Listen to how I
started and how I reached here.

I woke up around four this morning and, while preparing myself
to depart, I received an urgent message from Commander Massoud
saying that I should reach him as quickly as I could. Perhaps he
thought that I would get bored, not proceed forward, and return
to Pakistan, which I would not have done.

Although he mentioned in his message that the situation was
extremely bad in his area, with intense daily bombings by the
Russians, I decided to go as quickly as I could toward him.

I left everyone else in Panjshir, in the good hands of Commander
Najmuddin. I did not tell this to all of the British television team
as I did not want to alarm them. I simply told Andy that they
should stay there until they get a message from me or Commander
Massoud to come to Takhaar, or wait until Commander Massoud
comes back to Panjshir, and then they can interview him. It might
have been hard for them to wait and watch me move on but it had
to be this way.

Commander Najmuddin provided me with a horse and a good
horseman named Noor Ali. He also provided me with a small
contingent of freedom fighters for my security. I did not have
many things to carry except my camera and my notebooks. I again
thanked Commander Najmuddin and, at this moment, I especially
conveyed my thanks to his wife and his family too. By saying *hai
maidaan o tai maidaan*, which means 'O ground, I will beat you', I
started my journey.

* * *

After two hours of hiking among sharp rocks and big boulders, we crossed a relatively high and difficult pass with no name, or at least Noor Ali did not know it. It was layer after layer with a steep slope. The pass was such that as soon as you thought you have reached the top, another higher peak would suddenly appear in front of you. Thank God, we then came upon some Panjshiri summer pastures and encountered Pashtoon tribesmen, the sight of which was a real source of comfort for us. Their corralled horses were handsome, tall, happy, and even fat.

At the bottom of the nameless pass, I felt very cold. I waited until my horse arrived, put on my sweater and coat, then went a distance on horseback. We traveled until we reached the village of Khaawaak. No one lived there. The whole village had been bombed and destroyed.

A little further along, there was an old fort which had also been bombed and deserted. At 8 AM, we reached Chownee Khaawaak, which was once a sort of caravansary, built in fact by my grandfather in 1908. Everything was destroyed, bombed, and deserted.

I am currently in a nomadic tea-tent and Omar Gul is its owner. There are some women here as well. A young child, the same size as our little Mahmud, is playing with his small goat. His name is Tora Gul. These *kochie*s, or nomads, are from the Pashtoon tribes of the Laghman province and every summer they come here with their animals. From here, I intend to go toward Khaawaak, and from there to the Charkh-i-falak Pass or 'Wheel of the Sky'. The owner of the tea-tent insistently invited me to eat with him. Journey from here to the base of Khaawaak Pass takes three hours.

Today, there are many planes patrolling the skies. They dropped two bombs in the adjacent mountain and three bombs close to us. It was very loud and created lots of dust and smoke and sound. It had, thank God, no effect but delayed us by twenty minutes. Neither horse nor the horseman paid any attention to it. Omar Gul said, "The Russians bomb every two days."

Tonight, Noor Ali and I will sleep here among the boulders and rocks, under the starry sky of God, at the bottom of the Charkh-i-falak Pass, waiting and praying to cross it safely in the middle of the night. Omar Gul, the tea-tent shepherd, has already warned me of possible bombardment and the difficulty of the pass.

Monday, July 28
10:44 AM

I have crossed the Hindu Kush range. The Charkh-i-falak Pass was very difficult. After nine hours of difficult travel, I am sitting in the beautiful valley of Charkh-i-falak, among great boulders, writing to you. This valley is bigger than the Panjshir Valley and is extremely attractive.

The blue sky, the crystal clear river, the high mountains, the big boulders, the waterfalls rushing down from the side-valleys, the tall green trees, the wild flowers, the caressing weather, the small birds, the summer pastures, and the children of shepherds running behind their animals, welcomed my heart and mind after such an extremely difficult hike over the *Wheel of the Sky*.

Listen to how we climbed it and how it looked.

The hard route we traveled today is an ancient one, for centuries taken by merchants, conquerors, and ordinary travelers. Even the meaning of Charkh-i-falak, the Wheel of the Sky, was terrifying to me. We started our journey at 1:40 AM. For me, it was hard but was excited as it was the first time I was climbing this pass. In the beginning, the track was fine, with few rocks, but after an hour, it became very rough. The poor horse had great difficulty and I told the horseman to take the reins while I walked. Thank God, the horse's load was light. Twice the horse fell. Although he hurt his left leg, he was able to climb slowly. I also started to suffer from slight nausea and dizziness.

Noor Ali realized that I was not feeling well and gave me a small lump of natural salt to place under my tongue. It worked a little. It took us about two and a half hours to reach the bottom of the pass, which was littered with boulders and rocks. It was 4:30 AM then. Noor Ali gave me a small piece of bread, which was at least three days old. The weather became colder. There was snow on the peaks. I was thirsty but because of the extreme cold, I could not drink directly from the next mountain spring we passed. Therefore, I broke open my ballpoint pen, made a straw, and then I was able to drink from the freezing cold spring without causing ice burn. The cold had frozen my hands, face, and nose.

As we began our ascent, our horse moved with difficulty. He fell once again and badly wounded himself. Noor Ali suggested that we should leave the horse there and go on without the animal.

I could not accept this. After 20 steps, we both returned to try to help the poor horse. I could not leave the horse like that until he dies.

Noor Ali said, "If we kill him and go on, it is even better and easier for the horse and for us."

I could not do that either.

Thank God, at 5:45 AM, the horse, Noor Ali, and I managed to reach the top of the pass. It was beautiful. I could not believe my eyes. The sky was so close to the peaks that I could see its blue tinge reflected upon the snow. It was as if God has spread crystal-clear blue silk on some shiny white surface. I thought that if I had the choice, I would choose these colors for the flag of a free Afghanistan. We three were the owners of the mountain and the possessors of its beauty, sitting on the Wheel of the Sky.

I looked at Noor Ali and said, "Thank God we did not give up and brought the horse with us, otherwise, this poor travel companion of ours would now be standing lonely, waiting to die."

He patted his horse and thanked God too. I wanted to stay longer on the Wheel of the Sky when, the jets appeared in the sky and dropped some bombs. It disturbed our enjoyment of this beautiful vision with its breathtaking views. Twice the jets circled and dropped three more bombs very close to us. Three nights ago, they had bombed this area as well.

We rushed to make our descent. It was again not an easy task. It was very steep with sharp rocks. First, Noor Ali fell and hurt his foot. Then, the horse fell and could not move when his leg became stuck between two big boulders.

In the end, it took about four hours from the top to reach here, but if we calculate the time, starting out from Chownee Khawaak, it took almost ten hours of continuous walking. The pass had the longest, steepest, and hardest paths, with boulders and jagged rocks everywhere. If I consider Nooristan's Kantiwa Pass the king of all passes, then the Khawaak Pass is definitely its minister of defense. For me, both are the hardest and roughest, but both are unforgettably beautiful too. At this very moment, I am both hungry and thirsty.

I am sitting in a summer pasture on the northern flank of the Khawaak Pass. Noor Ali has gone to see if he can find something to eat. Noor Ali is a good man. The main difference between him and my old horseman is that Noor Ali does not have a 10-year-old son and my mind is more at ease.

Welcoming Children

Kezer Village, Khost, Baghlan
5:00 PM

If I calculate from early morning until now, we have been walking for almost 15 hours, and this is the second village that I have seen on the way.

The first was called Dara Deh. We were extremely hungry and tired when we arrived. The first person we met told us that a wealthy man named Haji Saleh was living nearby, and if we call him, he would give us a place to rest and may provide us with some food. I happily agreed because I knew Haji Saleh. Every time I was in Panjshir in the past, he always treated me with great hospitality. Therefore, I told Noor Ali to walk over and knock on his door, and inform him that I am here.

I watched as Noor Ali approached his house and knocked on the door but instead of my friend, his brother appeared and informed him that everyone had gone to the pasture and only he had remained home.

Noor Ali greeted him and requested hospitality on my behalf, but the old man instantly started shouting at him angrily, saying, "Why are you here? Why did not you take him straight to the mosque? Do you not know that everybody has gone up to the pasture?"

"The mosque is closed. No one is there, sir."

The man shouted back at him, "It is not my fault that the mosque is closed. That is not my house; it is the house of God."

"We simply wish, if possible, to get or buy some food. We are hungry and, as you said, no one is around to sell us food."

The moment he was about to close the door, I walked over and intervened, putting my foot on the threshold so that he could not close the door. I said, "Why are you shouting at this young man so rudely? If you don't give food, that is fine and we will move on, but why are you screaming at someone who humbly asks you for something?"

I was loud and curt but I was very tired and very hungry, and at that moment, my patience was wearing thinner than a sparrow's throat.

Here Noor Ali introduced me to Haji Saleh's brother. Then the poor old man became very humble, extremely kind, and exceptionally polite which made me feel like a shard of ice on the threshold.

With extremely modest words, he tried to compensate for his previous ones by inviting me into his home.

However, I could not melt my icy mood to accept his request. It was very hard for me to have food with someone against whom I had used very harsh words. I know that I made him very sad, not only by my bad words, but by not accepting to enter his home. He followed me at for at least a hundred yards as we walked away.

But never think that all doors are closed. As I was angrily leaving the village, I saw a sweet six-year-old girl on the way, carrying a small basket of fresh mulberries on her head.

With the breeze gently playing with her colorful dress, it looked as if a tiny beautiful bush was gently swaying with a basket of flowers on its head. She gave me a handful of fresh mulberries. Alas, her hand was too little to give me more. She said that she is taking the mulberries up to the pasture and refused to give me a little bit extra. I did not bother her because she seemed sweeter than the mulberries and I did not want to make her sweet mood sour. After asking her to sell me some, she very cutely said, "Do you not know, the mulberry is never for sale?"

The village of Kezer resembles the gardens of Paghman and Kohistan. Noor Ali is trying to look for someone to help us. At the bottom of the village, there is a ferocious river and high mountains on either side of it. When entering this area, I saw trees of white mulberries, apricots, apples, plums, almonds, walnuts, and sweet cherry. Another little girl had a basket full of apricots but did not give me any.

Now, I am sitting on the veranda of the village mosque. I pray that the mullah of this masjid (mosque) has not gone up to the pasture too. Since I see very few people in the village, perhaps only the mullah might be able to acquire some food for us. The sounds of sparrows come from every tree.

You can see an ugly drawing of a lion on the wall. In the mosques, we sometimes paint animals such as horses, lions, tigers, and birds, but we always avoid painting the faces of human beings.

The houses around this area greatly resemble the houses of the Kohistani and Qarabaaghi villages north of Kabul. They are small, muddy, but clean. In order to fix the broken glass in the windows, they have covered them with sheets of paper or newspapers. Incidentally, on one of the papers covering the window of the mosque, I saw a beautiful photo of Niagara Falls, from the Canadian side.

Just now, God has sent us someone named Hafeezullah. He is the son of Mullah Walee. He looks about 17 or 18 years old. In our country, one never knows the exact age of a person. We do not keep the date in which we are born. Our dates of birth are not registered anywhere, whether in the villages or in the cities. We are all home-born. Sometimes elders write the date in a corner of a Holy Quran, and even this is only possible if they know how to write. Sometimes they try to remember the season in which a baby is born.

For example, they say that he or she was born in the season of flowers, grapes, and walnuts, which are spring, summer, and autumn, respectively. Hafeezullah also did not know the exact date of his birth but mentioned that he was born in grape season. Another way that people try to figure out how old they are is to mention who was in power at the time of their birth. For example, they say that they were born when King Zahir was in power.

The Lion King

6:30 PM

We were waiting for something to eat when again Hafeezullah's face, flat like a cut apple, appeared. When I asked him if he had mulberries to give us, he generously said that all the mulberry trees are ours. By his generous offer, I presumed his family to be the owners of all of these trees.

"We do not own all the trees, but this house and all the trees around are yours, my dear brother. Eat as much as you like and be relaxed. You are our guest, and a guest, whether poor or rich, is a friend of God, sent by Allah for a good purpose."

I liked the way he expressed himself and appreciated the manner in which he offered it.

A white-bearded, one-eyed man with a wrinkled forehead passed with a bucket full of fresh apricots. I called out to him, "Hey, you are taking a basket of red apricots and do not even give a few to a sinless traveler like me?"

The old man shouted back, "Why do you ask in such a round-about way? If you are poor just tell me how many apricots you want. I do not care whether a poor man is sinless or a sinner."

He kindly offered me five.

I thanked him. "May God increase the number of the apricot trees in your garden by five times. Thank you."

A sweet small boy named Shair Paachaa, or *Lion King*, cracked the seeds of the apricots and both of us ate them, which were sweeter than the apricots themselves.

Noor Ali bought a chicken for 200 Afghani (1.40$) from a traveler and gave it to another little boy to take to his sister to cook for us. His name was Abdul Hay. He said that since his sister was sick and did not go to the pasture, she would cook for us. You know, my dear, after more than fourteen and a half hours' walking, crossing the Charkh-i-falak Pass, hunger is a difficult state of mind, tiredness of the body is even more so, and all you have is your heart to keep you from totally giving up. We have to move on and keep going. The war won't stop because we are hungry or tired.

Here, most children have gone to the summer pastures. Fortunately, a few are still here. If there is no bombardment in the pastures, these children feel happy or, as we say, their feelings become fat because they are up in the mountains with their families and goats. It is fun for the little boys and girls to sleep and wake up next to their goats.

Another boy showed up. He is a child with large eyes, a small body but a big head. His name is Zayer. He is called by other boys *kala kata* (big head). He hates when the boys call him this. He is from Panjshir. He is an internal refugee. His father has gone to Badakhshan to buy some sheep and goats.

He said, "I am happier here because there is less bombing than in my land. The jets are very scary. When they fly in the sky, I feel they only see and follow me. When I see them come, I hide in the caves and wait for a long time until I am sure that they are gone. I hate their sounds but my elder brother is not so scared. I know that the jets come to kill us. I tell my brother to escape too because the Russians come for nothing but to kill. Are you scared of jets?"

"Yes," I replied. "I am also scared of the fighter jets. They are terrifying and they come to kill. It is natural to be scared but when you are in the cave, do not worry about them."

The child keenly listened to what I said and instantly offered me mulberries. Although I thanked him and declined, he searched his small pocket and gave me some anyway with his tiny hand.

The Lion King then went and brought me some apricots and fresh mulberries. After eating some and talking to some other small children, I began to feel much better. When I asked the Lion King to tell me the names of the villages in this long and beautiful valley, he asked me, "What will you do with all these names?"

"It is good to know. It is useful for me and for others who may read it. In addition, I am writing these notes to my wife, the mother of my little sons."

A strange look appeared on his face and he said, "What is the use of writing to them?"

I smiled. "I feel like when I do this, they are with me. It makes me feel happy. My first son is six years old and one day when he grows up, he will read it. Maybe he will travel here and read it to you too. Wouldn't that be great? God has not only given us a gun to fight for freedom but also a pen to write for peace and love."

I do not know whether his little mind could understand what I told him.

He added sweetly, "There are many waterfalls. We go to them to wash. One corner of the waterfall is just for the girls. My mother washes our clothes there too. I go to the river to wash my hands and face every morning. My uncle has a net to fish in the river. My father takes our horses and our sheep to the pasture. I want to learn to play flute like my cousin. Whenever he goes to the summer pasture, he plays nicely for his goats and sheep. He makes good flutes out of reeds from the nearby reed fields. We have deer and even tigers in our mountains."

The Lion King was talking like a stream of water running calmly through a wild mint field. He will never know that he is one of the poorest boys in the world. He does not know that if he gets sick, there is no doctor or any medicine. He does not know that he does not have good shoes or nice clothes. He does not know that he is deprived of a school, even if only a simple place to learn to read and write, forget about toys and other childish luxuries.

Maybe he is luckier for not knowing. These poor boys and girls are even deprived of peace and security. Instead of flying kites for fun, they see flying jets bombing them from the sky. I asked the Lion King if he had any marbles so we could play together. He rushed to bring them to me. He also brought me five old walnuts and innocently said with a big smile, "Let us play!"

I enjoyed my time with the little Lion King.

Bazaar Day

Do Aabee Village
Garden of Jaan Mohammad
Tuesday, July 29
12 noon

A flat three-hour walk brought us to the village of Do Aabee, which is flatter and more beautiful than Kezer, with more people, huts, and shops, and a blue sky. By chance, today is a bazaar day in Garm Aow, as is every Monday and Friday. The bazaar was lively and cheerful with vendors, sitting on *chaarpaayee*s (summer beds), under old cloth awnings, sparse wares laid out on the ground, and four or five small mud shops.

Wahdatyaar, the head of the resistance financial office was waiting for me right in the middle of the bazaar. As soon as he told me his position, I realized that this is an area with some administrative basis. It means the freedom fighters have organized the area alongside their own war administration.

While I was talking to Wahdatyaar, the smell of fresh-roasted meat from the bazaar made me almost intoxicated. Wahdatyaar sensed this and said, "Come. Eat kebab, as my guest."

He ordered three portions of Seekh Kebab. I ate whatever I could manage. A man named Malim brought a very fine tea. This young man was once a teacher. His real name must have been different but people call him teacher. He was a funny man. He knew some poems as well.

While I was eating kebab, the most delicious barbeque in the world, Malim began to recite one of my father's poems. I think it might have been the first time that I did not take any interest in listening to a poetry recitation. I was so engrossed in devouring this tasty kebab that I could not pay attention to a Malim reciting even my own father's poems. It was not my fault, it was the kebab's. He asked me how the poem was. I said honestly, "I am sorry I did not pay attention." He said that it was a poem by my father. I told him "At this moment, for me, beauty lies in barbeque, not in poetry."

I encouraged the teacher by saying, "Having a teacher in these villages means having the future in your hands. A village without a teacher is like a man with no eyes and ears or a hungry man with no kebab."

He got a pen and a piece of paper and quickly noted this down. I liked seeing that someone was taking notes. It was the first time on this trip of mine that I saw someone other than the British television crew and I taking notes.

I asked Wahdatyar about the bazaar and about how people bring their limited goods here. The bazaar looked very poor but nonetheless was a beautiful sight to behold. Even turkeys, partridges, and ducks could be seen. The turkeys were really fat and fast. I saw about 20 to 25 of them running around. A tall, slim young man with a very long walking stick stood behind them. He was trying to stop the dogs from harassing his birds. They looked like two-legged goats with black and gray wings. The man who was taking care of them looked like a cave-less shepherd. I wanted to go to him and talk to him but the financial officer did not like this, so I dropped the idea.

An old woman was selling quroot. Another one had two beautiful, colorful roosters. An old man was selling a dozen or so small, handsome, and vibrant singing birds, in a very old cage. Someone else was selling second-hand or even new Russian army accessories, such as hats, boots, gloves, sweaters, socks, uniforms, torches, and even buttons and belts. I could not stop myself from going closer to investigate.

I talked to the little girls selling fish. One of them, maybe ten years old, told me that her father is a fisherman and catches fish every day. She was happy that this week her father had caught eleven.

A messenger came from Commander Massoud. His name is Jaan Mohammad. The moment I shook his hand I noticed his impressive features. His wide mouth, big nose, visible nasal passages, and a particular way of laughing were the first to attract my attention. In a few minutes, I found that he was a very nice, jolly man. He said that before joining the Jihad, he worked at the Kabul Hotel. He had contact with many elite and high-ranking people. He said he took care of guests better than anyone else. He said, "I am now amongst people who know nothing about these things. They are so poor and backward that they have not even seen the city of Kabul, let alone the Kabul Hotel."

He said, "Amir Sahib is anxiously waiting to see you." By *Amir Sahib* he meant Commander Massoud. He is called Amir Sahib as a sign of respect when we are talking to one another about him, or especially if we are talking to him. Sometimes people just call him *Commander*. I liked the way he talked. He seemed honest and friendly.

This place has one or two small schools. The people are mostly ethnically Tajik and they speak Dari. In the past, it was a very well-off village. The people were merchants who traded wheat and rice. The women wove rugs and some of them still might be doing it. I notice that the women wear different colored dresses than Nooristani women. Men are mostly attired in long green, brown, and gray-colored cloaks. They wear turbans or traditional sheepskin hats called *qarakuli* that are black, white, brown, yellow, and gray.

The food tastes and smells better than the food in the eastern and southern parts of the country. They have meat, beans, and different kinds of vegetables. The bazaar where I was before forms part of this village of *Doh Aabee*, or two waters.

Since Wahdatyar's home is close to here, he kindly invited us to his garden. On two sides, there are streams of water. I will stay here until 4 PM.

I asked Jaan Mohammad how we would proceed to the next town? He said, "There is a jeep waiting." I exclaimed, "Is that so, a jeep? The Commander's jeep? What great news!" However, he paused for a moment and said, "Khalili Sahib, the jeep is there but it does not have fuel. Now, since the jeep does not have fuel, you have to go by horse to reach the area of Yakha." Here in Afghanistan, we call any 4x4 a jeep. Although the Commander's is Russian-made, we also call it a Jeep. I hope we can find fuel in time.

I informed Jaan Mohammad that a very prominent team of journalists is also on their way to make a documentary about Commander Massoud. They are waiting on word from me to come here. They are in a hurry. Jaan Mohamed said that the commander is awaiting them too. I sent a very short letter to Sandy Gall asking them to leave as soon as they can for here.

Olang Zarda Village

We traveled by horse for an hour to reach here. When we reached Olang Zarda, an hour's ride by horse, next to the river, we laid out rugs and we performed the evening and twilight prayers.

On the way, I met a brave man called Doctor Saleh Mohammad. He had worked for eighteen years in the Health Ministry in Kabul. He has traveled all over Afghanistan to fight against malaria.

I asked him about the situation with malaria in Afghanistan before the war. He said that before the war, with the help of the UN and WHO organizations, we had reduced the prevalence of malaria in the north by 80 percent, but sadly, now it has increased again by 90 percent. He also told me that *sel* (tuberculosis) has spread much more than before, especially amongst the elderly and children. Women are the first victims. Besides malaria, he also gave me a long list of the names of other illnesses. He looked like a nice man and a hardworking paramedic.

Later, a group of educated and well-informed young people from the area came to see me. One of them was very sad and said, "Let us pray that the war ends."

Another asked me, "Do you think we can eventually win this war?"

I looked at him, replied, "I cannot even think that we will lose this war."

He said that he is educated and had worked in the Education Ministry. Another was once a judge and two others had worked in some offices in Kabul and the Baghlan provinces.

The judge said that it is almost impossible for poor people like ours to win a war against a superpower like the Soviet Union.

I asked him if we should give up.

He said not at all.

While addressing the others too, I said, "Be honest in choosing your goal. Do not worry and go on with one weapon. Hope."

He nodded his head and said, "You words are like poetry. I wish we could win the war with poems."

I told him, "Listen to me very carefully. If you do not surrender to the enemy and if you do not give up hope, even if you die before you gain freedom, you have won and achieved your goal. You are an educated person, go on, do not give up, work hard, trust your people, and mobilize them. Never worry about other things. For how long and how far can the unjust rule? For me, freedom is around the corner."

Before we could finish our pleasant and friendly discussion, our host called us for dinner, which was tastier than our discussion.

10

Poor Jeep, Poor Donkey, Poor Surgery

Wednesday, July 30
6:30 AM

I am now in a village called Saray Meerza. Just read how I started last night from the previous small village.

I was on my way to sleep when, all of a sudden, two men entered my room and informed me that the car was ready to take me to the next destination. To assure me, they showed me a letter too.

When I was sure that everything would be fine, I asked jokingly, "Is it the same fuelless jeep that Jaan Mohammad was talking about?"

"Yes, exactly. It is the same jeep but now it has fuel," one of them replied.

The men packed my clothes, sacks, and my camera in the fastest way imaginable. I was amazed how fast they do their work. I thanked them and told them to slow down and not to rush. They started to reply all at once, but one continued, "Since the engine is still running and we are not sure it will start again if we turn it off, we have to rush. It is an old jeep but the driver is very tough."

We started going down toward Massoud's grand Russian jeep. Actually, when I reached it, the engine was running and the men were happy to see it so. The first thing I saw by my flashlight was an old Russian four-wheel-drive, with no top, and full of bullet holes.

More interesting was the driver of the jeep. I knew him. He had been Commander Massoud's driver for a long time. His name was Gul Mamad but we used to call him Kaka, or Uncle. I jumped into the front seat and the jeep started moving. With an eye on the road, he told me, "Commander Massoud is eagerly waiting for you."

The odometer on the jeep howled 155,438 km, and it seemed to have stuck there. No one, including Kaka, could tell me when the odometer had stopped working. Even though it was an extremely bumpy ride, I shook hands with everyone, ten armed fighters, while Kaka was still roaring louder than his jeep at them. My first question to them was "How is *Amir Sahib*?

Almost all of them replied at once, "Fine. Fine!"

Kaka said angrily, "Is it not better that one answers, not all at once? The Holy Prophet advises every Muslim to talk one by one. If you do not know this much, how do you claim to be good freedom fighters? Jihad is not just to kill the godless enemy but to behave nicely too."

Mines, ambushes, and bombardments are just some of the possible dangers on the way, while riding in one of the oldest, ugliest, and dirtiest vehicles I have ever encountered. Since it was the only vehicle, it seemed more beautiful than a Rolls Royce to me.

One of the front lights did not work, and the other light was repeatedly turning on and off, for no reason. Kaka kept talking to me the whole way. The shadows made by the jeep's only headlight made the entire scene more terrifying. I should be honest with you. I did not know much of what Kaka was talking about. With the bumps and jumps of Commander Massoud's fuel-reeking Russian 4 × 4, it was hard to hear and understand what Kaka was saying.

Every two to three minutes Kaka was pushing me to the side with his shoulder, while trying to change gear from second to first, and back again. We never used third gear. After about 40 minutes, we reached an area called Yakha. All 10 fighters shouted in unison, "Kaka! Stop! Kaka, stop at the restaurant. We want to eat something. Please stop!"

Kaka stopped the car. I found that there was no conventional restaurant with four walls, but only a traditional, home-made stove heater, which was placed in the middle of an open field, next to the river. Many melons and a set of very old weighing scales had been placed next to it. Small and big rocks served as its weights. This, in theory, was considered a restaurant.

Kaka said that he had not eaten food and they fried a piece of meat for him. They bought for me a melon. Its price was 24 Afghani or 16 cents. It was not at all sweet. I tried a little of the fried meat that Kaka was having and it was extremely delicious.

The name of this village is Saraayi Meerza. Surprisingly, I found that Meerza himself is still alive. He is the owner of this village, the father of seven sons, and the father-in-law of seven young women. He welcomed me warmly. One of his eyes is blind. He is 70-years-old. He has a small garden, with patches of peppers, tomatoes, potatoes, wheat, and rice. Now I am sitting in his garden.

He is very kind to me. He asked me whether the war would be over soon.

I made him happy by saying, "Despite being old, you will see freedom and peace in your lifetime."

Cold War Theater: Resistance Caves

Shast Dara Village
10:30 AM

We arrived here about an hour ago. We are in the Shast Dara village, which is the central base of Commander Massoud in the north of the Hindu Kush mountain range. The high mountains, deep valley, and highly strategic location of this place, clearly show that it must be Commander Massoud's base.

In this place, Commander Massoud's men have dug *sumuch* (military caves or hideouts). They are as safe as the hideouts of the resistance in the southern parts of Afghanistan but much safer than the hideouts in other parts of the country. They are not just hideouts but can serve as traps in case the Russians attack with their commandos or ground troops.

The first to welcome me were Dr Fana and Dr Haqbeen. Both had many things to say, and were kind enough to generously offer me tasty tea with some raisins and walnuts.

My dear, right now, I am sitting in one of the *sumuch*s and talking to you. The men are overly kind to me. They are well disciplined and relatively better dressed than those in other places of the country I have visited so far. Here, there are fighters, advisers, a few medical doctors, as well as Commander Massoud's cultural, political, and logistical teams. The place I am in now is exactly the place where, one month ago, the Russians dropped 100 bombs and 1,000 commandos descended. Some fighters and civilians were killed.

In this valley, the resistance shot down some enemy helicopters, and a Soviet high-ranking officer was killed. Massoud was able to obtain maps from the downed helicopters which showed detailed plans of the Russians' would-be air strike targets.

They also told me that the mines planted by the freedom fighters worked very well against the Soviet commandos and, as a matter of fact, some of them descended right onto the minefields.

Anyway, the hideouts are spacious. One can easily move around the inside of the caves. There are three kinds of caves, which are chosen in such a way that they cannot be damaged by bombardment. In one of the inner caves, I found some small sacks of potatoes, onions, and a big piece of meat. They say they have rice and a sack of sugar too but I did not see them.

When I saw the resistance leaders' very limited supplies, which were not enough to last even two days, especially here in Massoud's main central base, I wondered how they could have such high morale with such a meager storehouse. I sarcastically told Dr Fana, "I did not expect our commanders to have such a large store of essential supplies in reserve."

First, he did not understand what I meant and then laughed loudly and said, "Do you know that we even have a sack of sugar?" Maybe his was also a sarcastic point.

I hope you will be able to read my tiny, hastily scribbled, and scatty handwriting in my small yellow notebook.

4:20 PM

From the beginning of the day when I reached here, all I have done is to talk to people and write. An interesting man of about 50 years brought a big watermelon and said, "The civilians do not like the Soviet Army. They simply say that the Russians are nonbelievers and have the same view about the Afghan communist puppet regime.

I know that many of the Afghan communists are not faithless but the perception is that a communist is a godless person. They consider the communist very immoral with no ethics, while all the freedom fighters are faithful and all of them are highly moral and extremely ethical."

I said to him, "I agree with you because of their ideology, all communists are faithless. You should know this fact that not all communists are immoral and not all our fighters are ethical. In both, you can find good and bad."

On hearing this, he looked at me and sincerely said, "I agree with you now. A freedom fighter commander severely beat his wife every night and no one could do anything about it. She was my daughter. He broke her hand and wanted to cut her ears. Now I have brought her back home. I also beat my wife but not that much."

Soon after, I met some men from the Kapisa and Parwan provinces. They said that the younger brother of a close friend of mine has become the head of the intelligence service of the puppet regime, in the Parwan, Kapisa, and Bamyaan provinces. His brother is a great friend of mine and belongs to a great family. We grew up together but, unfortunately, the war has made us enemies.

In the afternoon, they prepared for us white rice with pieces of meat. There is a well-known man here by the name of Dr Abdul Rahman. He is a medical doctor. He is around 35 years old. He is not practicing medicine here. He is very busy in the political mobilization of the people and other freedom fighter groups. I will probably talk to him later.

Shast Dara

11:00 PM

My dear, while the black bird of night spreads its wings over everything, we drink our tea in the light and under the shadows of the lanterns, and sit in a relatively large resistance hideout on clean mattresses and beautiful carpets. The men have taken off their boots. Everybody is trying to relax. The dim light of the lantern is creating shadows on the large and small bodies of Dr Rahman and five or six other local resistance intellectuals. It makes for a very special atmosphere and ambiance.

While the soothing sounds of the mullah's recitation of the Quran was still touching my heart and mind, I asked Dr Abdul Rahman if he had any cassettes of Afghan classical music, which we could listen to. Without replying, he quickly went to his ancient rucksack and took out an even more ancient cassette. From the worn-out look of the cassette, I guessed that he had probably listened to it 1,000 times.

We started listening. It was very soothing to hear songs sung by Saraahang, the king of Afghan classical music. I thought if the sound of the recitation of the Holy Book was coming down from the heavens, the sound of these classic songs was ascending to the skies. The music brought me back to the old days of my childhood and the time when I was a student. The spiritual poetry of one of the songs that touched my soul went something like this:

I am the soul of the lovers and the lovers are my soul.
Tonight, I am the guest of God and
God is a guest of mine
Tonight I am the souls of the lovers,
The lovers are my soul.
The world dances in front of me.
Everything from the earth to the sky has become one.
Everything has become love.

We all liked the music and listened for almost an hour or more. It made my heart and soul relax. The echo of the tunes and the play of the shadows on the walls made it feel very special.

While still listening to the music, I started a discussion with Dr Rahman and other friends. I told him that the time will, inshallah, come that we capture Kabul, enter it with our green and white banners, celebrate our freedom for seven days, and then what? Are we doing anything now to prepare ourselves for that time?

Abdul Rahman said that that is exactly what Commander Massoud was saying as well. "I have heard him say many times that the day will arrive when we install our heavy weaponry on the mountain peaks of Kabul, move forward, attack the heart of the city, and destroy the palace of the cruel communist oppressors. Then we have to bring peace and security for our war-ridden people. Are we working for that now?"

I told him, "Commander Massoud is very right, Doctor. Once we gain freedom, our goal should be to bring peace to the hearts, minds, homes, gardens, mountains, villages, cities, towns, schools, and even the mosques of the people. War is the cruelest lane to liberty, but peace gives us the best chance to see a light at the end of that lane and enjoy our freedom. We should all fight for a free and peaceful Afghanistan. War is necessary when there is no freedom, but peace is essential when there is freedom."

As I was still expressing myself, Dr Abdul Rahman cut me off, took off his glasses and cleaned them forcefully. I could see clearly the flickering reflection of the light from the lantern upon his shiny, bald head.

He put his glasses back on, touched his fist-sized black beard with his left hand, glanced like a hawk at all the men, lit another cigarette, and addressed us saying, "What you said makes sense that we must work harder and waste no time. We intellectuals have to be closer to Commander Massoud and not allow religious and fanatic elements to be by his side. Fanaticism and extremism are dangerous. They are like 'snakes in their sleeves'. They are 'water under the carpet'. They are scared of their own shadows. They are suspicious of every new thing."

Between these tedious and hot political discussions, I was also listening to the words of the singer coming from the cassette player. He was singing a folk piece about the time our people fought against the British. It was so beautiful that I asked Doctor Rahman to light a cigarette for me too. The doctor is a chain smoker. Listen to the poetry of the song:

Oh my beloved, stop your sweet caresses
Take your gun,
The British are behind the line of fire?
Kabul is burning.

Shast Dara

Thursday, July 31
4:30 AM

Last night after saying goodnight to everyone else, I went to another cave to write some things to you, and it was around midnight that Dr Abdul Rahman called me to help find a space amongst the boulders for me to sleep, and luckily, we found a relatively flat place.

While Massoud was in the nearby mountains, the freedom fighters were working hard, the Russians were planning their operations, the world was watching us in the light of their own interests, the cold war was in the fifth gear, and the poor people of this village were dreaming of freedom and hoping for peace, I told myself whatever happens, let it happen, and went to sleep.

Let me talk a little bit more about last night and how the fighters manage to sleep in such a rough and rocky area. Each person looks for a relatively flat space for himself, spreads a cloth underneath as a mattress, pulls a patoo over his face and lays down to sleep.

They take a rock, cover it with their combat jackets, and use it as a pillow.

Despite all these hardships, perhaps they sleep deeper than those who sleep in five star hotels in Switzerland. This type of sleeping arrangement is a direct result of the particular circumstances of men at war, for they have no alternative due to abject poverty. They have no quilt, no pillow, no extra patoo, or blanket. One flashlight is shared amongst five to ten fighters. The lucky ones have one pair of shoes for a whole year or until they are totally worn out. They have one or two changes of clothes and one or two pairs of socks to last a year. They have one woolen hat to cover their heads until they are killed or they die.

I was lucky because a small rug was given to me to sleep on.

Anyway, I slept well but got up very early in the morning when Kaka Mamad Gul arrived and announced that Commander Massoud had finished his work and that he might come down from the mountains of Firring today.

I met an interesting old man whom I would like to tell you about. I never thought that I would bump into him here, so far away from his home or mine. He is an old man, maybe in his seventies. He is from the Aashaawa village, which is to the immediate north of Kabul. I know you remember this man. He was actually a very well-known cheese seller in Kabul. He is the one who for years used to come every two days from his village to Kabul in order to sell his homemade cheese. His thin and flute-like voice could be heard every morning shouting, *Aashaawa Paneer!* (Aashaawa cheese). He used to go from door to door, calling to his customers and selling his round palm-sized lumps of cheese. They were full of dust, not very clean, but quite delicious.

I insisted that he briefly tell me what circumstances had brought him here. He said, "My family had a long tradition of cheese making. My wife, my daughters, my nieces, and some other women from the neighborhood used to make it together. We all knew that there were people in Kabul waiting daily for our cheese.

"The people of Kabul loved it, and they loved the way we used to call out to them to come and buy it. Our customers were women who, hearing our calls, would rush out of their doors to buy our product. We knew all our customers by name. One day, while my son and grandson were on their way to Kabul with one or two sacks of cheese, the Russians bombarded them and both were killed. They were not the target but they were unfortunately caught in between. The blood of my son and little grandson made the white cheese red.

"When I heard the news, two things made me very sad. The first was that I would not be able to see my beloved son and my sweet grandson again. The second was those deprived Kabul cheese buyers who would no longer hear the loud voices of my children in the mornings as they called out, "*Aashaawa cheese! Aashaawa cheese!* Come and get your *Aashaawa cheese!*"

He stopped here because he saw me in tears.

Dr Rahman became worried, and interrupted us, "What is wrong?"

I told him, "Doctor, life is nothing but sweet and sour memories, and the war pushes them deeper down. Let us thank our tears for bringing them up again."

My dear, tell this story to my children and tell them that their father always loved Kabul, even its poor cheese seller. When I see Massoud, I will read this story to him too. I am sure he knows this old cheese seller because he was also brought up in Kabul.

8:00 AM

Breakfast has finished. I am now sitting on the eastern river bank where a long line of around twenty donkeys are arriving from the direction of Ishkamish district, while on the other side of the river, I see another thin line of innocent donkeys moving northward.

Their loads are filled with food and other items meant for sale to the resistance. I know it is a war, and in a war, you do not distribute sweets, you throw bombs.

For me, it is interesting to imagine what the donkeys think of this war and how barbaric we must seem to them, bombing and killing each other.

These supply donkeys may ask each other simple questions like, "Do we not carry their loads? Do we not help them get their supplies faster to their destinations? By transporting these supplies, do we not help them to stay alive? Then, why do they kill us?"

These poor donkeys do not even know who their friends and foes are. They may hear the roaring of a fighter jet, and all of a sudden, they are engulfed in fire. They may also ask, "If such means exist to swiftly carry vast quantities of heavy bombs, then why do they not employ them to carry their food, clothing, and medicine, instead of using us?"

The answer from another donkey would probably be very simple,

"My dear friend, they are human beings. They destroy the houses and properties of one another, but we animals never do such things. They are more savage, wilder, and crueler than the wildest and cruelest of animals. Have you ever heard of a tiger burning the house of another tiger? Of course the answer is no."

Last year, on my previous trip through Nooristan, I looked at my poor donkey who had been wounded by a land mine on a mountain pass. He was bleeding profusely. He was scared. He could not move further even an inch. His eyes were filled with blood. His leg was broken. His belly was bleeding. We could not help him at all. There were other mines on the path in front of us and attack helicopters were flying all around us. My donkey's owner did not have any other choice but to take the load from his donkeys back, kill the donkey, and leave.

Just before the owner was about to shoot the donkey, I looked into its bleeding eyes and said, "Which one of us should be called a donkey? You? The Russians? Or all of us?" He knew the answer but did not say anything. Maybe he wanted to die in silence. By the way, the tearful eyes of the donkey's owner as he prepared to kill him, hit my heart harder.

By the way, smoking and using *naswaar* or chewing tobacco is forbidden amongst the freedom fighters of Commander Massoud. Anyone who violates this will be fined 300 Afghanis or about $2. You know that I have smoked one cigarette every night for the last seven years and I cannot stop or reduce it. However, the commander knows this but does not want to fine me. Dr Rahman, our chain smoker, is also exempt.

5:45 PM

It has been a relatively long day for me.

In the morning, I asked Dr Fana and he kindly provided me with his tube of toothpaste, which was almost out of paste. The tube was flat. I laughed and asked, "What can I do with this?"

He replied, "Just press the tube from the bottom upward, and surely, you will extract a little."

I shouted, "It is perhaps easier to chew the tube itself. There is nothing in there."

He laughed and said, "Khalili Sahib, that is up to you, but be careful of your teeth."

I tell you something that you may not believe. Here amongst the ordinary caves, we have a cave, which is supposed to be a kind of medical clinic-cum-operation room. Oh, I paid a visit there. It was worse than the hideout in which they keep potatoes. They told me that it was a surgery room or cave. It was small, dark, dirty, squalid, and humid. There I found two lanterns, a broken gas light, and some very old and primitive surgical tools.

However, despite all its Stone Age conditions, by a miracle it has worked and even helped some of our wounded soldiers. We do not have any other choice. We are human beings too, I think. We need a medical clinic for all eventualities, and we have to use whatever we have at hand.

Three weeks ago, they performed an appendix surgery in that hideout or medical cave. I talked to the man who had undergone the operation. The surgery was performed at night, under lantern light. He was fine. I saw his wound, which also looked okay.

However, this is not true with every case. If you ask me why I did not go and ask those people who had undergone surgery and still had pain and suffering, I would simply tell you that I tried but I could not find any of them left on this earth. They have gone to the other world, to join friends who had been operated on in the same kind of medical caves. It is simply a matter of luck if someone survives.

I asked the doctor how he feels. I received his answer through the stream of tears rolling down from his innocent eyes.

"Khalili Sahib, I cannot watch a freedom fighter or a civilian dying of blood loss and leave him like that. No doctor can do it. I try my best. I know I cannot help them, as I want. Before and after any operation, I pray and ask God to help both of us. I am myself not an experienced surgeon at all and my limited surgical instruments are so primitive that they look like old kitchen tools. What can I do? While performing these operations, I feel like a butcher in a dirty butcher's shop."

I don't want to write more on this topic. It is a long and painful story in this part of the world, and perhaps in most countries of the East. We are born with pain and we die with pain. Peace and happiness live in the deepest corners of the valleys of our dreams. It is no one's fault but our own.

11

Little Saleha: Onward to the Commander

Friday, August 1
6:30 PM

At 4:30 AM this morning, four fighter jets revealed to us their noisy wings. First, they dropped flairs to tag their target. They were right on top of us. Our men prepared themselves. The jets were very high, maybe about 3,000 meters or even more. After about half an hour, they flew overhead and bombarded our area, each unloading what seemed like every one of their rocket caches. The thunderous and deafening sounds of the rockets exploding echoed all around us. Thankfully, no one was killed or injured. Dr Abdul Rahman rushed toward me to see how I was and I assured him that I was fine. My dear, this is war and bombardments are a real part of it.

I was just informed that Sandy, Andy, and Noel have arrived here as well. I told the young freedom fighter who had brought them to instantly take them into one of the caves, just in case there were more bombardments. I also immediately told Dr Rahman to assign some men to take care of the foreigners. I added that Jaan Mohammad should be instructed to help the group because he knows Sandy and Andy very well. I talked about Sandy with Abdul Rahman regarding his important mission.

I had not finished talking to him when another intense Russian bombing started very close to us. We rushed toward the office cave of the doctor to take refuge. Despite the roaring of the jets and the loud blasts of the rockets hitting the ground, I thought to myself that at least something positive had come out of the intense bombardment around us and it was that we were able to discuss the topic of how to deal with the air power of the Russians.

Dr Rahman and I talked about the rumors of getting Blow Pipe and Stinger missiles, which are both surface-to-air guided rockets; one is British and the other is American. We discussed the prevailing conviction that if they give us these anti-air rockets, we would be able to recapture our skies from our enemy.

The bombardments ended while we were still talking. Dr Abdul Rahman went somewhere to work while I took the opportunity to take a short walk to the river to get some fresh air. Next to the river, I watched a line of poor donkeys carrying food, wood, or weapons. I took some Super 8 footage for about 3 minutes.

* * *

My dear, I am back now, sitting in a cave and writing to you. All around this area, there are unexploded bombs, mines, and even toy-mines, which are very dangerous, like snakes in the grass. Whenever I walk here, while I enjoy watching small children playing in the fields, my soul is gripped with the worry of what may happen to them if they step on one of these mines. It is in the nature of the children to go out and play.

Look at the generosity of our enemy: they provide for our children toy-mines in the shape of butterflies. Their only purpose is to terrify the whole village, force the poor villagers to abandon their villages and become refugees. When I see these little children with simple but colorful clothes, they look to me like beautiful butterflies with no wings. A shepherd named Naseem told me that the communists have spread hundreds of these toy-mines to terrorize the civilians. What a tragedy for the children and their mothers! What a cruel use of science!

Yesterday I saw a poor little girl with one hand. Her name was Saleha. Although about eight years old, she looked like a four-year-old. Her father told me that a year ago she touched a toy-mine, injured herself, losing her right hand, and had been in coma for a month. Since then she is terrified of everything and does not touch anything, which looks like a toy.

I talked to her a little and gave her a candy. She could not unwrap the candy with one hand. I helped her. I told her that the fingers of her only hand are beautiful and her teeth are pretty. She was sad that she could not eat her food with her right hand because she did not like eating with her left.

With the innocent glance of a beautiful broken-winged bird, she softly said, "I always hide my missing hand from the other children. When they look at my stump, they either laugh or ask many questions, which makes me even more sad. Maybe they are right. I know. I look ugly with it."

When I told her that her goat looks pretty despite the fact that it did not have fingers, she became happier. She had a great smile but a sorrowful glance. I gave her another candy and told her to give it to her mother. She said nothing and did not take it. The father tenderly caressed his daughter's beautiful unkempt hair and told me that her mother had lost her life a year ago from a lung ailment, a week before their little daughter touched that evil toy-mine. I thought, maybe the mother was luckier not to have seen her child in such a miserable condition. Like little Saleha, we have hundreds and hundreds of little mine victims all over Afghanistan.

A bit later I had the opportunity to talk to some men from the Central Units. They were talented young men. They wanted to go to school and they were dreaming of even one day going to college too.

Tonight, they promised us that they would prepare potatoes. God willing, Jaan Mohammad has brought pepper with him. My Super 8 camera was not working and I fixed it. One of the battery coils had rusted and did not conduct energy to the batteries. I put a piece of metal over it and it started to work. Imagine, a person like me who has never been able to do anything like this and has never been a handy man, repaired a camera. Say bravo. It is a miracle, at least in my case.

My dear, you never know what will make you feel better in a war. Thank God for small things.

Valley of Khwaja Sultan Shayra

The Takhaar Province
Saturday, August 2
8:30 PM

I was not able to write to you today, the main reason being that I hurriedly started my journey in the morning in order to reach Commander Massoud and, on the way, two Soviet jets bombarded our location heavily for a very long time.

Listen to what happened from morning till now. At 6:30 AM, we left the Shast Dara Valley. We had to cross the river as fast as possible to avoid further possible bombardment. The river had no bridge. The waters of the river were higher than my chest. It was a beautiful blue river with relatively dangerous rapids. For me, it was harder and scarier to cross because I do not know how to swim. The water was very fast and ice-cold. I had a genuine fear of falling into the river and drowning.

The problem was not just my fear of the water but how to hide it from the others because, amongst the fighters, fear or phobia is considered a cowardice. You always have to show that you are not scared of anything. Even Doctor Rahman, despite his medical background, has the same opinion that phobia is a kind of cowardice.

We crossed the river holding each other's hands tightly. Since I had not taken off my socks, I slipped twice. I was almost gone, taken by the water. The river stones were very slippery. I was scared and called out to the others to help me, and they did.

Dr Rahman and his friends, even though they were going to another valley, had to cross the same river with us. I shouted to him, "Can you swim in case the water takes you away?"

He boasted, "I swim like a fish."

When he was talking to me, suddenly his glasses fell off his face into the river. I was surprised to see that, in no time, the doctor dived in after his glasses. Not five seconds had passed when he emerged from the ice-cold water with the glasses in his hand.

He was very happy and shouted proudly, "Don't worry, Khalili Sahib, I found my glasses."

*   *   *

At 10 AM, two jets, four helicopters, and two SU-25s began their bombardment. They created hell straight through until 6:20 in the evening. The bombardment was so heavy that we had to find shelter to escape the firestorm. The thick smoke and intense fire came so close to us that I thought we were done for. Thanks to the caves and big boulders, we were sheltered and protected from injury.

Luckily, while escaping, we stumbled upon an excellent hideout, which was one of the Central Unit's bases. There were about ten armed fighters inside. They knew me and, to my surprise, they had tea, sugar, and even rice to offer us. It was a good break, a time for tea and a piece of bread. One of the fighters told me that we should not worry about the bombardments too much. I asked him the reason. He aptly said, "If the Soviets have bombs, we have boulders to give us shelter. If the Soviets have guns we have God."

Anyway, we finally left the hideout and it took us 12 hours of continuous walking to reach here. I am now in a summer pasture, which belongs to Baay Mohammad. He is a nice man. He does not have much to offer to our stomachs but has a big smile to boost our spirits. His children are not here.

Since his first wife was *sanda* (barren), he married a second time. He was not lucky with the second wife either because she has also not been able to produce any children. I told him that it might be his problem rather than his wives', which he did not believe at all. He argued, "A man can never ever have a problem of this sort. A man is a man. God has created him strong enough to produce as many children as he wants."

He himself was a tall and very big man.

When I told him that I have two boys, he said, "If you, with such a small body, could have two boys, why should I not have ten?"

"If you believe so, go on marrying all the girls in the village, and yet you may have no children."

He said with a laugh, "Maybe."

Right now, I must sleep because in the middle of the night and at 2:00 AM sharp, we will depart toward the Namakaw district, where finally I will be able to meet Massoud. The weather is good and my health is fine as well.

Valley of Namakaw

The Takhaar Province
Sunday, August 3
2:30 PM

My dearest, at last I am here, the place where I will see Massoud. I am in Namakaw, a district in the Takhaar province. Last night, I woke up at 1:30 AM. I grabbed the flashlight and my pistol from under my pillow. I gave my rucksack to my donkey owner and departed.

The monotonous things now awaited me: the sounds of the horsemen, the neighing of the horses, men saddling up, the braying of the donkeys, the light of the night stars, as well as cold, hunger, thirst, birds, boulders, and bombs. I had only a few pieces of candy, which were my only source of comfort.

It was two o'clock in the morning that we started toward the pass, step by step. The weather was cold but once I got on my way, I felt so tired that I thought I had a slight fever and might not be able to follow the narrow tracks. I also felt that I could not control my balance. In the beginning, each step of mine was as heavy as a boulder and each step forward needed the power of an elephant. Since my donkey seemed thinner and weaker than me, I did not ride it. I used the flashlight so much that I drained the batteries completely.

Thank God, at four o'clock, the sky began to brighten. The beautiful breaking of dawn was a blessing for me. It gave me higher morale and better vision. It was so beautiful that instantly so many poems came to mind. It was 4:30 AM when we performed our dawn prayer and, immediately afterward, we began our climb toward the pass. The closer we came to the peak, the harder our journey became. My donkey fell and injured itself, which slowed our journey further. Later unfortunately, a horse fell off the cliff and broke both his leg and his neck.

At 5:30 AM, we climbed right to the top of the pass of Sultan Khwaja. While nothing in comparison to the passes we had climbed before, this one was difficult nonetheless. To avoid possible bombardments, we speedily descended from the pass.

At 7:40 AM, we reached the first pasture, which was owned by a Gujur tribesman. The Gujurs are mostly nomads and predominantly live in the east of the country. The name of the pasture owner was Mohammad Omar. He was very humble and kind. He could speak a little Farsi and Pashto too. He brought me a bowl of food.

My dear, the descent has not been kind to my New Balance shoes. I think next time I should bring an extra pair of shoes, although no pair of shoes can give you a guarantee on these mountains.

We left the generous Gujuri pasture and, after about three hours of relatively difficult terrain, we reached, at 11:30 AM, the bottom of the valley. We hurried to the end of the path, though no water awaited us there to quench our thirst. Overall, the path was not that arduous. It had an elevation of 3,500 meters.

At the foot of the valley, the pastures and their owners began to appear. They were kind enough to bring us yoghurt, butter, bread, mulberries, apples, and tea. Their bread and butter were excellent. The weather was fantastic. I left them and was quick on my feet because I knew that the next stop would be the headquarters of Massoud and I would have reached my destination.

4:00 PM

My dear, I am now having tea in one of the headquarters of Commander Massoud. As I told you before we are in Namakaw.

The minute I arrived here, the tea was ready. There was also a message from Commander Massoud which read, "Khalili Sahib, last night intense bombardment blocked us from coming down the mountain. In a day, I will be with you. Take your time. Be careful. There will be more intense bombardment and the Russians might send some special commandos. I heard that you are in a rush to return to Pakistan soon. My advice to you is: Please do not be in a hurry. We are not too far from each other."

12

Commander Massoud

Monday, August 4
8:30 AM

My dear, finally, after almost a month of traveling to see Commander Massoud, last night we spent some time together. We stayed awake for most of the night and talked. It was 2:30 in the morning when we stopped talking and went to sleep. He was absolutely exhausted.

Yesterday, he had come from the Farkhar district and instantly sent word that I should come to see him alone.

The message read: "Khalili Sahib, it is my wish to see you as soon as possible. I am waiting eagerly. We have a lot of things to talk about."

It was around 8 PM when his bodyguards came to pick me up. I dressed and departed immediately. I arrived there in no time.

Massoud was sitting with his men. He had worn plain white traditional clothes, a *khaki* military vest with various large and small pockets, two ballpoint pens on the left side, and a palm-sized radio on the right side. A big glass of tea with five sugar cubes on a white saucer lay in front of him. On his wrist, he wore his distinguished watch, which a friend had bought for him as a present. As usual, he looked very refined with his high, pointed nose, long arms, bony body, big black eyes, and clean marble-like teeth. His very thin beard and even thinner mustache were no different from last year.

Of course, he had on his head the same typical Massoud hat that he wore tilted in his own unique way. Commander Azeem, Commander Gadaa, and some other northern commanders were there. Commander Azeem is the one whom I sent to London for treatment to have his wounded hand amputated.

The minute Massoud saw me, his beautiful smile beamed from far and he shouted, "Khalili Sahib, welcome! May you not be tired. A good friend shows his face on a difficult day. O Man of God, welcome! Everyone here knows that I was waiting and looking forward to seeing you since you started out from Chitral. I know how hard, high, difficult, and cold the mountains must have been. Even horses cannot make this kind of journey in a proper manner. May you not be tired!"

After hearing these welcoming words of his, I passed the other commanders and went straight to him. We shook hands and hugged each other. I kissed his face twice, the way we Afghans greet each other. Massoud does not like this but I did it anyway and he also warmly welcomed it.

I said, "Yes, although the paths and passes that I have taken were extremely indeed difficult, the desire to see you made the high passes lower and the rough paths smoother. The path you are on has so many political ups and downs, as well as so many military gains and losses. Thank God, together we go and together we win."

In a friendly, welcoming spirit, he replied, "You are right but, thank God, we are all taking this path together, hand in hand, shoulder to shoulder. We have to push forward and break all the barriers that stand on our path to victory."

I immediately cut him short and asked, "How are you? How is your health?"

"Thank you. I feel better than ever," he replied with a genuine smile on his face.

To me he looked brighter than a year before. As usual, his hair was very tidy and his clothes were clean. Then he calmly told me, "We will have food and, afterward, we will sit alone and talk more. Do not worry, Khalili Sahib, if our discussions are long, the summer days are even longer."

*   *   *

My dear, we had a long day talking with commanders and the common people. It was night. There were two lanterns instead of one in the room, which attracted me the most. I do not know why. The five by four meter room was cluttered and crowded because everywhere Massoud goes, his bodyguards, men, and commanders follow him like a shadow. The mattresses were very old, the two windows were like small portholes, the door was short, and the ceiling was full of leak marks. There were no curtains or electricity.

We ate some boiled rice, big pieces of meat, and a little wild spinach, and then the men were excused and both of us spoke until 2:30 at night. Beforehand, I had thought that we would not talk about hard political topics for at least tonight, but I was wrong.

He right away started asking political questions. In the beginning, I was reluctant to talk about politics but I could not say no to him.

Our discussion was both hard and soft. On the harder side, we talked of the condition of our party's activities in Pakistani exile, Professor Rabbani's political leadership, his executive committee and, above all, our relationship with the ISI or Intelligence Service of Pakistan. We talked about how and why the ISI was trying to spread all kinds of negative rumors against the Commander.

I told him, "My political office has indeed encountered many problems dealing with the ISI. We do not know whether they are our enemies or our friends. I have to be very careful not to allow them to create problems for us. They never trust us, but the leader of our party advises keeping some legitimate relations with them. The ISI does not like the fact that we have strong and independent commanders. Whenever possible, they always try to go through the back door, in order to influence or provoke our commanders or deputy commanders against us."

In this regard, Massoud commented, "Professor Rabbani is right to advise you to keep some relations with the ISI but we have to be very careful."

We then spoke of our regional and international contacts, especially with the United States, Iran, Saudi Arabia, Egypt, France, Britain, Germany, and other European countries. In the context of our international contacts, we spoke of Professor Rabbani's trip to the United States. Massoud was listening very keenly to everything I was telling him.

Then as usual, we had some more tea with some almonds and raisins. It was a nice short break from our deep political conversation. Since he is interested in cameras, especially video cameras, he checked out my Super 8 with great enthusiasm.

I jokingly told him, "Handle it carefully. It is not a gun. It must be very new to you. It needs a lot of sophistication and at least a week of training to handle it properly."

With a genuine smile he replied, "If it was really sophisticated and delicate, then you would not be able to use it either."

We both laughed.

"Khalili Sahib, whenever we meet, you are very short and precise about the internal and external politics relating to the war. I grasped the core of what you were saying and inshallah, we will talk more about them in the next few days."

Despite not being in the mood to talk at length, he briefly touched upon the work that he has done on the military front and the general situation regarding the war. He even allowed me to take notes of what he has been doing in the previous months in relation to his organizational work in the areas he commands. His whole aim and goal is to bring about order in the northern part of Afghanistan.

He said, "I concentrate mainly on thirteen northern provinces. These provinces are located to the immediate north and south of the Hindu Kush mountains. My most urgent goal is to unify the scattered groups and forces of the resistance in order to make a united central force. For the time being, I may not attract other parties to join Jamiat but to coordinate our activities against the common enemy."

In relation to the enemy, he continued, "Without unity and coordination, it will be very hard to win the war sooner than expected. The enemy has one command and one strategy; we have lesser unity and almost no strategy. The enemy's resources are limitless but our's are much less than we require. In a guerilla war, we need not just to organize our warriors but to mobilize our civilians too. This is why I try my best to mobilize the people in their own areas. If you lose the people, you lose the war. I am purposely training some young educated fighters to do this job and also ask my commanders to always keep good relations with the common people."

Somehow, he produced some honey in a small bottle to share with me. "Do you know the difference between pure natural honey and common, impure honey?" he asked me jokingly with a sarcastic smile as he poured very carefully directly from the bottle onto my unclean saucer.

"Yes." I answered with a loud laughter.

He went on to say, "Along with everything else, we need an army for the future of Afghanistan and my goal is to lay the foundation of that army today. No doubt, it takes time, money, and a lot of sacrifice but we have to start it now. Today's organized guerilla force should be tomorrow's army of a free Afghanistan."

While he was well informed about the central part of Afghanistan, he asked me repeatedly about other parts of the country and the situation of the freedom fighters there. I told him in brief about my repeated political expeditions in the south, east, and west of the country and explained how they fight there against the enemy. I said that they are not well organized but very much willing and determined to fight to the end. I mentioned many names of the commanders of those areas to him and asked, if possible, for him to make contact with them.

He has the idea that we have to be as close as possible to the Pashtoon commanders of different parties. He said that he has already built close relations with some important Hazara and Uzbek commanders and that the political office of Jamiat should be closer to all other parties of all the different ethnic groups. He repeatedly and confidently told me that, ultimately, we would win the war, but we have to work day and night to prepare the nation and ourselves for that day.

He then went on to talk about the power of his intelligence service. He said that he has built an effective spy network to infiltrate the enemy. He mentioned that some of the Kabul regime's commanders are cooperating with him and have helped him to learn more about what is going on within the regime's army and police force. While I was not paying close attention to this point, he drew my attention repeatedly to the importance of the intelligence service in the war.

He mentioned Dr Abdul Rahman and two or three others who are working very effectively in this field and added, "A war without intelligence is like a room without windows."

Before he started talking about other subjects, I asked for a little bit more honey. He gave a bit but not more than the first one. On seeing this, I laughed and told him that even generosity has a limit, especially when it comes to pure honey.

He also talked about the strong and weak points of the Russians and the communist regime in Kabul and said, "They are united and have a plan, are determined, well equipped, and rich but they do not have the support of the people. We are determined and full of faith, we fight for a great cause, and have the full support of the people, but we are not united, not well equipped, and are very poor. Despite our deficiencies, we win because God, people, and time are on our side."

I liked the way he put it.

Besides other things, he told me that he was concentrating on his upcoming operation against the Farkhar government garrison. He confidently told me, "This will be the first government garrison that is captured by resistance fighters. It will, inshallah, enable us to boost morale and provide experience for the offensive phase of the war."

It was late—already about 2 AM—when we stopped this line of discussion.

In his usual friendly manner, he himself changed the topic by saying, "In the next few days, we will have sufficient time to talk about war and politics but for now, Khalili Sahib, let us read poetry. That is what relaxes us and fills our hearts with joy. Politics never ends, life does. Let us take care of the second, first."

One of the wonderful things we always do when we are together is to recite poetry.

Massoud does not have poems memorized, except for a few, but he understands the essence of a poem when someone recites to him. He enjoys it a lot. While listening to a poetry recitation, he keeps very quiet and even closes his eyes and listens to each verse with all his heart and soul.

He laid down on the mattress, put a thick pillow under his head, poured a cup of green tea, and called his body guard to bring more raisins and a few sugar cubes. He asked me to lie down on another mattress across him and start reading, saying, "Whatever poem comes into your heart, please recite it." All of a sudden, the following poem by Hafiz jumped from my heart:

Come, come! Oh my Beloved!
Bring me a cup of wine,
Our Life is fast, founded on the wind,
The castle of our desires is founded on the sands
Believe in no promise,
from the promise-breaking universe,
This old widow is the bride of a thousand grooms.
Under the blue sky
I am a slave of the one who is not dependent,
Upon anything, upon anybody.

He sighed in appreciation and repeatedly murmured the phrase *not dependent upon anything, upon anybody,* and asked, "Are we not fighting because of that, Khalili Sahib?"

I replied, "It is deeper than that. It is not only a question of freeing a piece of land but freeing our hearts as well."

He winked at me and said, "One at a time."

After reading poetry, it was time to sleep.

On my previous trips, we always slept in cave-like hideouts but this time we were in a room, albeit a very poor one. Inside, there were usually the two of us and one or two of the Commander's closest bodyguards. Our host, Maulavi Shaheed, brought Massoud a red velvet quilt and for me an ordinary brown one. His quilt looked much better than mine did. He caught my glance at his beautiful red quilt, immediately switched the two and gave me his. Massoud is always kind and generous to me.

I was happy to get the velvet quilt, which had beautiful green flowers sewn on top. It was soft and thick enough to keep me warm.

With his usual smile, he said, "This is for you, Khalili Sahib. You can use mine."

I looked at his sleeping bag and jokingly said, "I do not know which one is more comfortable, this beautiful red velvet cotton quilt or your soft, thin, and warm sleeping bag?"

He quickly replied, "Let's exchange then again; I will use the quilt and you can use my sleeping bag."

To this I said, "No, no, I am joking." We both laughed.

The room was about four to five meters squared, in a muddy two or three room house, with two small windows. Although it was a poor room, it had a great view. We left the lantern half-lit in the corner and went to sleep. Before going into the world of our dreams, for some minutes we talked about our families too. In the morning, his bodyguard complained that we talked too much.

We woke for the dawn prayer at around 4:30 AM. He never misses any of the five daily prayer times. He loves the dawn prayer the most. I went back to sleep for an hour or so. He also has the habit of going under his blanket and taking a short nap after morning prayers. When I woke up, people had already come from the Parwan and Kapisa provinces to meet Massoud.

After breakfast, he excused everyone and sat down with Commander Gadaa, Azeem, Yahya, Shaheed, Wadood, Zabit Saleh, and some other commanders. He gave them their mission, to take the government garrison of Farkhar, and revealed the plan of attack. Gadaa and Azeem were listening with particular attention.

Massoud drew a very large model in the sand and as he walked around it with a long stick, which he used as a pointer, he showed them the locations and positions of the men, rockets, .50 calibers, mortars, and BM12s. Commander Gadaa had questions, which Massoud answered.

My dear, I am busy and cannot write to you every hour. I will try to write to you either in the nights or in the mornings. We will have our lunch and after doing some other work, we will go with Massoud to Namakaw and stay in the same place that we were last night. This is the plan but it may change.

Village of Zawaryong: Valley of Namakaw

Tuesday, August 5
8:00 AM

Last night, once again, Massoud and I stayed up until the late hours.

Let me tell you a couple of his personal and interesting habits. When he talks, he never wants you to move your head, body, or even blink. You have to stay motionless and concentrate with all your mind and body on what he says. The minute you touch your pen or look around, he stops talking.

Listen to another one. While he is explaining something, he repeatedly says, "Did you understand or not?" He wants you to repeat exactly his last sentence or even the last number he has just mentioned to you. For example, he says, "I have made four bases in Takhar," and he immediately asks, "How many bases?" You have to say "four bases," otherwise, he will not continue. All I mean is that he wants you to understand everything he says. It is understandable that, in a war situation, people's lives are in danger and he wants to be sure that his men fully understand what he says and what he means. Thank God, he excuses me from this routine.

He is a true leader, and indeed, you can find the attributes of leadership in him. He uses his heart and mind when he talks and penetrates the hearts and minds of others because he tells the truth. I also should admit that I do not even touch my pen when he is in that mood for talking. He adds power and beauty to the simplest words he uses, through the honest way he expresses himself.

Once, I was very quiet and silent, listening to him, he asked me "Are you with me?"

I said, "Go on. I am always with you." And he knew I meant it.

The weather is very dusty now and last night it was cold as well. The mosquitos were kind enough not to bite us. Before we fell asleep, we both got into our sleeping bags, turned off the lantern, leaving one of the windows partly open. Everything was silent.

For five or ten minutes, I could not sleep and I knew that Massoud was not sleeping yet either.

I calmly asked him, "Commander, in the last two or three days, you told me so many things about your activities on the ground, but please tell me honestly, do you really believe that we can defeat the Soviet army?"

He did not answer for a few seconds and then replied, "I believe with all of my soul, spirit, heart, and mind that we will be victorious." The room seemed to become even more silent as his words faded into it.

After a minute, he sat up in his sleeping bag and asked me in a deeper voice, "Did you hear me, Khalili Sahib?"

"Yes, I did, but tell me, do you have any time limit for reaching our goal of freedom?"

Quietly and calmly he replied, "I cannot answer that question because I do not know."

I sat up in my sleeping bag as well and said, "Okay Amir Sahib, I agree that we will win the war but what do you think will happen after?"

With a kind of unique intensity, he went on, "That is exactly why we should work very hard to lay the foundations of peace in a post-war Afghanistan. It will not be easy at all. Every post-war situation is harder than even the war itself, especially in Afghanistan with its strategically difficult geographic location. Undoubtedly, the fight for freedom is difficult but when you finally win freedom, you need stability and stronger leadership."

While falling into a deep sleep in my shepherd-like sleeping bag, his last sentence was echoing in my ears: "Let us now concentrate on winning freedom, but post-war stability needs a stronger political leadership."

I should not forget to write that last night Commander Massoud met with Sandy Gall and his team. He spoke with him and his team for about two hours and gave him a long interview. He respects Sandy Gall and Sandy Gall respects him. He knows both Sandy Gall and Andy. Noel created a great artistic war ambiance for the interview. I liked it very much. In a smoky room with a small window, low ceiling, old mattresses, large pillows, in the light of the lantern, the flames of a candle, and our flickering shadows on the walls, Noel had made it as theatrical as if we were on Broadway. It was a sight to remember forever.

Massoud said that if Sandy wants, they could follow him for the next four days. Sandy Gall was very happy and accepted. He will follow Massoud until the Farkhar operation. Massoud will, God willing, stay here for five more days with his other commanders, and after that, we will all go for the operation on the main government garrison of Farkhar.

Village of Naqshee Dara

From morning until now, which is 2:30 in the afternoon, I spent most of the time with Massoud. It was more or less a routine day for the Commander. A poor old man had come from the Shaawa village to talk to him. A group of fighters from the Baghlan province had also come to get help from the commander.

Next to a small river, we decided to have some tea and talk for a while. It was an ideal place to be alone. His bodyguard brought a flask of green tea and some raisins. He asked them also to bring us some candy; however unfortunately, at that moment, there were none. The rays of the sun were soft on my skin, not too hot and not too cold. We crossed the river on foot so that we would also be further away from the guards. As usual, he had on his khaki vest and a pair of worn but polished Czechoslovakian boots.

Just before he was about to start speaking, I asked him what operation had been the most important for him since the beginning of the war? Without any hesitation, he answered it was the operation of 1984. I remembered that it was the time of the ceasefire with the Russians.

"It was a political, military, civil, and intelligence operation," he went on. "For the most part, my forces were weak, immobilized, not very well equipped or trained, poor, and inexperienced, at least in comparison to the Soviet troops. The first thing that came to my mind was if the Russians attacked, it would have been nothing short of a complete massacre of my forces and of the civilian population in my valley. On the other hand, the perception was that I was strong, organized, experienced, well-trained, well-equipped, and well-funded. I was in a dilemma. Now the Russians wanted a ceasefire.

"As you know, I had two people in the Intelligence Ministry of the communist government in Kabul named Tajuddin and Kamran.

They clearly told me that the Russian reasoning behind the ceasefire was to ultimately attack the Panjshir valley and the Shamaali plains, and destroy my forces. I had to act. I called the Counsel of Religious Scholars, my fighters, commanders, and the elders of the people. After a week of discussions, the majority gave me their consent for a ceasefire.

"The day of the signing of the ceasefire arrived. Soon after, high-ranking Russian officers came to the Panjshir valley and we signed a ceasefire agreement. We both wanted more time. They needed time to prepare for an attack and I needed time to train my men more and lay down defensive positions."

"As soon as we signed, the propaganda against me started. Everyone called me a traitor. The Russians were secretly spreading the rumor that they had bought me and I was their puppet. For my part, I showed everyone that I was upholding my side of the ceasefire. In the meantime, I started to send false reports to them through my double agents that we were not preparing for battle and that everything was normal in the valley.

"Six months passed. I received concrete intelligence that the Russians were ready for their attack. They had all the intelligence they needed about the Panjshir valley and my forces. I was the one who had given them all the military maps of the positions and coordinates through my double agents. The Russians were going to drop commandos on each and every one of my 34 military bases throughout the Panjshir valley. Their plan was to kill and capture as many of my men as possible, confiscate their weapons, and conquer my valley. They were confident they would win.

"My strategy was to evacuate the common people from the valley in such a way that the Russians would not know. If they did, they would instantly attack before their planned date.

"The safety of the people was the most important thing. There were probably about 150,000 people living throughout the valley. The mountains were full of snow and the weather was very cold. Would the people agree to leave their homes and their valley? Would they cross the mountains with their women and children to the other side of the Hindu Kush range? The brave and loyal people accepted. It was going to be an unprecedented evacuation. It had to be done and it had to be kept secret.

"On the military side of things, I told my men to plant hundreds of mines in the places around our military bases where we thought the Russian commandos would descend. All along, we never let on that we knew they were going to attack.

"We got word from Kabul that, in three days, the Russian siege would start. I immediately called the commanders of each base and told them to make sure that their populations were evacuated, except for the few that were kept back to show that everything was normal.

"On the day of the attack, first came the reconnaissance planes flying overhead, and then the loud thundering sounds of dozens of attack helicopters could be heard heading toward our location. The skies of the Panjshir valley were soon filled with these sinister flying machines.

"Now, it was time to see if my plan would work. Would they land where I guessed they would? Would our forces be able to defend their positions? Would we have many fatalities?

"The helicopters began to descend and the attack started. The shadows of their combat choppers fell upon each corner of the valley as they circled and dropped their men. Each one was filled with fully armed commandos.

"One group of helicopters landed in the part of the valley where the local population had their homes. Simultaneously, the others landed behind the fighters' bases. As their feet hit the ground, they triggered the mines my men had planted weeks before. My fighters, who had taken defensive positions around the drop zone, gunned down those who did not step on the mines. The Russians were being destroyed. My plan was working.

"It was then, through the distant sounds of exploding mines and machine gun fire that the Russian generals realized they had fallen into my trap. My people were safe, their commandos were ambushed.

"As we watched all of this unfolding, Radio Kabul was announcing over and over again that my forces had been defeated, I had been killed, and the Panjshir valley had been overrun. They did not know yet that our poor fighters had successfully defended against the attack. Those Russian commandos who could retreat did so. Those that could not were either wounded or killed. Thank God, my forces suffered very limited casualties and total victory was ours."

He had finished his story but was too humble to boast about his victory. I asked him which part of the whole operation was the most decisive. With a very determined and sincere voice, he said, "The people's support gave us the strength to fight better. We fought for our people and we won for them."

Massoud thought for a moment and said, "Write in your diary that there was an old man with a sick and injured son. They were evacuated one cold night with hundreds of others. He struggled to climb the snow-filled mountains with his son on his back. People offered to help him but he refused. With his back hunched from the weight and his body exhausted from the climb, he crossed the excruciatingly high Wheel of the Sky Pass."

"When they crossed the pass, everyone was exhausted. Each person tried to take rest somewhere. The children were running around, happy to be no longer climbing. Suddenly, a loud mournful cry erupted so great that it seemed to shake the whole pass."

"Shocked, everyone looked and saw the old man tenderly laying his son on the ground. He gave him a kiss on his forehead and looked at him for a long while. People gathered to see how the boy was doing, still hearing the loud cry of the father echo across the mountain top."

The old man looked around, tears flowing from his eyes, and said, "I kept two things secret in my heart in order not to bring down the morale of the women and children: the death of my beloved son and the cry of my own soul."

"It was here that the father announced that his son had died on the other side of the mountain. Everyone cried for both and they buried the son where his father had tenderly laid him down. One day, if we have time, we will go to see the grave of that young boy and tell him about the bravery and heroism of his father for the love of freedom."

In tears I said, "Love and sacrifice were born together."

*   *   *

Another group of young educated men had come from Kunduz to join the ranks of the resistance. After being done with the affairs of the common people, the commander asked me to accompany him to a meeting of about twenty selected elite commanders of the North.

When we arrived at the meeting, Massoud told me to explain to his commanders our political efforts in the West and the view of the world in relation to the holy war. He also insisted that I should tell them that the Americans would eventually give us stinger missiles. While giving them a summary of our affairs, I could see that every one of the commanders was very eager to know more about the topics I was talking about. Their questions on the policies of the West and Pakistan in relation to Afghanistan were very interesting.

Then, the commander, in his usual way, took off his wristwatch, placed it in front of him and started to say, "The time for scattered fighting, party politics, thinking individually and operating separately, is over. We have to believe sincerely in mobilizing the people and organizing our fighters to make them believe that they are one in the same. The enemy is united and we have to be united too. The government in Kabul does not sleep and tries to do whatever it takes to defeat us."

He stopped for a few seconds, looked at each of his commanders and continued, "We have to do more. We have to reach out to other parties and encourage other commanders to support our efforts. We cannot do it alone and should not do it alone. Success lies in the unity of the resistance fighters. No doubt, it is a Holy War but blessings do not come without moving forward. The Russians are bringing thousands of soldiers and spending millions of dollars to win the war. We cannot defeat them until and unless we are organized and united."

After giving a long and very moving speech, Massoud talked to them about his operation on the Farkhar garrison, which will be launched in a week's time. He reiterated that it would be the first time the liberation movement will attack a garrison or an established enemy base. He called it a new phase in the anti-Soviet war.

When Massoud ended his talk, his commanders were very energized from his words and were shaking each other's hands and talking as though they had already won the Battle of the Garrison. As I looked at these young fighters, I asked myself: Why is Massoud so respected, supported and believed by his fighters? The only answer that convinced my heart at that moment was that he is faithful, honest, and trustworthy; talks from his heart; and directly touches the lives of the people in a positive way.

He is always objectively optimistic and ends his talks with certain standard sentences: "Let us pray and ask for God's help. Let us work harder to win this war. May God be with you till the end of the road."

Last night, Jaan Mohammad made the most delicious French fries. It was as tasty as the ones our cook, Shah Walee, makes at home. I am busy today and may not be able to write to you. Wait until I am free. God knows when.

Hanging Stars, Sweet Memories

Wednesday, August 6
8:00 AM

My dear, we are still in Namakaw. Last night around 10 PM, Massoud and I decided to sleep on the roof of the house because inside was too warm. When we took our sleeping bags up to the roof, we both stood for a minute and took in the natural ambiance. His bodyguard, who is always with him and is allowed to stay with us during our private meetings, brought a thermos of tea. When he began pouring tea for the commander, Massoud immediately told him to give the first cup to me.

The bright, shining stars in the deep, dark sky, the sounds of the river in the distance, the rustling of the leaves on the branches, and the soft winds reaching us from the mountains made me realize that it was a fantastic decision to sleep on the roof.

Naturally, with such an ambiance, our roof talk was also nicer than our room talk. Massoud who had also been moved by the beauty around him, turned to me and asked, "Khalili Sahib, what do you feel at this moment?"

As we both looked up toward the stars, I answered him, "To me the darkness of the night resembles the war dominating the minds of my people and the silver stars are symbols of hope, shining in their hearts."

With such a wonderful atmosphere and mood, Commander Massoud turned to me and said, "Khalili Sahib, let us not talk only of war tonight but of other more interesting things."

I happily agreed. We laid down our sleeping bags. I sat down on mine and Massoud laid down on his. We were maybe two meters apart. The commander looked at the little stars above and, without hesitation, started talking about his childhood, as if the silvery shiny balls in the sky had transported him back to a time of peace and wonderful memories.

His eyes seemed to linger on one tiny star and, with a certain feeling of nostalgia, he said, "What a sweet childhood we had with our parents, siblings, relatives, friends, our Kabul, our gardens, our vineyards in Parwan and Kapisa, our mulberry gardens in Istalif and Panjshir, our orange orchards in Jalalabad, our holiday festivals, our poor stadium, and so much more."

After hearing his words, the curtain over my mind also dropped, and as my childhood memories played out before my eyes, I added to this train of sweet memories: "Our hunting in Parwan, our picnics in Paghman, our trips to the Qargha lake, our Independence Day celebrations, our cheese sellers and knife sharpeners at our doors, the beggars on the street, the smoky kebab stands, the young girls walking around, the kite fighting, and the bazaars filled with customers. You are right, Commander, it was a special time in our lives and now, thinking back, we should admit that we took it all for granted."

As soon as I stopped, he started again, "As you know, Khalili Sahib, I went to the Istiqlal High School. It was such a wonderful school with very smart and gifted students, great Afghan and French teachers, and an atmosphere of youthful learning. They taught us French there and we all competed to be the best students in our classes."

I instantly asked him, "That was a school for the royal and the rich, how was it that you went there?"

With a broad, mischevious smile, he answered, "Because, besides the royal and the rich, highly intelligent students from nonroyal families were also accepted."

"If they accepted highly intelligent students, then you must have been an exception to the rule."

We both laughed.

"Commander, I went to the Nadiria High School and even though they taught English, they did not have that many highly intelligent students."

With another mischievous smile forming on his face, he said, "Then that is probably why you were accepted."

We both could not stop our laughter this time and it seemed as though our laughter had intermingled with the passing breeze heading toward the heart of the valley.

We then talked about art, music, and culture. He mentioned as he had done many times before, "Khalili Sahib, I will never forget when I used to sit in front of the radio every night from nine to ten o'clock to hear you recite poems on your popular radio show. I have such fond memories of those times, sitting with family and friends to hear the poetry which you would choose to recite for us."

My dear, he was referring to my program called *Zamzama-haayi Shab Hangaam*, or 'Murmurs of the Night'. He was talking of such a distant time, long ago. So much has happened between then and now.

His bodyguard interjected and said, "My apologies, Commander, but I also used to listen to the same program. It was nice to hear Khalili Sahib recite poetry on the radio but it is even nicer that now I can listen to him recite the poetry in person. Thank you for allowing me to stay for your talks."

Then the commander mentioned his mother, and a fog of sadness seemed to cover his face. He said, "I lost my dear mother only eight years ago. I do not remember a single prayer which I have not said for her. She is always with me. She was a dominantly confident woman. I miss her, Khalili Sahib."

We both stopped talking. It seemed an appropriate time.

As we lay on our sleeping bags, it was as though absolute silence had surrounded us. The sounds of the river, the rustling of trees, and the howling of the breeze were all muted somehow, leaving us to our thoughts. Our conversations ended there. We had been talking for two or three hours but now sleep beckoned. As I adjusted myself in my sleeping bag, I noticed that the starry night had been replaced with some thin, white clouds. The commander's bodyguard could not take our long conversation and had fallen asleep a long time before. His snoring kept me awake for a few more minutes as I am sure it did Commander Massoud as well.

*   *   *

Almost half an hour later, after I had fallen asleep, I felt a few small raindrops on my face. I knew that Massoud had probably felt them too. We both kept quiet in the hope that they would stop and the heavens would not rain down upon us. As sleep slowly beckoned, I first imagined that I was home and our little son Mahmud was playing around me. I turned my face and yet some drops of a gentle rain were keeping me from sleep. Before opening my eyes, I came to realize that it was the wet fingers of rain touching my face, not the little fingers of my little son. Since it was so soft and gentle, I let the rain lightly slap my face for one or two more minutes. It had a sweet scent.

At this point, I could not tolerate it anymore. I took my sleeping bag and went down from the roof. As he watched me going down, Massoud shouted aloud, "What a brave freedom fighter! Just a drop of rain and he is scared."

I told him, "I know you are brave enough; enjoy your sleep."

Not a few minutes passed when he and his bodyguard came down too, pretending that he did not want me to be alone. As it was obvious that the rain had forced him down too, I told him calmly, "Do not worry, you are still brave."

*   *   *

Breakfast was ready about 6:30 AM. When we finished eating, Massoud went for some meetings in the other room.

The weather is clearer today. I can see now through my dirty, old window that many fighters are coming in from the four provinces to participate in the attack on the Farkhar garrison. Some of them are even wearing camouflage guerilla uniforms, which is a clear sign of progress for the resistance.

My dearest, I talked to Commander Yahya and Commander Hashimi. They are both very young and very dedicated fighters. I asked them what they feel like after they have won a battle. Commander Yahya replied first, "Yes, it is true, we sometimes fight looking into the eyes of our enemy as we kill him. But as I do after all my battles, I just walk away from the field. I do not like looking at the dead bodies of our fallen enemy. The killing of any one is cruel to me but what's done is done. We are all here for a purpose and that is to fight and to try to defeat our enemy"

Commander Hashimi, with vengeful pride in his voice, said, "When I see the dead enemy soldiers lying on the ground, filled with blood, I hear the screams of a thousand Afghan women and children as they are killed or wounded by the rockets of these cruel enemies. This is war and we will kill them until they leave. I feel no remorse. I feel good because I have done my duty."

I only saw the feeling of revenge in his eyes, heart, and mind.

Maybe this is the real meaning of war, when forgiveness is totally lost. This is not a personal flaw of Hashami's or of others' but maybe it is the cruel essence of war that makes all of us act and feel like this. War is the worst option but, if it is the only option, there is no other way but to fight. This is why I am here to encourage people to fight for freedom, not forgiveness. What other way do these men have to achieve freedom? This was what Commander Hashami meant when he said, "You cannot win a war with love and forgiveness." Maybe he is right, God knows.

*   *   *

Let me tell you the story of poor Ibrahim, the foot-runner who prepares tea and cooks for us. Six months ago, on a beautiful spring morning, under the blue sky of the village of Chil Khirman, some small children were playing around, here and there, like charming butterflies. Beautiful goats and sheep were running about in the nearby meadows. The women were busy cooking food and making *naan* bread, around their *tandoors* or ground ovens.

Five or six white-bearded men of the village were busy picking weeds and channeling the streams to their cornfields. That day the sun was warmer and more beautiful than on other days. The birds were chirping; the dogs too were running and playing just like the children. Beautiful spring flowers of yellow, green, blue, and purple colors were everywhere.

It was around 11 in the morning when a Russian attack helicopter appeared in the sky, bombarded the poor village. In ten minutes' time, everything and anything was engulfed by hellish fire and blood. No longer did any sound come out of that small village. There was complete silence. No laughter of little children and no bleating of goats or sheep could be heard.

Without regard for anything, Ibrahim started running toward the bombarded village to find his wife and children. He arrived and saw everyone drenched in smoke and blood. His wife, his children, his father, his mother, his four brothers, and his sister were all gone. What a tragedy! The bloodstained pages of his family life were entirely erased from the chapters of time, forever.

Ibrahim was crying like a child as he was telling me his agonizing story. While I was also in tears, I asked him to tell me more about when and how he got married, maybe it would help him through his pain.

"About four years ago, I saw her in one of the cornfields in my village. She was busy working with her family in her own cornfield. That day was a beautiful day. I will never forget it. Without thinking of anything else, I rushed home to tell my mother and my sister about the girl in the cornfield."

While he was wiping away his tears, he said, "A month passed. I used to go to her cornfield almost every day in an attempt to try to see her again. My mother, my sister, and two other women went to her home. When they returned, my sister told me that the girl had also seen me in that beautiful green cornfield and she liked me too.

"Luckily, the family of the girl accepted our proposal, or *khaas-t-garree*. That night when my mother returned from my would-be wife's house and congratulated me, I was so happy and excited, I felt like an eagle soaring high in the sky.

"When I rushed that day toward the village after that dreadful bombardment, I could not think of anything else but that green cornfield, my shattered dreams, and my burnt desires. As you were reciting some poetry to the commander last night, even though I did not know the meaning, it went deep in my heart."

Who could bring back the laughter of his wife and the sweet smiles of his children to that cornfield, poor Ibrahim's *love field*? I shared this with Commander Massoud as well.

He calmly said, "War creates tragedies and I cannot even listen to these stories anymore. May God bless them all."

6:00 PM

Tonight will be my fourth night here, in the village of Namakaw. I have benefited from the time spent here, more than ever because selected groups of freedom fighters have been arriving from all corners of the north to join the battle of Farkhar. Despite whatever is going on, let me tell you that my thoughts are always with you and the only thing that makes me feel closer to you is when I am writing.

We are still waiting for the remaining groups of fighters to arrive from different provinces of the north to take part in the operation on the garrison.

Earlier Jaan Mohammad, the so-called Chief of Protocol, found a fishhook and went to catch fish for us. I also went along with him to the small river that runs through the village. There were many fish, both big and small, but the fishhook did not have the power to catch the bigger ones.

I jokingly told the Chief of Protocol that his fishhook was weaker than he was.

He quickly replied, "Khalili Sahib, we need to catch a fish, not a dragon."

We caught about eight small fish, each of which was the size of my extended palm. They were spotted trout. The spots were black, brown, and red.

I sent a message to Commander Massoud, asking him to kindly come down because I am not feeling well and cannot travel to the upper valley where he is currently busy with more preparations for the attack on the garrison. I did not go up with him mainly because he walks very fast and I would not be able to keep up. It is definitely a bother for me when he walks so fast but it is more of a bother for him to slow down to my pace.

Once I told him, "Commander, you are going so fast as if freedom is around the next corner and you would miss it if you do not rush." He turned, looked at me and simply said, "That is exactly how I feel. Freedom is as close as the next corner or the next peak."

Luckily, Massoud accepted that he would come down himself, instead of me having to go up. It is now 7:30 in the evening. I do not think I mentioned anything to you about the village where I am staying. It is a small village. By chance, an old man visited me whose name was Akbar. Despite being illiterate, to my surprise, he was able to compose poetry. He told me, "There are probably only about 30 to 40 mud houses in this village; most of the time the people stay in their pastures. They are mainly from both the Tajik and Uzbek ethnic groups."

*   *   *

I forgot to tell you that yesterday, in the late afternoon, we had a delicious coffee with Commander Massoud. His bodyguard always carries Maxwell instant coffee for him. It is always Massoud himself who prepares it in a special way that only some privileged Kabulis used to do before the war.

He first puts two or three teaspoons of warm water in a cup, then adds a teaspoon of instant coffee powder and finally a tea-spoon of sugar. Then he mixes and presses the contents of the cup with the back of his spoon to the sides of the glass for at least three minutes until the mixture of the coffee and sugar becomes white like milk. At this point, he fills the cup with boiling water, stirs, and the coffee is ready. It looks like a cappuccino with no milk and no chocolate on top.

He did this with a special kind of pride evident in his facial expression. With great satisfaction, Commander Massoud told me, "I know that you also know how to make a coffee like this."

I said, "Commander, I think that you have forgotten that I am the one who taught you how to prepare instant coffee like this in first place."

He smiled and said, "In that case, you should take the first cup." I did not accept and told him that I would make my own.

"I hope you won't break your finger or crack my cup. It is not easy, Khalili Sahib."

The coffee tasted very good. Besides the commander, no one else drinks coffee. He is the only one.

One of his bodyguards told me, "The only thing the commander does that I do not like is when he drinks that black stuff. It is nothing but a waste of sugar."

I forgot to tell you that today I gave 10,000 Afghani or $70 to the office of the resistance. I only brought 50,000 Afghani ($357) with me from Pakistan. I need 40,000 Afghani for my return trip, but right now, I am 35,000 Afghani short. Thank God, we can go on even though we have such little money. It is the cause that pushes us forward.

Let me finish writing. In an hour's time, Commander Massoud will be coming here. Until he arrives, I will take a bit of rest. Bye for now.

Nightmares, Day and Night

Village of Da Barneek
Thursday, August 7
6:30 AM

My dear, I am in the village of Da Barneek. You know better than anyone else in the world that, on Wednesday nights, I have nightmares. Listen to this funny story, when a nightmare created a nightmare.

Last night was Wednesday night. Commander Massoud and I had talked for a long time about different topics as we usually do at night and we were tired so we decided to call it an early night. Thank God, there were no mosquitoes to keep buzzing in our ears. The atmosphere was quiet and the only sound that could be heard was of the cool breeze coming through the window and the occasional snoring of the Commander's bodyguard. I slept a deep sleep for about two or three hours.

All of a sudden, I heard Massoud screaming, "Khalili Sahib! Khalili Sahib! It is just a dream! Wake up! You are dreaming."

I suddenly woke up, realizing that my friend was trying to help me out of an awful nightmare. When he saw that I was awake, Massoud started to laugh loudly at me. To his guard, who was sleeping nearby, it must have sounded so strange to hear suddenly the loud laughter of his commander, at such an odd time of the night. At this moment, Massoud switched on his flashlight, which seemed so bright that I had to cover my eyes for a second.

While the white beam of the flashlight allowed me to see Massoud's face, he said with a smile, "Khalili Sahib, you had nightmares last year as well."

Massoud's bodyguard who was watching from the corner of the room interjected, "Sir, it is nothing. We say that 'the darkness has pressed upon your chest'. Do not worry, pray that God is the most powerful and go to sleep."

Commander Massoud allowed his bodyguard to finish speaking, looked at me with an ever wider smile, and as he clicked the button to turn off his flashlight, in the complete darkness of the room, he jokingly said, "Do not blame the nightmares for your own fright. Be brave and let the nightmares be scared of you."

You know what happened later? Early in the morning, before prayers, I heard the screams and shouts of Massoud himself. His bodyguard was on extreme high alert, now that it was his commander who was screaming. He was up and ready to attack whatever enemy might have entered our room.

I quickly shouted at Massoud, "Commander, wake up! Wake up, Commander! It is just a dream. You are fine."

Massoud jolted awake. He was looking around the room as if to find the reason why he was screaming in his sleep and said, "It is the first time that this has happened to me, but why now?"

A few minutes later, when we got back into our own sleeping bags to sleep for a while longer, I jokingly said into the dark room, "Do not blame the nightmares for your own fright. Be brave and let the nightmares be scared of you." I heard the Commander laugh softly to himself.

In the morning, when the bodyguard was telling the story to the other men, I could hear them laugh loudly at his words. It made me laugh too but the problem was that they were blaming me for the nightmares of their Commander. Men will be men.

My dear, leave last night's story of our nightmares to one side and listen to this one that Commander Massoud told me himself. It is the story of Commander Azmuddin who is one of his political intelligence officers.

The wife and only child of Commander Azmuddin had been internal refugees in Worsaj for a year. After one year, Commander

Azmuddin decides to go see them. With a lot of effort, he gets permission from Commander Massoud. He goes speedily along the way on foot, so all the quicker to have his family in his arms and to rain kisses on his child. After all, he has been counting every night for more than 360 nights to see his small family. With no telephone, no postman, no radio communication, and no way to even see a photo of them, it was a great day for him to have the chance to come home. He was dreaming of seeing his baby take his first steps in front of him. He buys a simple toy for his boy and one or two gifts for his wife.

He reaches home. His young wife rushes to greet him. This is one of the happiest moments for all of them. Sounds of welcome and joy fill the house. He runs happily to kiss his son. His wife is highly excited and has no words to express how she feels at the sight of her husband playing, kissing, and talking sweetly to their little boy. The sky, the flowers, the trees, the grass, and all of nature seemed to be celebrating in her happiness.

They all go inside. She gets her husband's combat rucksack to put it in a proper place in the next room. Commander Azmuddin shouts to her that he has put some simple gifts for the two of them in the rucksack. Their son frees himself from the embrace of his father and runs after his mother. The sounds of the little one's excitement and of his mother's laughter fill both rooms.

All of a sudden, her unlucky fingers hit a hand grenade in the rucksack. By chance, the needle of the grenade is loose, her gentle touch pushes the needle out of its place and, in an instant, it explodes.

Commander Azmuddin hears a loud explosion and runs to find what has happened. He is horrified to find the bodies of his beloved wife and his sweet child smeared and soaked in blood. Not an hour has gone by that the young wife who was eagerly waiting for him to come home, dies in the arms of her husband. His little son does not die but is severely injured.

Azmuddin, who had just lost his beloved wife, could not stay for more than one or two days with his injured son, mainly because he had lots of work to do back on the Salang Highway. He left the house for the war with a weeping heart and no loving wife to greet him when he returns.

Listen to another true story. It is the story of Shaaniyaaz. He is a bodyguard and friend of Commander Massoud.

For the last six years, he has been responsible for carrying Massoud's backpack, preparing his food, shining his shoes, washing his clothes, keeping his important documents, taking care of his guests and doing all sorts of random jobs for him.

For about a year, Shaaniyaaz was asking Commander Massoud to allow him to go for a few days and see his young wife and recently born child of about three months. There had been no time available for him to take leave and his request to go home was always rejected by the commander. Four days ago, Massoud suddenly gave him permission to immediately go and see his family. Shaaniyaaz was very happy and excited that the commander had allowed him to go home for a few days.

He puts on a new combat jacket and trousers, polishes his shoes, buys some candy and simple gifts for his beloved young wife. His friends tell him to start his journey the next morning but he cannot accept and says that he will rush home and walk the whole night without stopping. He walks for more than nine hours with no rest to reach her.

Early in the morning, he reaches home. He is so happy it seems he has grown wings and flown there. With all his heart and soul, he eagerly knocks on the door of the house. His father-in-law opens the door. Shaaniyaaz impatiently rushes into the house to see his wife. The house is empty. Shaaniyaaz looks into the eyes of his father-in-law, which are full of tears.

He grabs his hand and shouts, "What has happened? Tell me! Where is she?" The father-in-law recites a verse from the Holy Quran, "We come from Allah and we return to Him."

As Shaaniyaaz stares into the empty room, he asks in a low and sad voice, "How did she die?"

With tears falling onto his beard, his father-in-law says, "The Russians bombarded our village and our home. Your beautiful baby son died from that attack. She was very severely injured. For two days, she was bleeding. Until her last breath, all she asked for was you. We sent a quick message to Commander Massoud to inform you, but you came too late, my son."

Without saying another word, Shaaniyaaz takes his rucksack and walks out of the house. While walking with tears in his eyes and pain in his heart, he is thinking of nothing but her. On the way back to his commander, he might have been remembering the night they got married, his wife's lovely smiles, and the few sweet days they enjoyed together. While walking alone, he is just with God and the beautiful memories he has of her.

Walking the whole night, he is exhausted and sits to rest a little. He opens his rucksack to get something to eat. Oh what a tragedy! He finds the gifts he has brought for his beloved wife. Amongst the gifts, he sees the candy he brought for his little son. He touches it and breaks the silence of the night by loudly crying, "Oh God, tonight I wanted to share these presents with my beloved family." His broken-hearted cry could be heard for a very long distance.

My dear, these two sad stories brought you and my children to my mind. What else can I do to fill my heart but to write notes to our little sons?

My little Mahmud,

My heart is restless when I think of you. You are six years old now. I am sorry that most of the time I have left you and your mom alone, since I have been busy in the liberation war of my country. Any time I see a small brown child, you come to mind. When I see naughty goats with their small sharp horns, small bodies, thin and shiny feet, jumping from stream to stream and from stone to stone, I remember you. On the mountaintops, when I see heavy snow, I wish to have you with me. Everywhere I go and everything I see, I remember you.

Being far from you and your little, naughty, and troublesome brother Majdood saddens me. You are my good little son. May God protect you and may a day come when, with the will of God, you become a faithful young man, proud of being an honest Afghan and a good Muslim and, above all, a better human being. However, always stay moderate, never go to any extreme, and never try being a fanatic. Even though you are born in America and you opened your eyes to the skies of that beautiful country and people, your native land is Afghanistan. Be good to both, the country you were born in and the motherland of your mother.

Your father

My cute and sweet little Majdood,

I do not know you well. You are just 18 months old. With you, my love, I did not spend more than a few months. You do not know me and you call me *Uncle* but you should know that there will come a day when you will be my friendly son and will call me *Dad*.

Village of Namakaw

Friday, August 8
5:30 PM

Last night, Commander Massoud and I talked at length about some serious issues and as usual, we changed to lighter things such as peace and poetry.

I did not do much today but things are moving along. I talked with a nice man whose name was Sayed Ahmad. He is smarter than many of the commanders I have met so far. I found him more a cultural man than a political person. He had a very soft heart. He didn't like the Russians at all but was relatively balanced on his views about them.

Let me tell you something very different from war and the Russians. Today, I bumped into a friend who is a French journalist. His name is Pierre. He says he is a photographer too. We call him Hussain. Hussain has been involved with us for the last five or six years. He has good relations with most of the Afghan parties in Afghanistan and Pakistan. He has a good typical French character, but in the meantime, he acts and talks like we do. I do not know his full name.

In France, we have many friends. A few writers and analysts from different countries, usually Americans and Europeans, also visit our war zones and write about them. Commander Massoud respects them and is very kind to all of them. He knows that I respect them as well. I told him the following story.

It was a cold autumn day. I was in Kantiwa and in a rush to go to the north. Haji Ghafoor, the Commander of Kantiwa, told me that there was a foreign woman in a very serious medical condition. I went instantly to see her. She seemed to be on her deathbed. No one was there except a poor old Nooristani woman to take care of her. The Nooristani woman could not explain what was wrong with the dying young foreign woman who was a doctor or a paramedic.

The doctor said that she is in a sort of half-coma. She could not understand and could barely talk. She was lying on a dirty Nooristani traditional felt-wool bed. The room was very small and dark, with no windows. It was like a cave larger than a grave. Under the Nooristan blanket, she looked like a dying bird. She was a European girl, French I think. I could not recognize her well because the pallor of her face was sickly, as yellow as the sunflower, and her eyes were as yellow as an autumn sunset. They were half closed and she was in tears. She had been in the Badakhshan or Kunduz provinces helping poor people for a year or more.

I gave her a little water. She recognized me. I moved closer to her to be able to hear her voice. She was moaning like a feverish baby. She was talking in broken English. When she saw me, a beautiful half smile formed on her dry lips. She was so happy to see a friendly face. She thought she would die because her liver ailed her greatly. I told her that she will be fine but she had to go to Pakistan as soon as possible and promised that I would find someone very soon to help her to do so.

While I was holding her cold hands, she told me, "If I die, please do two things for me.

I said, "Anything, please tell me."

"If by any chance, you find my family, tell them that I loved them. Second, get the list of medicine from my bag and please buy the medicine and send them to the North because I have promised those poor women and children that I would send them the medicine they need."

When I heard her last requests and how selfless she was, I cried too. Thank God, she did not die and was hopefully able to keep her promise to those poor women and children and take them some medicine. I always consider these types of people unique and extraordinary. They are the conscience of their nations. They are the spirit and soul of their peoples. Sadly, I do not remember her name. Anyway, thanks to Pierre who brought this story to mind.

*   *   *

A friendly chat is always sweeter than anything. Today Commander Massoud and I had that sort of chat. He told me about his childhood and how much he liked all things that are related to the military.

"When there was no one around, I would wear my father's hat and salute myself in the mirror. When I would be outside, I liked to play soldiers with the other boys in the area. I was their commander and they were my men. I also liked to be the leader of the boys in the neighborhood and prevent the bad boys from harassing the girls."

"Somehow," he continued, "I was always the one the children came to when they needed help. Besides kite flying and marbles, I loved to hunt. The problem was that we even had to hide our flying kites from our parents as our parents thought that flying kites was a waste of time. I never remember a day or a week when a friend did not fall off the roof while kite flying."

I told him, "Except for the military hat, which my father did not have, I also grew up with the same interests. What else did we have to do in Kabul?"

"I was also very interested in football. I was not as good as I wanted to be but I loved playing."

I reminded the commander that I was much better at football than he was.

He laughed and said, "If there are no witnesses, anyone can claim anything."

13

Battle Preparations

Saturday, August 9
9:30 AM

Things are going well. Commander Massoud is busy with battle preparations.

From a half-broken window, I am now watching Baaz Mohamad, the horse owner, who is standing beside his very thin and sick-looking horse. He seems very sad and is looking to the sky, as if asking God to help his poor horse. Oh, I see that the horse could no longer stand and has just fallen onto the ground. Let me call Baaz Mohamad to see if I can do anything. Wait, my dear, I will talk to you later.

I am now back again. I went down to help Baaz Mohammad. Luckily, Ibrahim joined me to help. Baaz lamented, "This horse is my whole life. He has been on so many long journeys with me. He has always been strong on the mountains and well behaved on the ground. When I load him with lapis lazuli, I choose each stone so that it does not have sharp edges. Now my poor horse is not feeling well. I do not know what I should do?"

I asked, "What can I do to help your horse?"

"The only thing you can do is to pray for him and for me."

We all tried whatever way we could to assist. Ibrahim, our helper, also used his own methods to help the horse of Baaz. All of us worked for at least an hour, after which the horse got a little better and got to his feet again. Baaz became a little happier.

* * *

It is about 11:30 AM. After helping Baaz with his horse, I am now trying to convince Ibrahim, to make me fresh tea, although he is not in a conducive mood. In order to avoid making tea, he advised me that too much tea is not good for one's health.

I laughed and reminded him of a proverb: "If you ask the lazy to do a job, he offers you nothing but fatherly advice." When he heard the proverb he said, "Please call me even a communist, but not a lazy man." He begrudgingly went off to make some tea.

God has his own ways. Now let's look at how the story of the horse unfolds.

I am looking now at a little child about the same age and size of our six-year-old son Mahmud, through the same broken window of the same poor room. Baaz, the horseman, is not there. The child has a black, dirty woolen hat on his head. His *kalaush*, or Russian rubber winter shoes, is at least two sizes too big. They are not only large but very old, with three holes in each one. Two big patches on his brown shirt are visible.

He is just now putting a bucket of water in front of the sick horse. Now he drags an old dirty and torn maroon carpet toward the poor sick animal. It is too heavy for him and I can hear him panting for breath. He finally reaches the horse and lays the carpet upon him very gently. The horse is calm and quiet. Sometimes he flicks his tail in the air. I can now see the horse nuzzling the boy with his head and nose. The boy does not even mind if the horse nudges him hard. The boy takes something from his dirty little pocket and tries to give it to the horse but perhaps the horse does not like the smell.

The boy tries again. Still the horse rejects the offer. I can hear the boy saying, "Eat it. It is very tasty. Eat it, you will feel good."

I cannot see what the boy is offering the horse.

A scrawny and dirty little dog approaches them. The dog is careless. He jumps about and bothers the horse. I hear the cute little boy telling the dog, "Don't come forward. The horse is not well today. Do not bother him. Let him rest. Go away, go away." The dog obeys.

Everything is silent. It seems as if God has sent this tiny little boy to take care of this horse, which looks at least 20 times bigger than the child.

It is a beautiful sight. The boy is now cleaning the horse with his little fingers and it seems as though he is cleaning and count-ing the horse's hairs, one by one. What a kind and merciful heart the boy has! He picks thorns from the horse's tail and cleans it with his little hands. Oh, his fingers seem like a small comb or a tiny brush.

The child hangs around the horse for about 20 minutes. Somehow the horse is standing comfortably now. Maybe he is enjoying the sweet caressing and nursing of the small child or maybe he wants to thank the boy by showing him that he is fine.

The boy told his dog "Look, the horse feels fine now. Do not do anything to upset him. Do not bark loudly. He may get disturbed. Let us go."

Whoever he is, may God bless him. Thankfully, I was brought a cup of tea. It smells very tasty.

4:35 PM

Today I've had much more time to write to you, off and on.

By now, you should know why I am here and cannot move toward Badakhshan. It is mainly because we are waiting for the operation on the garrison. Freedom fighters flow here like rivers from different valleys. Each one is armed. Their weapons are mostly Kalashnikov and Kalakov machine guns. Having a Kalakov means that a Russian has been killed and his weapon has fallen in the hands of a holy warrior.

So far, groups from Taliqaan, Panjshir, Sanjan, and Dur Nama have arrived. Tomorrow, groups from Badakhshan, Nahreen, and Ishkamish will follow. Lines of donkeys have also arrived with important supplies and there are still many more donkeys expected to arrive bringing more. One or two central units of Commander Massoud might also take part in this operation. This will be a grand preparation for the first united operation of the liberation movement against an established communist government base.

Before, the freedom fighters were attacking outposts and mountain posts that were very much smaller than the base they plan to attack in the next few days. In the past, the fighters of one village or province would attack a government installation, but now, Commander Massoud is going to include warriors of five or six provinces in a united attack plan. United we will be victorious.

God willing, everyone will arrive for the operation on the garrison of Farkhar at the latest by the day after tomorrow. They will wait for Massoud to give them their final assignments and the overall military strategy of how they should participate in the attack on the garrison.

Today again, from one to three in the afternoon, I spoke about different aspects of the war with Commander Massoud. He talked about military tactics used by the soviets and the resistance. Our tactics have so far consisted of ambushes, attacking outposts, launching some rockets on established enemy bases, planting anti-tank mines, mobilizing people, and increasing the scope of their intelligence. On the other hand, the tactics of the Russians have consisted of locating the enemy, bombardments, launching long-range artillery, planting anti-personnel mines, using ground forces, capturing an area from the hands of the freedom fighters, and maintaining the big cities with two or three security belts protecting them. He also said that the Russians have recently started to drop limited numbers of special commandos to cut or block the retreating lines of the resistance.

Massoud gave his ideas very frankly about how we should reduce our dependency on Pakistan. He believes that the more dependent we are on our neighboring countries, the more problems we will have, now and in the future. He believes that we, if possible, should get direct help from the West rather than through our neighbors. He said that it is even better for us not to get help from the West, if it is through the ISI of Pakistan.

I told him that we would work along this line but the West is not in our hands. They have their own policies based on their own interests. Although our common interest is to fight against the soviets, they have their own ways of how to achieve this. We cannot control their policies. As for the ISI of Pakistan, right or wrong, the West watches us, reads us, analyzes us, pleases us, displeases us, helps us, and evaluates us through the eyes of the ISI. They are the closest of allies.

Massoud is relatively objective and has a longer-term vision. In the beginning, when you hear him speak, his ideas seem simple but later you realize that they are practical and useful. I am going to be writing to you less because I fear my notebook will run out of pages.

Since I have become busy with events of the day, I sometimes forget to carry my yellow notebook with me as I move about and have to use some extra sheets of paper to write to you and then later I transfer my words to the yellow notebook. Maybe it is not so strange for an Afghan.

Preparations Go Well

Sunday, August 10
3:30 PM

I was very busy and could not write to you since morning.

Once again, last night was spent with Commander Massoud. Until late in the night, we talked. We discussed different wars, violent and nonviolent. I told him that Afghans outside Afghanistan are also struggling in their own way against the Soviets. We spoke of demonstrations and, in particular, about my actions in the United Nations against Gromyko, the Foreign Minister of the Soviet Union. He already knew the story, but still he asked me for the details, and I explained everything to him.

You remember, in 1980, after the Russians had invaded Afghanistan, we were in America and we held a small demonstration at the United Nations consisting of newly expatriated Afghan, who numbered no more than 50 or 60. I was their leader. I went in and sat in the gallery as the United Nations session began.

When Gromyko started delivering his speech, I threw hundreds of small flyers of a bombed and burned Afghan woman from the gallery down upon the members of the United Nations and shouted, "He is a liar! He is a liar! The truth lies in the flyers!" This is when the United Nations' guards rushed and arrested me.

Massoud listened very enthusiastically to this story and seemed to hold on to each word that I spoke. He was more interested in how I was released. We talked about life in the West and American movies. Surprisingly, despite being at war, he was in favor of more movies with love and humanity, rather than war and killing.

It is getting warmer and I am getting bored with collecting and relating so much news of the war. By the way, I should tell you that when I remember you, the beats of my heart drive me to reach my pen and write to you, more and more.

* * *

Today, there seemed to be a bit more work. In the morning, freedom fighters from various southern parts of the Hindu Kush Mountains came to see Massoud. Some of them were even equipped with old British muskets. They wanted me to ask Massoud to give them some new weapons.

Later, when Massoud arrived, I conveyed their message to him and asked him to talk to them directly. The Commander addressed them, "*Watandar* [compatriots], should I show you the easiest way to get weapons?"

All the men shouted, "Yes, Please. That is why we are here."

He looked at each one of them and then with a more intense voice said, "Attack the enemy posts and capture their weapons. This is actually the basic rule in a guerilla war, this is the way things have to be. You have to use your enemy's arsenal until you make yourself self-sufficient."

Incidentally, and immediately after that meeting, a message reached us that Commander Najmuddin from Badakhshan has captured about 200 pieces of weaponry from an ambush against the enemy. It was a good example for the men.

Then I decided to sit and talk with a famous commander from the Panjshir valley. He is Commander Panaa, who has been a commander on the Salang highway. He has captured much *ghanimat*, or booty, from the Russians.

He is a young man around the age of 33. He has a dark complexion, is of average height, and sports a thin and trimmed beard. He is brave and knows guerilla tactics well. What I liked in him was that he never believes that he will lose any battle. He thinks he will always be a winner. He asked me what a fighter should be like when he is in a war zone. I said, "He should be honest, brave, and never forget that freedom needs sacrifice."

My dear, it should make you happy to know that the horse of Baaz Mohammad, which was being taken care of by the small child, has become better. Do you know how? In this village, a local traditional veterinarian recommended that one kilogram of butter mixed with seven eggs should be given to the horse. They laid the horse down and forcibly gave the horse the mixture. The horse was back to normal in about four hours.

Baaz Mohammad is happy and today he has let his horse go free so that it may graze in the wild grassland.

I asked him, "Did you tell this to that little boy who was taking care of your horse?"

He said with a smile, "Of course, he is my son."

When Baaz Mohammad left, I saw the horse through the same broken window and I said to myself, he is lucky that he is healthy and free. I hope a time will come when I see my nation as free and fortunate as this horse. May the time come when a caring hand shall help the poor children of this land.

I told the story and my wish to Massoud and he said, "What a poetic wish. Include my wish with yours as well. Let us end your wish with an *Amen*."

Warriors Arrive

Tuesday, August 12
6:00 PM

Yesterday, in the early evening, the brothers of Massoud, Ahmad Zia, and Ahmad Wali, also arrived from Pakistan. Both have become very thin. Massoud was seeing his youngest brother, Ahmad Wali, for the first time in six years.

The minute the Commander saw poor Wali, some brotherly teasing started. He is such a nice and innocent looking young boy. He studies in London. I was on Wali's side in order not to allow Massoud to tease him too much with his jokes. Wali is about 23 years old. They are both younger than him. Massoud has real authority over them because he is older and his brothers know what he is doing for Afghanistan.

I think I have not told you that poor Andy has been tormented by a boil on his hip for the past five days. He has touched the boil so much that it has now become like a hole on the left side of his lower hip. Jaan Mohammad, the Chief of Protocol, put hot onions on it but it did not really work.

I talked to Andy a little. He was not feeling well.

"Tell me on which hip is the boil, left or right?"

He looked at me with a confused expression on his face and said, "What kind of question is this? What difference does it make which side of my butt hurts?"

I replied, "In our tradition, if you have a boil on the left side, it brings luck and you will become rich, and if it is on the right side, its unlucky and you will become poor." He laughed and said, "Even if it makes me the richest, I still hate this damn thing."

I translated Andy's words to Jaan Mohamad.

While laughing like the 'sound of girls clapping', he said, "For a nonbeliever, it doesn't make any difference. Left or right, lucky or unlucky: he is still going to hell."

I told Andy what Jaan Mohammad said and Andy replied sarcastically, "Maybe he is right but please bring the hot onion and get rid of this damned crater before I'm sent to my fiery hell."

Andy has become so close to us Afghans that we always consider him as one of our own and there is no holding back with words or jokes.

All the groups have arrived and, God willing, there is a chance of leaving tomorrow or the day after.

Ibrahim, our helper, is busy preparing breakfast. He announced that there is no bread or sugar. I am not that hungry anyway. When I woke up, I remembered this beautiful piece of poetry and I do not know why. Now, listen:

Tell the nightingales of the garden
My beloved is sleeping,
Do not sing aloud.

I shared this poem with Commander Massoud and asked him which birds he likes the most.

"In the sky, the wild ducks flying high in a single line," he said. "But on the ground, the partridges look beautiful to me. What about you?" he wanted to know.

"The migrant cranes of Kabul, in the spring," I replied. "And homing pigeons."

I told him a sweet story. "My father was sitting with the King, watching a Buzkashi match in Kabul Stadium. The players were on beautiful horses, trying to get the dead sheep into the circle. The king asked my father what he thinks of the game being played in front of them.

My father kept quiet.

The king insisted that he say at least something about how he feels while watching.

He quickly answered, "I see an animal, riding another animal, pulling another animal."

Torture by Communists

Wednesday, August 13
5:30 PM

Work was moving forward like any other day.

For the first time, Commander Massoud was using the BM12, which is a category of Russian surface-to-surface rocket launchers that covers longer range of 9 to 10 km. It has twelve rocket rounds mounted on a metal base, which is bolted onto two wheels, thereby making the BM12 mobile.

A young commander called Zabit Saleh prepared the BM12 for testing. They fired 12 rounds. Each round is about half a meter long. The rockets travel in an arc and not straight. It was very interesting and loud. The men were extremely happy to see that they have something very special and new in their arsenal. Massoud gave the command to start. The sound of this BM12 filled and echoed through all of the valleys and mountains.

For some seconds after the test, everyone fell silent. At that moment, Commander Massoud stood and slowly walked across the front of the newly tested weapon. I was a bit far away and could not hear what he said. It made me happy to see the fighters were all laughing and shaking hands with one another.

I walked over to the commander. I shook his hand and congratulated him. We were all excited that the new weapon had passed the test. I instantly thought how ironic are such moments in our lives when we become so happy to receive and test something with such a great capacity for killing. Whatever it maybe, this is war and in a war, what else can make you so happy but a brand new weapon? I'm sure Massoud must have thought something similar as he looked at this weapon of killing.

While leaving the test area, Massoud saw that my camera was in the hands of a young boy and instantly said, "Khalili, how come you trusted your sophisticated and beautiful camera to a young and unsophisticated boy?"

I said, "Don't worry. I have already made him sophisticated by training him a little." We both laughed.

His name is Ghulam Hadi. He is about 19 years old. He is very slim. He looks like an ancient Greek laborer. His eyes are green and his hair is blonde. He was imprisoned in the Puli Charkhi prison in Kabul, when he was in the tenth grade. He spent three years in a prison cell with two of his classmates and now he is with the Liberation Movement.

He had some horrible stories to tell, especially of the torture tactics that the communists used there. He told me, "Khalili Sahib, every week, they introduced us to a new torture tool and tested it on us. The Soviet advisors were always watching us as we were tortured, beaten, abused, slapped, spit on, electrocuted, hung from different extremities, starved, and shouted at. We were given very little food. While beating me, the interrogator shouted that we were supplying information to freedom fighter groups, the evil rebels, and if we denied it, he would break our necks. We just kept quiet."

His emotions stopped him from talking but I asked him to go on.

He said, "We were kept there for three years without any investigation but, thank God, the beatings were not as bad as they were in the beginning. Since we were very young, they beat us once or twice a day while the poor elders were beaten much more. After three years, they released two of us. Early one morning, they took us out of the prison, brought us to the center of the city, and told us to clear off. Unfortunately, later I found that the third boy who was with us had died in prison."

I slapped his back and said, "Now, you are with us. You will go with me to Badakhshan. You will keep my rucksack, take care of my notebooks, and learn how to use the camera."

His first attempt at learning how to use the Super 8 camera was taking footage of the testing of the BM12. I do not know whether it was a good start for a young boy or not. In a war zone, I think it was.

I accompanied Commander Massoud to the room where Ahmad Zia had brought for his brother some personal gifts which included a small radio, binoculars, nail clippers, some medicine, a knife, a flash light for reading, and 10 million Afghani, or $70,000, but believe me, the whole amount was distributed by Massoud within five minutes. Still, we owe 50 million Afghanis, or $357,000. He only allotted four million Afghani, or $30,000, to internal refugees scattered around the northern zone. They also distributed money to the provinces of Badakhshan, Parwan, and Kapisa. Just imagine the gap between how much we need and how much we have.

The expenditure of the northern zone is staggering. Besides strong leadership and a stronger will, challenging a superpower requires money too. Without money, it is very hard to push the wheels of the war to victory. If peace is nationally valuable, war is economically expensive. It is sweet to give your life in the fight for freedom, but it leaves a bitter taste when you see a friend starving on the battlefield.

Besides the machinery of war, the civilians need our help too. At least they need food, medicine, and clothes. Children must go to school and that requires money as well. In these two days, our food situation has become worse. We have only bread and tea with no sugar. We make do without.

I bought one packet of candy for 30 Afghani, or ¢20 US, which I am secretly throwing into my mouth one by one; otherwise, the friends here will finish them off in a minute. Jaan Mohammad told me that by tomorrow, Inshallah, we will get wheat flour, sugar, and, if possible, cooking oil and even some eggs. When I asked him about sugar, he said that I ask for too much.

Commander Massoud does not like expensive things. He prefers to wear the clothes of a regular freedom fighter and rarely has anything special that people would notice. Maybe this is one of the reasons that his fighters and the common people like him. Interestingly enough, amongst all the personal gifts of his, Massoud was most proud of his flashlight for reading.

I forgot to tell you that yesterday a very unique young man visited me, who is called 'Payk', or 'fast messenger'. He is from the Balkh province. His job is to take messages as fast as possible to others. He always travels on foot and never uses a horse or donkey. Some say that he is as fast as a galloping horse, as quick as a summer fox, and as rapid as a winter wind. He is about 26 years old. He shaves his beard and grows a thin mustache. He can travel very fast from Mazar-i-Sharif to the Panjshir valley and Peshawar.

Let me put this into perspective for you. We make the trip by foot from Chitral to Panjshir in twelve days and he does it in five. This is a very fast pace by any standard. He told me that he travels 60 to 70 kilometers a day on these trips, never less than 15 hours. By car, we travel maybe around 500 kilometers in around 8 hours to go from Kabul to Mazar-i-Sharif but he can do this trip crossing mountains in less than nine days by foot. On the road, it is easy but crossing these high mountains, mostly in the Hindu Kush range, on foot and at such a pace, is very difficult indeed.

The fast messenger has hundreds of stories about his trips. He is a real survivor. He has escaped from wolves, tigers, and many enemy ambushes. His slender body seems to be nothing but skin and bone. He has fox-like eyes. The commanders write their letters on pieces of cloth and stitch them to his combat jacket. He runs day and night to get the letters rapidly delivered to their destinations. If he would have been caught, the communists would interrogate him and later maybe kill this fast messenger of the resistance. He told me "I sleep little, eat little, and talk little. In the mountains, I always remember God and on the ground I remember the Prophet."

I gave a long letter to this fast man to carry like a galloping horse to Commander Malim Atta, commander of Mazaar. I advised the fast messenger to be as steady as the clouds of autumn while running as fast as the winds of winter.

Last night, we heard on BBC Radio that resistance operations upon the city of Kabul have increased. Five BM12 rockets damaged the embassies of Russia and Poland in the capital.

BBC Radio is very important to the Afghan people. People listen to its Farsi language broadcast every night, very attentively. The common people do not trust the British because of past wars but they trust BBC broadcasts in such an extreme way that if the BBC were to announce that 10 plus 10 is 25, the people would accept it. Commander Massoud always listens to the BBC News with his small pocket radio. I asked him, "Do you trust BBC?" He answered, "I try." I know BBC does not favor the Russians in Afghanistan but they try very much to be careful when they talk about us too.

5:30 PM

It is 5:30 in the afternoon. I see in the distance that Commander Massoud has found some time and gone to a corner to be alone with his younger brothers, Ahmad Zia and Ahmad Wali. After all, they have traveled all the way from Pakistan and London to visit him. They are probably talking about their sisters, brothers, parents, other family members, and the good old days. Massoud's father is alive but his mother passed away some years ago. He is not married yet. We all have this problem of separation. We are always far from our loved ones. We always miss them and more so, we miss family life.

While Massoud is talking with his brothers, at a distance I see a small child who is busy helping his father harvest wheat, between the weeds and the thorns. He is chasing cows, grabbing their tails to guide his plow in order to separate the seeds from the stalks. He is about eight or nine years old. He seems very thin and is barefoot. His green jacket is full of colorful patches. Despite the weather being warm, he is wearing long rubber winter boots. Even his boots have at least three yellow rubber patches on them. He looks very confident, as if even with his tiny body, he is the lord of all the animals. Strangely, he has an old dirty whistle around his neck but I do not know why.

A few moments ago, another child of about the same age, brought me a spotted trout in the hope that I would buy it and I did so. I gave him 40 Afghani's, or ¢27, and a piece of candy for the fish. He happily ran back toward the yellow field until he reached the boy with the whistle around his neck. Maybe they are brothers and he is going to tell him to come and get a piece of candy from me as well. Unfortunately, I do not have anymore.

Anytime I see a child, I remember our little sons, Mahmud and Majdood. It is natural. I was murmuring the following quatrain, on and off since morning. Please read it.

I remember you, day and night,
I forget everything, even my sight
Without you,
I am a memory forgotten
A heart broken,
I am a candle, with no light.

Thursday, August 14

Preparations for the operation are going well and moving successfully forward. Tonight, in the middle of the night, we are going to depart toward Khusdeh Village and from there, God Willing, we will continue toward the theater of our operation.

I took some good pictures of one of the groups from the north. In the afternoon, I went to the river, performed my ablutions, and washed my clothes. Ibrahim insisted that he would help me but I did my own washing, which was not more than a pair of socks and a shirt.

Tomorrow is Eid Qurbaan, our sacrificial festival of Eid. I am sure that the operation against the garrison will commence after Eid celebrations.

14

Celebration before the Battle

Eid-e-Qurbaan
Friday, August 14

My dear, Eid Mubarak! (Happy Eid) to you, my mom, my father, and my children! Without you, Eid is like a flower with no fragrance, and a sky with no blue.

I am speaking to you from Khusdeh, the first village in Farkhar district. We left early in the morning and arrived here at around noon. The pass was not that high and the path was not that bad. The valley of Farkhar is one of the most beautiful valleys in the northern parts of Afghanistan. About 15 years ago, it was a summer resort of the then king, Zahir Shah. It was famous for its trout and horned deer.

This is our first stop before going to the area of our planned operation. The minute the fighters arrived here, they were divided into different houses. The common people accommodate them in their homes so they do not have to sleep outside. It is their way of contributing to the war effort. None of the fighters celebrates Eid because they are far from their homes.

The local children are wearing new or washed clothes for Eid. Around their eyes and on the eyelashes, they have the black color of *surma*, a natural eyeliner. On occasions like this, women, men, girls, and boys also use this natural powder to make artificial moles on their cheeks, chins, and on the corner of their lips. They get it from the mountains of Farkhar. Most of the children have colorful handkerchiefs pinned to their shoulders. They are going to their relatives' homes.

Two or three women hold their shoes on their heads in order not to get them dirty from the mud so that they do not look bad when they reach their relatives' homes for the traditional Eid greetings. Just before they reach them, they wash their feet in the stream and put their shoes on again. Shoes on their heads show how poor they are. Whatever, they look beautiful, at least to me.

Women wear *chadari* or *burqa*s and the girls have long scarves or shawls covering their locks of hair. Some older women use either horses or donkeys to take them to their relatives' homes. A few carry small baskets filled with colored eggs, fruits, or homemade cookies to take as gifts. Those who have sugar and rice at home, make rice pudding but they mostly cook the meat of sacrificed goats or sheep.

Boys carry colored eggs and make themselves ready for *tukhum jangi,* or egg fighting. We fight with everything, even eggs. The boys are given one or two boiled eggs, one of them holds out one end of his egg while the other hits the end of his own egg against the first child's egg and whoever's cracks, loses. Then the boy with the cracked egg flips it over and the fight is repeated. Whoever has both egg-ends cracked, loses his egg to the other child.

The commander of the area gave me a colored egg, and, instantly, a sweet boy challenged me to an egg fight. He won my egg by guile, using his own rigged egg. The boys are very smart. They use a needle to puncture the egg, empty its contents, fill the egg with wax and when it hardens, it is ready to trick people. I liked losing to that little boy, even though I was tricked. The little boys and girls get money or *Eidee,* which is a gift from the elders. If you do not give them that, they ask you repeatedly until you are forced to do so. It is a lovely tradition.

In the past, our Eid celebrations were different. We had more enjoyable times. In Kabul, in those days, we children had more fun, toys, sweets, balloons, bubble gum, kites, and marbles, with no horror in our hearts and no terror in our minds. Today in Kabul, as here, the children have more fear and horror because of the war. No doubt, even our own rockets being launched on Kabul, while terrifying the Russians, bring horror to the hearts of the poor children too.

Last year during *Eid,* as you have read in my notes, I was in Gandeel, a village in the southern province of Kunar, an ethnic Pashtoon area. They had great Eid celebrations too. The people did whatever good they could to keep me happy. I was the only guest in the whole village. They had their special dances and fired guns into the sky to celebrate these holy days. The men were dancing in the open fields, maybe the women in their homes.

The children were wearing new or washed clothes and they had *surma* lines around their eyes too. Their *surma* lines were deep blue, while here in the north they are black. The children had the same colored eggs for fighting. The Pashtoon villagers would also apply different colors to their sheep and goats. It is also a tradition to put *surma* around the eyes of those animals that are specially selected to be sacrificed on this holy day. This is what Prophet Ibrahim did to his son, Ismail, when he was taking him to be sacrificed to God.

The Pashtoon women wore long, colorful dresses of black, deep red, and purple hues. Attached to the front of their big decorated turbans, the men sported a hawk feather or a single rose. They looked as if they had small white rose bushes with a single red flower perched on their heads. Some of them wore long gowns with old, rusted swords hanging from their belts. They had rooster fights and dogfights too.

In both cases, whether in the north or in the south of Afghanistan, the war has created horror in the hearts and minds of the people, especially the children.

I hope that you have made new clothes for our sons, Mahmud and Majdood. This is our tradition as well as a religious duty to dress our children in new or washed clothes. After all, it is the sacrificial festival.

Today because of the Eid celebrations, the people look happy but deep in their hearts, they worry about the upcoming attack on the garrison. They know that their boys are preparing for a big operation against the government. We could not observe Eid prayers, since we were concerned the government might bombard us as we prayed.

Commander Massoud decided not to start his offensive on the government garrison during Eid.

He told me, "It is a holy day. We should let people enjoy their *Eid* and celebrate as much as they can."

I think it is a good decision. One or two days do not make much of a difference.

Anyway, however the poor people feel, good or bad, calm or agitated, we sent our freedom fighters to block the paths leading to or exiting from this village because there is a chance that someone might report us to the Soviets or the Soviets may come to this village. God forbid, if they find out that we are preparing an offensive, they may start bombing our positions.

Ahmad Zia, Ahmad Wali, Jaan Mohammad, our foreign friends, and I have taken shelter in a small garden, which belongs to a man named Qaari Mawjood. In front of me, there are two grapevines, two sour cherry trees and one sweet one, three walnut trees, one *sinjit* tree, three peach trees, a few poplar trees, and a beautiful old weeping willow. To the north of us, there is a cave where we may take shelter, if a bombardment starts.

The weather is quite warm. We are waiting in the hope that someone brings us food from the Eid celebrations. Once again, my dear, *Eid Mubarak*! Happy Eid!

4:30 PM

The old *panja chenaar*, or poplar trees, in front of us, look extremely beautiful. Gently and gracefully, the winds comb their green locks. With their wrinkled trunks, the old poplars look like graceful grandmothers dressed in beautiful green and white gowns. Oh my God! The goats and sheep look like grandchildren grazing in the shadows of their grandmothers. Although our eyes feast on the heavenly scene of the poplar trees with their green dresses, silver-colored leaves, white trunks and sky-reaching branches, we are still very hungry. No empty stomach enjoys beauty. Ah, thank God! The food is on its way. I will write to you later.

We had our lunch. First, Qaari Mawjood, the owner of this beautiful garden, brought some delicious dough to drink. Then, three handsome, bearded men brought big pieces of roasted meat and small pieces of fried liver. Another villager brought us tea, candy, and sugar cubes. They repeatedly poured black and green tea into our cups. The roasted meat was most delicious. God bless the soul of Prophet Ibrahim, who was the creator of Eid of the Sacrifice, and thanks to whom we now receive so many different kinds of food for lunch today!

All the roasted meat and fried liver tasted wonderful to us on this special day but I wish I knew how the poor sheep and goats feel about this day when they are sacrificed for the sake of God. The pieces of bread were large, round, warm, and delicious. The wheat bread was so tasty I thought Prophet Adam and Eve might have baked it on purpose to exchange paradise for it. A God-sent freedom fighter brought for us green onions and fresh chili peppers too.

Qaari Mawjood said that his garden, which was without doors or walls, belongs to his father. He has a black beard and a shaved moustache. He is educated but I do not know to what extent; at least he can read and write well. He is clean and tidy. He has a very innocent and kind face, which looked like he had not committed a single sin in his whole life.

Just a moment ago, I saw a bunch of very small children from this area. They were wearing brightly-colored clothes of scarlet, crimson, green, and yellow shades, with flower patterns that were even brighter. Pinned onto the shoulders of the boys' were handkerchiefs of red, green, and orange colors, hanging down to their little elbows. Most of them wore *kalaush*es on their feet. The difference between the girls and the boys on this festival day is that the boys get eggs for egg fighting while the girls do not.

I asked one of the girls the reason. The little nine-year-old told me, "Eggs and guns are for the boys. Dolls and gum are for the girls. God has created us like this."

15

Battle of the Garrison

It is eight in the morning. It is the second day of *Eid-e-Qurbaan*. We are still in Khusdeh village. Throughout the area, the local people have become aware of the preparations for the garrison operation and of the arrival of the fighters. They are very worried.

One of them is Gul Agha. He is the son of the spiritual elder of Kanda Kaw, is a good man, and works very hard to help people in different ways. He is doing almost everything for the resistance. He is from a very respectful family. His father was a known Sufi. He rushed to me and asked me if I needed anything.

When I asked if he could remember something from his father, he eloquently replied, "The wise man is the one who believes that each breath is an arrow to hunt happiness. The smart man is the one who is patient, whether he is sad or happy, rich or poor, or sick or healthy."

He gave me a handful of almonds and advised me to eat them only when I face a danger. To be honest, I had them the minute he left.

Commander Massoud is busy dividing the men into different groups and assigning different tasks to each, before deploying them to the battleground. Commanders like Yahya, Wadood, Panaa, Azeem, Ahmadi, and Amaanare going back and forth to complete or fix the last parts of the preparations for the operation against the garrison. I can hear the sounds of test-firing of the .50 caliber rounds.

Fifty donkeys are being made ready to take ammunition and weapons to the area of Karaanee, meaning the district headquarters of the government. At least fifteen hundred pieces of wheat bread and forty kg of meat will be needed for five hundred men on the day of the battle. We need four to five hundred *mashk*, or rubber barrels for drinking water, for just one day of the operation. The men have to install the heavy weaponry in fixed positions on the ground and on the sides of the mountains; while at the same time, the attacking forces have to take their positions.

Commander Yahya told me, "The operation starts when these heavy weapons rain down fire upon the first three government forts and then, undercover fire from these heavy weapons, the ground forces will attack. Face-to-face combat will occur only if the government soldiers do not surrender. Ground troops are armed with hand grenades and Kalashnikovs. One of the main problems will be mines, therefore we have to demine the area as our forces move forward. There are hundreds of mines already planted around the fort."

According to the plan, the operation should not take more than two hours. It is impossible not to notice Massoud in these final days of preparation. He looks slightly concerned, although he shows a strong face to his men. I told him that he looks tired but he instantly denied it. Do you know why he is bit concerned? It is because: (a) it is the first united offensive against a government garrison, (b) the groups are still undergoing training and are not really battleworthy, (c) it is the first combined and coordinated attack from all different parts of the north, and (d) we have very little experience in this kind of offensive attack.

After all, we are entering a new phase in this war, from a defensive to an offensive one. It is the first time that the freedom fighters of the north will be tested to see if they can defeat an established Soviet garrison. The garrison is the first step, then a province, and then the capital. There is a long way to go and it needs a lot of work and patience. God help us.

At this moment, I am writing to you from a mulberry garden. Last night, we slept under the mulberry trees. There is no sign of bombardment yet. Maybe the Government troops are also busy with their own *Eid* celebrations.

Today in the morning, via radio broadcast, I heard a speech by Ustad Rabbani, the leader of Jamiat, concerning his trip to America. In his speech, he praised the help of America and other Western countries in Afghanistan and condemned those hypocritical Afghan leaders who receive the largest help from them but at the same time condemn our allies the most.

At the end of his speech, he eloquently addressed the West, "We will ultimately defeat the Russians. Afghanistan and other Soviet Republics will be freed from the grip of the Soviets. Stay with us to the end. God is great."

Khaf Dara

Thursday, August 21
3:37 PM

My dear wife, I have some very good news to tell you! The operation went well and it was successful! Commander Massoud was victorious!

I am very sorry that I was not able to write to you in the last five days. I was indeed very busy day and night and, anyway, your notebook was not with me. I had only taken with me the notebooks in which I wrote of serious military events and details. However, I was taking some short notes in separate sheets of paper for you as well. Do not lose them. As for how the operation went, though it is a long story, listen:

It was the second day of Eid that we departed from the village of Khus Deh for another place called the Dasht Khus Deh. At sunset, we reached a relatively large ground banked by a deep blue river and surrounded by many old, majestic, and fantastically beautiful poplar trees. Most of the fighters had gathered there. They were armed with machine guns. Their ages ranged from twenty to thirty. Their boots were old, ripped, patched and very different from each other. Most of them wore the round pakols, or hats, popular to resistance fighters. At least to me, they looked very determined and confident, although they were all the poorest soldiers in the world.

When I saw the threadbare appearance of most of our men enthusiastically heading toward the operation zone, I remembered some advice from my father which consoled my heart and filled it with hope: "Son, for a fighter, it is the rich heart which matters, not the poor hat."

Massoud asked me what I was thinking about and I quoted my father to him.

He instantly said, "Khalili Sahib, God bless your father. At this moment, it is only the blessing of God and the poetry of your father which can fill my heart and the hearts of my poor men."

More than 400 freedom fighters, armed with mostly captured Russian weapons, were waiting for their order to depart toward the operation area. The air was thick with anticipation for the operation. Everyone knew what they had to do and everyone was ready.

The evening prayer was interesting for me. When we were praying, it seemed as though the various weapons of the freedom fighters which were placed in between them, were also praying to God. It was a very special scene.

The touching of the sun's rays like arrows upon the lofty rocks of the mountains, the dancing of the clouds over the passes, the sounds of the wind through the corn fields, the neighing of the horses, the chirping of the sparrows from atop the old poplar trees and the dreams of the faithful men for freedom, filled my mind and heart with an unforgettably special feeling. The dark shadows of the mountains looked glorious in the near distance. I wish I had the power to understand the language of the mountains, birds, and wind to tell me the story of the past and even to foretell the destiny of the future.

After dusk, we came along with Commander Massoud to the nearest summer pasture to take rest and had food there. At night, around 2 AM, in Jamiat's old and creaky car, which was more like a Russian lorry, we departed.

The next day at around three-thirty in the afternoon, we started heading toward the area of operation. A lower mountain overlooked the government garrison. At five in the afternoon, we reached there. That area is called Chishma Garm. The mountain has many pistachio trees.

Ahmad Zia, Sandy Gall, Engineer Arif, one or two others, and I accompanied the Commander himself. He had his binoculars, ready to command every aspect of the operation from this position on the mountain. Engineer Arif was handling the Russian communication radio, R105, for him. The weather was perfect.

*   *   *

At 5:30 PM, by the firing of BM12, the operation started. It seemed like hell on earth, at least to me who has never used a weapon except for hunting. Heavy weaponry was raining their hellish fire upon the forts. There were four high-walled forts, targeted one after another. After the BM12s, the cannons, mortars, and .50 caliber weapons started firing upon different targets.

The position of the enemy was as follows: four strong forts belonging to the military, police, and intelligence service, seven outposts on the top of the mountains covering and protecting the forts, three hundred and thirty four soldiers, 76 mm desert guns, and some mortars. Commander Zabit Saleh was doing very well. The roar of .50 calibers, mortars, and cannons blasting from all sides was very loud.

Within five minutes, one-handed Commander Azeem captured the first outpost, which was located on the top of the mountain. First, the plan was to take the outposts on the mountaintops. Four outposts fell into the hands of our fighters in less than fifteen minutes. It was done very precisely. When the cannons of the Commander Massoud started firing, the different ground forces started moving forward. All Commander Massoud's plans were being played out in front us.

Commanders Azeem and Panaa captured the first and second forts and while attacking the third one, they were stopped by enemy fire. Two of our boys stepped on mines and both were killed which slowed down the advance of the other men.

Taking advantage of the two casualties, the enemy started their counterattack. Their fire was heavier than ours was. We lost two more fighters and about six were wounded. Massoud was busy, ordering his men what to do and what not to do. Engineer Arif, the communications man did a good job. Andy and Noel were with the fighters, filming. Armed with their cameras, they were as brave as the Afghans.

When it started getting darker, once again Massoud ordered his men to move forward under a new wave of artillery barrage. Their advance was swift and they captured all of the outposts, including three poorly built forts, except for one. The last fort, which was run by the intelligence forces of the enemy, called *khaad*, kept our men under constant and heavy fire. At that moment, unfortunately, our ammunition and cannon shells had been used up.

It was seven in the evening. Massoud himself started to rush down from the mountain. We ran after him. Massoud 'walked like the wind', as Ahmad Zia put it.

In no time, we were right in the middle of the theater of operation. The battle down on the front line with the fighters was extremely loud, with constant gunfire, repeated mortar fire, and the screams of the men to one another. It was as if we had entered another world. Some of the commanders, after seeing Massoud running down the mountain toward their positions, immediately came to give him their battle reports.

He ordered that the operation be slowed down and the commanders wait for further orders. He had correctly assumed that the mines would martyr more of his men. The commanders went back to their men and gave their orders. Andy and Noel were still on the frontlines with them. The thick smoke of gunfire spread everywhere. The battle continued but at a slower pace until two at night. The enemy outpost that was covering the intelligence fort resisted very well and showed great bravery.

According to Massoud, the first phase of the operation was successful. Fifty-three enemy soldiers surrendered and a great deal of weapons and ammunition was captured. Sufi Mayraaj, one of Commander Massoud's trusted bodyguards, was martyred.

We went to take some rest but early in the morning, we returned to the battlefield. The fighting had ground to a halt. The Russian helicopters' rotors appeared around nine in the morning and the bombardments started. Massoud ordered his men to once again start the attack on the remaining posts. This was our second day and the second phase of the offensive. The enemy bombardment grew heavier.

The ground trembled from the impact of their rockets. Four attack helicopters attacked us in unison with rockets and machine gun fire to show their strength. Our men did an even greater job on the second day. Their attacks seemed more swift and precise.

History was being made in front of us and I was standing next to the man who was the director of this epic scene. Commander Massoud was calmly and confidently ordering his commanders, telling them how to move forward in the field. We moved forward as our forces moved closer to the enemy.

At one point, we saw that the Russian fighter jets and attack helicopters, which had tried in vain to turn the battle in their favor, turned their tails and left. The commander saw this as a good sign. We were all very happy.

Once again, I could see Andy right on the front line, taking footage of the offensive. He was fearless. Then the screams of the men, the sounds of the guns, mortars, and rockets went silent. We were informed that the remaining intelligence fort and the police outpost had surrendered too. A hundred and fifty nine prisoners fell into the hands of our men. A large amount of ammunition, weapons, and food supplies were also captured and instantly sent to different villages so that they may be kept safe from possible counterattack by the enemy.

We won the battle. I shook the commander's hand and congratulated him on his victory. As we were looking at the battlefield, filled with smoke from the guns and bombs, and at the men celebrating their victory, the commander, now in a very happy mood, smiled and said, "Thank God we have won the Battle of the Farkhar Garrison."

I looked at him, "Commander, let us pray that we win the war too."

*   *   *

The battle is over but now listen to the story of the prisoners. A large group of these prisoners were being taken somewhere by the fighters. A most cruel and merciless police commander was one of them. He was in chains. His name was Najib Ra'd. He had no hat or boots and his face was covered in blood. Parts of his clothes were ripped and his sleeveless shirt was stained with blood as well. Other prisoners looked even worse than the police commander did.

There were women and children who were crying, lamenting, weeping, and begging for amnesty. Seeing these trembling and distraught women and children made me very sad. Even though I know that their husbands, brothers or fathers have been the real cruel killers of our time, watching an innocent child shivering at the sight of his father in the hands of the enemy was painfully tragic, at least for me.

It was even more painful when I saw a small girl holding on to the back of her father's shirt so tightly that there was no blood left in her little knuckles. Another child was crying in her mother's lap. A woman was asking the men to be kind to her husband. She had four little children running behind her and a small three-year-old boy sat in the arms of his captured father. His small, worried eyes gazed at his father anxiously and as they walked by, I could see his tiny hands were dripping with the blood he was trying to clean from his father's face. Another little boy with tears in his eye was pleading with one fighter not to push his father. An old woman, the mother of a communist soldier, was crying like a baby, pleading for the release of her young son.

I asked an armed man, "Why is this old woman and the other women being taken as prisoner? Leave them alone this instant. Let them go."

He told me, "They are not prisoners. They are coming of their own accord to be with their captured sons or husbands but do not worry, they will be looked after."

Unlucky is the one who is a prisoner in the hands of his enemy.

Commander Massoud immediately instructed that the prisoners, and especially women and children, should be treated with respect. He shouted loudly, "Be careful about the prisoners. Do not let the women and children accompany them even if they want to, but if they insist, let them go along and take care of them. Do not even push or shout at them in front of their fathers or brothers. They are like one of our own."

Thank God, our men obeyed the orders of the Commander. I could see that they were indeed treating the women and children with a special kind of respect. I was happy that the commander's men were well behaved, even when they were angry.

Later I told Massoud, "Look at the power of love. It is the first time that I see people volunteering themselves to be prisoners. Look at them; even though our fighters do not allow them, they still push to be close to their men, whatever the circumstance. Love is boundless."

The communist police commander, Najeeb Ra'd, captured by Massoud's men, was always considered to be one of the cruelest enemy commanders, who has killed many men and abused many innocent women. An ordinary civilian told me, "This police officer even used to bite the flesh of the innocents captured by his men."

I told him, "Whatever wrong they have done, we should be careful and take a lesson that the rule of justice is the cruel and unjust ultimately fall into the hands of justice. As the common saying goes, *chaa kan aakher da chaas*, or 'the well digger is ultimately devoured by the well'." My dear, here the well digger is symbolism for the unjust and is not just a poor honest well digger.

Although Commander Yahya assured me that he is always careful about captives, he asked me apprehensively, "What rule is the best in this situation?"

Remembering the little boy with his tiny, blood-drenched hands holding onto his captured father, I told him, "Justice and mercy. The rest, God knows."

Commander Massoud heard this and said, "In that case, God shall give us reward in this world and in the next."

* * *

My dear, read this interesting story. Last night, when the offices of these traitors were being burnt, a middle-aged man walked toward us. His name was Maulavi Ahmad and his father's name was Peer Totak. While watching the red flames of the burning fort blazing toward the sky, he started shouting repeatedly, "Thank God. God is great."

Someone told me that he is the owner of this fort. I called him and asked, "Why are you thanking God while watching your own fort burning to the ground?"

He simply said, "Because the enemy is no longer sitting and living there. No longer will it be a place to torture innocent people."

While Commander Massoud heard my exchange with the man, he looked at him and said, "I am sorry. You are right. If this fort is not burned, tomorrow the communists will come back, and bring their soldiers to burn the houses and crops of our people, and will make this fort their base once again. I hope we can rebuild it for you one day."

The man eloquently replied, "I do not think you will build it again but I hope that at least from this place our homes are not rocketed and our people are not tortured again."

I looked at the commander and said, "What a great lesson he has given us." With a smile slightly forming on his face, the commander told me, "If this is so, write it in your notebook, Khalili Sahib."

Interestingly, from one of these forts, besides other booty, our men brought out about 100 bottles of vodka, which were immediately smashed.

I asked Andy why he did not buy them? He laughed and said, "I am Polish, I do not like Russian vodka."

The next morning, Soviet helicopters filled the skies and bombed the area extensively. In the evening around sunset, they returned to attack us, killing two fighters, three civilians, and wounding four others. Unfortunately, Commander Hashimi, the head of the resistance of Farkhar, and Commander Wadood were amongst the injured.

* * *

I should not forget to tell you that something very special happened that 'made our hearts like a garden, our minds like a divine field of flowers' and filled our eyes with tears of joy. Sometimes, simple things touch our hearts and this is about that simple thing.

Yesterday, we were all sitting in a kind of hilly garden. The weather was perfect. The sky was brilliantly blue. Massoud, some of his commanders, some political and religious people, and I were sitting together. Everyone was talking to one another about all kinds of everything. Massoud was laughing loudly at the various stories and was trying to banter back and forth with some of his more friendly commanders. When he is happy, he does not care who is around and what he says. It seems as though he expresses his heart to the heart of others.

We were all happy. We had no military operations on the way. The small children of the village were playing around us too. Some of them very eagerly wanted to listen to us.

All of a sudden, an old, slender, white-bearded man, with a long walking stick in one hand and a sort of cloth bag in the other, appeared. He approached us slowly and at his own pace. In order to keep his balance, he was holding his walking stick very tightly and precisely placing it where he thought best supported his weight.

He walked directly toward us, which immediately attracted my attention. I could see that Massoud had already noticed him as well. One of the Massoud's bodyguards approached the old man, asked him what he wanted and who he wanted to talk with. Without stopping, the old man pointed his walking stick toward Massoud. The commander seemed to be attracted by this action of the old man and shouted, "Let him pass. It is okay. Let him come."

Again, the old man very solemnly moved toward us with his slow and careful steps. Maybe he made about 15 to 20 more steps until he finally reached us.

He greeted the commander, "Salaam!"

The commander greeted him with more humble words and asked, "Please sit, Uncle. What can I do for you?"

The old man chose to sit on a relatively flat rock. He took his breath, looked into the commander's eyes and, with words which seemed to come straight from his heart, said, "May God bless you. My son informed me about the victory of our boys and I came to congratulate you and more so to thank you."

Commander Massoud thanked him in one or two beautiful sentences, and went on, "Uncle, what can I do for you?"

The old man replied, "Oh, what can you do for me? I am an old man. I have seen many ups and downs in my life. I am a faithful Muslim and I always pray for my people, wherever they are in Afghanistan. My wife is also very old. We had one boy that we lost in an enemy bombardment. We are now living with his two orphaned children and his widow. My wife and my son's widow gave me a present for you and I am here for that reason."

The old man opened his cloth bundle, took out three necklaces made of real pistachios and gave it to Commander Massoud. Let me explain, my dear, that the locals de-shell pistachios, string them up like necklaces, and keep them for the winter. He presented three pistachio necklaces with his trembling hands to the commander.

Massoud took the necklaces, touched them, looked at me, and while all three hung around his fingers, he said, "Are they not beautiful, Khalili Sahib?"

"Beautiful may not be a sufficient word for this. We have to find a more beautiful word to describe this necklace, which carries with it an important message that the mothers of our motherland support our cause. If I am right, then victory over the Soviets is under the shadow of these necklaces and at the gate of this garden."

Do you know what happened next? Commander Massoud kept one of the necklaces, gave me the two others and said, "One is for your father the poet of our land and the other for your wife, the love of your heart."

With this, the whole Farkhar operation was successfully completed.

And now, my dear, I bear a necklace made of pistachio from me to you.

16

Onward to Badakhshan, Cradle of Old Culture

Friday, August 22
4:00 PM

I am now in Mashtaan village, which borders the Badakhshan province. About five in the morning, I woke up and saw that Massoud was sitting upright.

He asked me, "Why don't you stay one or two more days."

I thought about it a little and told him that there is too much work to be done and I have several conferences to attend in America and Europe. We talked as we walked up and down the riverbank. We also talked briefly about the difficulties of working with a self-interested and self-serving ISI. While Massoud accepted that working with them was often unpalatable and he would prefer more direct help from the West, he said for the time being we should at least try. At last, he said that he would try to meet me again if I returned on time.

Massoud ended by saying, "I have radioed Commander Arianpur and he is waiting for your arrival."

We said our goodbyes and went on our way.

I left in a captured Russian truck which we had used some days before. It was huge, dirty, noisy, and slow, with torn seats and a strong smell of petrol. Sitting in that type of truck was in itself like being in a garrison battle. The difference between the two was that, in a garrison battle, you may achieve a great gain but in this one you are always at a painful loss. In an old vehicle like that, the outside weather did not make any difference because there was no place for air to enter and circulate since it was filled to capacity with fighters, their weapons, ammunition, and supplies.

The driver recognized me, started talking very loudly about war and peace, and ended by reciting a beautiful folk song. I thought that if sitting in this truck is a loss, talking to its driver is definitely a gain.

With us we had wounded warriors from Kishm too. They were in a lot of pain. One of them had a severe head injury. He was about twenty years old. His name was Shah Jan. He was only a boy and newly married. Excruciating pain prevented him from talking much. I gave him two painkillers. I did not have more. An old man gave him an apple. Another fighter had a very serious leg injury and a high fever. The other fighters sitting with us were fine, and were happy that they had been able to help capture the government garrison.

After one or two hours, the truck became like a family home to all of us. I was offered some pieces of cornbread. Ultimately, that huge old engine brought us safely to Mashtaan Bridge, which was on the main road from Farkhar to Badakhshan. Upon reaching the village of Mashtaan, I got down from the truck. After eating a little food and having tea in a small teahouse, we started our journey once again on foot and, after some time, we came to and crossed an old wooden bridge.

On the way, the weather was a little warmer but the beauty of the valley attracted my heart so much that I did not care about how hot or cold it was. The minute I entered the valley, a young man by the name of Ahmad Amini welcomed me and instantly recited a beautiful quatrain of my father's:

O sweet spring, you are flowing so gently!
Whose message do you bring, where from do you come?
You are like tears streaming from my eyes,
Quietly, softly, slowly and calmly.

I hugged him and complimented him by saying, "*Bah bah bah,* what a wonderful way of welcoming me to your beautiful historical land of great poets. You showed me that your land has always been one of the cradles of our civilizations and one of the birthplaces of the Farsi language."

Ahmad is the District Attorney. Immediately, he brought me some tea and a sort of local warm dessert by the name of *laala*. They make that natural dessert out of the bulb of a special wild flower. They dry the bulb of this flower, grind it, and make it into flour. They cook it in a special way. The color of this sweet dish is white and it has the texture of chewing gum. It does not need sugar or any other sweetener.

Some respected religious people kindly joined us. I enjoyed listening to them and reading for them some Rumi poems. They liked the one that goes:

My life?
Nothing but three stages.

I was raw,
Became ripe,
Then burnt.

Bakhtangan

Saturday, August 23

Yesterday, we traveled two and a half hours and reached this first summer pasture of the Kishm Valley. On the way, the weather was extremely cold and I could not hold myself from shivering, since I did not have a sleeping bag. I thought that I might have malaria. Two freedom fighters, who were with me, asked the owner of a nearby summer pasture if they could borrow a mattress and blanket.

Luckily, the owner of the summer pasture recognized me and brought a number of blankets that he had collected from the other tents or *kappa* in the pasture. After having a piece of bread and a little butter for my dinner, I found a flatter place to sleep. The shepherds thought that I had a high fever and put five thick blankets and one woolen rug on top of me. In no time, I was covered deep in the blankets, up to my throat. I did not even take off my shoes. All in all, I could not move an inch from under these heavy blankets and within five minutes, I started to sweat and fell asleep. I woke a few times, noticed that the moon was of a pure white color, shining silver light on to the surrounding mountains.

The shadows of the boulders and trees at a very far distance looked like they were moving toward me. It reached to the point where I was a bit frightened. I shook my head and thought that I might be having a nightmare but I was awake. Once again, I imagined that slowly and gradually the rocks were moving toward me.

Now the early morning weather is very good. The sprinkling of dewdrops has made everything around me fresh and beautiful. The wild and sweet smell of nature fills the deepest corners of my soul. Despite having less sleep last night, I feel great.

Today, I had a chance to ride my new donkey. I liked him. His color was black and white. He had a bell dangling from his neck that attracted my eyes more than his handler, who had nothing around his neck. While I was comfortably riding it, I was thinking of two famous donkeys in our history. One was the donkey of Jesus Christ and the other was the donkey of Mullah Nasruddin. People know hundreds of stories about these two famous donkeys. In our culture amongst all other animals, these two are celebrities.

Though my donkey was behaving very well, I said, "If you are not as good as the donkey of Jesus, at least you are like the donkey of Mullah Nasruddin." I hope he has understood.

Besides the short stories, we have bundles of poems and jokes about them. They have been and they are still the sources of popular and great sayings and proverbs. For example, if an Afghan comes across an idiot, he would use this verse of a poem of Sa'di, 'Even if you take the donkey of Jesus to Mecca, on its return, it would still be a donkey'.

The owner of my previous donkey was called Mir Alam. The name of my new donkey handler is Israfil. He is a nice young man and it is worth talking to him. He has a yellow beard and a very thin moustache. He is tall and slim. He looks more like an Italian commercial model. While walking behind his donkey, he talks to it as if his donkey understands what he says.

I first asked him if he knows anything about the two famous donkeys. He replied in such beautiful way that I admired him very much.

He said, "Anybody who does not know about the donkeys of Jesus and Mullah Nasruddin, is a donkey himself."

Thank God, I knew a little about them otherwise I would have been included in the same category.

In addition, he quickly added, "But sir, whenever you mention Jesus, do not forget to say 'peace be upon him' because he is a Prophet."

To make him happier, I repeated the words 'peace be upon him' a couple of times.

Mashtaan Pass

August 24, 1986
6:20 AM

It is 6:20 in the morning. Now, we are on the peak of the Mashtaan Pass. After 55 minutes of easy walking, we reached to the top.

Although the village below is very poor, the pass itself has a great view. My donkey, the two fighters, Israfil, and I have stopped here to take a breath.

My Dear, I wish that in the future, we build a bedroom here with a mountain view window to watch the ballet of the sunrise, right from our bed. What a beautiful morning it would be when the soft fingers of the morning mist, wake us up to a dreamful day. Now in this early morning, the golden sparks of the sun's rays have created a unique beauty as if they are playing hide and seek with each other and the morning breeze is gently moving the fog to allow the arrows of light to shower the valley.

My clothes have become very dirty and filled with sweat. The weather is a bit cold in the night and it is possible to handle it with a shawl or patoo but during the daytime, the sun is caressing my skin softly, kindly, and warmly. Let me not forget that there was a village before Bakhtangan village, which they called Farmaanqully.

First Summer Pasture of Badakhshaan, Dasht-i-Haram

August 25, 1986

It is eight in the morning. This place is called Dasht-i-Haram. When I entered this beautiful valley of Kishm, the sweet scents of the wild herbs and the green wheat fields welcomed me.

I am now in the first pasture of the valley of Kishm. The place where I am now is located in the west of the province of Badakhshaan. Despite the fact that I did not walk much and rode the donkey all the way, I do not feel good. I am extremely happy to be in this valley, which for years I have desired to visit. I hope I am able to have some tea here and then move forward to the next village.

When I arrived to the first one, a nice shephard kindly welcomed me. His name was Abdul Qadir. Without asking, he brought us a cup of tea with no sugar or candy but kindly provided us with a piece of dry and crunchy bread. It was very hard to eat but I managed. I should not forget that on the way, I had fallen asleep for a few minutes on my donkey and almost fell off.

In this place, the *kappa* or tents are made of reed. Some villagers have regular tents as well. The weather is beautiful. You cannot imagine my dear how the sky is so blue, beautiful, and clear. The mountains beyond me are filled with snow but the mountains next to the valley are dusty and gray. The clear waters are like the waters of Nooristan. The yellow sharsham flowers and the purple colored clovers give a unique beauty to the valley.

Host is Out, House is Open

Mir Kaan Village
House of Haji Latif
August 26, 1986

It is now 10:20 in the morning. This is Mir Kaan village. We are now at Haji Latif's guest room. It is a 7×8 meters sized beautiful room with two mountain view windows. One of which has a glass pane and the other has only an old newspaper. A nice rug with a deep red color and small diamond patterns is laid on the ground. A dish or *aftaw lagan*, especially used for washing hands is in one corner and a clean towel is hanging on the wall above it.

The room has foam mattresses with red covers along the walls and a big hard pillow on each one of them. I see a lantern hanging on the left wall to use at night. In the middle of the room there is a big spittoon used for tobacco spits.

No one is here to help us. As the verse on the wall said, 'the door of the house is open' but sadly, at this time, the owner is not around to give us food, tea, or water. We have to wait for someone to get us something.

While waiting for the Haji, another guest with his 12-year-old son also joined us. The minute the father recognized me, he rushed out to find the would-be host or owner of the house. It had not even been five minutes when Haji Latif, the owner of the guesthouse appeared. He is a big man with a black and gray beard. Despite his face being full of old small pox marks, he has a kind and caring complexion. Haji Latif, in the second year of President Daud Khan had gone for the pilgrimage to Mecca which is why he is known as Haji. He said hello, then welcomed us and humbly asked permission to go find us some food. In less than a minute, he was gone.

I washed my hands, prayed a little, listened to the singing of the Sayra bird and I am still waiting for Haji to bring us some tea and hopefully something to eat as well. I will write to you later.

Sabz Dara, Kishm. House of Haji Sayed Amanuddin

August 27, 1986

Yesterday, we stayed in the village of Sabz Dara. I had a chance to talk to some people including the family of the home we stayed in. Even though it took him an extremely long time to bring us food and tea, he was a generous host. My dear, I was so tired that I decided to rest and write more to you today.

All day today, I have just been walking in the valley and talking to the people about economic and military issues that I will not bore you with but in the evening, after dusk prayers, I asked Jamaluddin and Mabud about the socio-economic affairs of the people in the area and of their social organizations.

He told me the following story. It is a very interesting one, which shows how their judicial system works and how the verdict of the judges could be stronger than the sword of the commanders. It is very promising. I hope, one day we can expand on it because I do not think that in most other areas controlled by the resistance we have the same model. It impressed me a lot. This is what Mabud told me:

A woman had an ugly affair with her brother-in-law. This was going on for a full two years. It was a highly untraditional, unIslamic, and an immoral relationship. Somehow, the poor husband found out about this shameful act. While he could not believe it at all, he had started to be suspicious of her. The woman having felt her husband's newly suspicious nature provoked her lover to kill his brother, otherwise she would end her love affair with him.

It must have been a horrifying night. In order to prove his love, he went to his own brother's house, viciously killed him with a sharp axe, returned to his beloved and showed her the very weapon he had used, which was stained with the freshly murdered blood of his own innocent brother. The woman kissed the bloody axe and congratulated him for his sincere act of dedication and bravery. She hugged her lover and said, "Tonight will be our most pleasurable night."

After some weeks, this horrible story was somehow disclosed to everyone and the freedom fighters arrested both of them.

Commander Arianpur, the chief of the resistance in the area, immediately summoned the two accused and asked them to tell the truth of what occurred, minute by minute. Surprisingly, the woman gave the commander all the details of what happened that night and explained everything right from the beginning to the end, in a very cold and callous way. Commander Arianpur who was not a judge but the leader of the commanders in this area, asked the woman three times, as is customary in Islamic law, if she provoked her lover to go and kill his brother. The woman admitted three times that she had in fact provoked him.

Then Commander Arianpur called the lover and asked the same question. The lover confessed that he was having an affair with his sister-in-law and that he was the killer of his own brother. So here, according to Mabud the storyteller, Commander Arianpur did not issue a verdict to hang or stone both of them to death. He simply said, "This is not my job. I am not a judge. These two must be put on trial." He called two available judges along with some religious leaders for this purpose. He was sure that both would be executed.

The day of the trial arrived. The court was a simple room in a poor mosque. Everybody was there. The judges sat under the arched alter. The religious people took their places close to the judges. Some of the commanders and other limited fighters were also present and Commander Arianpur himself was one of them. All were sitting cross-legged on the bare ground of the mosque.

The eldest judge asked if the two accused to be present in the mosque. They were.

He first called the male accused into the room and asked, "Have you committed this act of adultery with your sister-in-law?"

"Yes, I did."

The judge immediately asked, "For how long?"

"Sir, for almost two years."

Everyone was nodding with contempt.

The judge asked his third question clearly and loudly, "Have you killed your bother?"

"Yes, I did."

The judge lowered his voice a little and asked, "Did you kill your brother with your right hand or with your left?"

"I killed by brother with both of my hands, left and right."

The judge asked simply, "What did you use to kill him?"

"I used an axe."

The judge asked no further question to the male accused.

Now, He called the second accused. A veiled woman entered the room.

The judge ordered her, "Show me your face."

"I am a Muslim woman, I am not allowed to show my face to just anyone."

The judge shouted, "It is a trial and I am the judge. Show your face to me and to the witnesses to prove your identity."

She agreed and let the veil drop and showed her face.

The judge asked the killer, "Do you know this woman?"

"Yes, she is my brother's wife."

The judge turned back to her and asked, "Have you ever had an extra-marital affair with this man?"

Confidently, "No sir, I have not."

Everyone in the room started murmuring to one another. The judge raised his right hand and signaled everyone to be quiet.

He looked at each man and asked, "Has any of you been witness to this woman and this man having an extra-marital affair?"

No one said a word.

The judge then asked the woman a second question, "Did you tell this man to kill your husband, who was also his brother?"

Even more confidently, "No sir, I did not."

At this moment the most powerful man of the area Commander Arianpur stood up and said, "She admitted three times to me that she did have an affair with the killer and did tell him to kill his brother. She is lying to you now."

The judge turned to the commander and while looking directly into his eyes, said, "Commander, that was not a trial where she admitted this fact to you. She is now sitting in a trial and in front of a judge. Please sit and let us continue."

The judge pointed to the killer and asked the woman again, "Have you asked this man to kill his brother?"

"No sir, I have not."

Another commander stood and shouted, "I swear she has done it and she did provoke the killer to kill his brother."

The judge looked at him and said nothing until the man sat down.

As the Judge turned back to the woman, he took his handkerchief out of his pocket, cleaned his beard, wiped the sweat off his forehead, raised his voice and very loudly said, "This is my third and last question. You are standing in front of a judge and I am one of the flag carriers of the Prophets, do not lie to me because I judge on what you tell me. Have you provoked this man to kill his brother?"

The woman with her unveiled face, sitting in front of the judge and others once again said, "No, I have not provoked him, sir."

The judge now turned to the people in the room and in a stronger voice asked, "Is there anyone in this court who can bear witness that this woman provoked this man to kill his brother?"

Once again, Commander Arianpur shouted out, "She told me herself that she had provoked him."

The judge looked at the commander and said, "This woman has not confessed to me in this court to have done it. Have you, yourself, seen her doing so?"

Silence fell for at least three minutes in that small room of the mosque. The judge consulted very calmly with the other judge and the religious people around him. Everyone expected that the verdict would be the stoning to death of the woman and the hanging of the killer. The air was thick with anticipation.

He then brought his attention to the accused man and very calmly said, "You are guilty. You will be hung because you admitted to this court of killing your brother."

A sigh of relief filled the room. The men watching were now even more confident that the judge would rule in favor of her being executed as well. The mosque fell silent again.

The judge put his right hand on the holy book, looked at the woman for a few seconds, then addressed the room with a confident authority and said, "She is not guilty. She cannot be stoned to death because she did not admit to her crimes in front of me and this court. In addition, there is no witness and sufficient proof to tell me that she has done so. Therefore, she is free."

My dear, the story is not finished yet. According to Islamic traditions, the parents of the victim have the right to forgive the killer if they want. The sad and unusual part of this case was that the parents of the victim were also the parents of the killer.

When they were asked, the parents said, "We forgive him because he is the only son we have left."

Everybody in the room where I was sitting was silent when Mabud finished the shameful story.

Jamaluddin was the first to comment, "I will never forget that trial and never forgive the judge for such a wrong judgment."

I told Mabud, "This story is in indeed very moving to me because of its human touch and its judicial dimensions. I still believe that in a war situation like this, it is the gun and the decision of a strong commander that rule and not the verdict of a weak judge. I am happy to see that, at lease in one place, even in a war situation, a judge's rule can be so strong."

Jamaluddin interjected and said, "Commander Arianpur and the rest of the fighters did not like this judgment at all."

The tailor which I had hired to sew a pair of clothes for me was also listening very carefully and while cutting the blue fabric for me, said loudly, "The judge is the judge. As long as he is not taking bribes and he fears God, his decision should be respected."

The shopkeeper, Haji Fazluddin said, "Although our judge has always been an honest and wise one, the killer should have not been left free."

A typical young fighter who was listening as well said, "The woman should have been stoned to death."

At that moment, I thought of how the hundreds of women living in this area might have judged the accused, for her or against her. I wish knew.

After lunch, I went to visit a boys' school of this village. They were sitting under a big old green poplar tree. I tied my donkey to a rusted nail on its giant trunk. The boys were of 10 to 12 years of age. They were excited but I did not know of what, my donkey or myself. It was again a painful sight to see. Blood fills one's eyes seeing the poverty of these boys. Their shoes, their shirts, and their overall appearance were very poor. Some of them were barefoot. Their clothes were full of patches.

My dear, now listen to what happened while I was in the small and poor class.

I very proudly told the cute boys, "Write *azaadee* or freedom for me."

Only two little boys started writing.

I abruptly asked the teacher, "Why are only two of the boys able to write?"

While poor eyes of the boys were focused on me, in a soft voice, the teacher said, "Mr Khalili, they can all write but in the whole class, we just have two pencils."

I was ashamed of my question.

My Dear, when we gain our freedom, it will not only be with the barrels of guns, firing their thousands of bullets at the enemy but also with the tips of those two pens. I pray that one day millions of kids have schools to attend and endless pencils to write.

Now let me stop my writing. Although the people around me understand it, it is not good that I keep writing in front of them. I will talk to you tomorrow through lines of my notebook.

17

Afghan Steel Factory

Tuesday, August 28

It is twilight now. I am in the village of Karas Deh. While being on this journey, it relaxes my soul to write to you. I hope you like what you read. An hour before I asked the fisherman of the valley, who is at the same time a .50 caliber gun operator for the fighters, to bring his fishing net and go with me to the river for some fishing. The river with its wild rapids was running down from the village toward the city of Kishm. The small shepherd boys along with their small goats were coming down from the dusty mountains. Their tall and thin shadows made the meadow look more crowded.

While waiting for the fisherman, I saw that a small boy was playing his flute, made of reed. He had made his six-holed-flute all by himself. He was a beginner in playing his handmade instrument. Although he was a novice, to me, he sounded better than the greatest flute players of India.

Hopefully later, someone will bring us some food and tea. It is very cold and I am very tired today, so I think we will stay here for the night and start our journey again in the morning. Hopefully it will be warmer tomorrow and we will be able to get some horses to ride. Kiss my boys Mahmud and Majdood for me.

Village of Farmanqulee

August 29, 1986

In the morning, we left the village of Karas Deh. They had baked two fish for me in a *tandoor* or a clay ground oven for breakfast. From Karas Deh until here it was about 3 hours walk. We are going to eat our lunch here and afterward we will travel for another 20 minutes to reach the village of Jar Shah Baabaa.

I am sitting under a big, old green poplar tree with Maulavi Maroof. A cold wind could be felt coming from between the patches of clovers, through the Poplars and willows trees. I talked to Maulavi Maroof and found him an extremely anti-communist and a fanatic, religious man. After finishing a brief conversation about politics, religion, and spirituality, we started again to the next village.

It is 6:00 PM now. A few minutes ago, I reached this village, which is called Farman Qulee. I quickly did the *asr* or early evening prayers. I am sure by now you know that this war has so much worries, so much wanderings, and so much goings on here and there. I am so sorry that whenever you open these notes, you find nothing but poverty. Let us hope that if war divides us today, peace and prosperity will link us tomorrow.

My dear, Jamaluddin took me to a very interesting place in which metal dishes, bowls, horseshoes, and jars were being made. It was a small mud house, which was also being used as a work place. The owner of the house was a blacksmith. He was a very simple man. His name was Maulavi Samad. He has been doing this for many years. Despite not being a Muslim cleric in any way, he was calling himself Maulavi. I don't know why.

There were molds, frames, pieces of burnt metal, and ashes, scattered everywhere. You could see pieces of destroyed tanks, planes, and helicopters in his small, 6 × 6 meters, workplace. There was also a mud ground oven, which are still used by the blacksmiths in Afghanistan. When a helicopter is shot down or the fighters destroy a tank, the people bring the pieces to this blacksmith. He buys them.

So far, in the valley of Kishm, there have been six military planes or helicopters shot down and most of the pieces were brought to this workshop.

The blacksmith told me, "The best pots, horse shoes, and spades are made of the metal from the wreckage of helicopters and planes." He also had pots that were 5 kilos and he sold them for 1,000 Afghanis or 7 dollars.

I took my time, looked at everything, and showed my appreciation for each piece to the maker. He looked like a very talented man. Two or three boys were helping him. The room was small, dark, and filled with ash. It had a small window, which seemed highly unhealthy.

This man and his workers had a higher morale and spirit. They seemed very happy as if no war going on outside their workshop.

I asked him, "So you must be really happy when a helicopter or plane is destroyed by our fighters, right?"

He said very smartly, "I am not happy when they are destroying our small homes but I am happy when the fighters destroy them and I use the pieces in my small workshop."

I asked my traveling companion, "What should we call this room?"

He laughed loudly and said, "Khalili Sahib, this is our only steel factory."

I told him, "I love your answer. From now, I will remember it as the only Afghan Steel Factory. Let us pray that one day we do not get our steel from the killing planes but from under the earth of our own land."

Mabud calmly said, "What a nice dream."

I asked Jamaluddin to provide more young workers to learn ironwork in this amazing "Afghan steel factory".

18

Back on Rocky Track—Village Justice

Tuesday, September 2

My dear, I was very busy over the past couple of days talking to different commanders and elders of the area, which I have written about in my other notebook. It is all very detailed and would probably bore you. One day if I am killed and you or my boys want to have the details published of what we have done, feel free.

Let me also tell you that two days ago, I decided in the village of Tangi to not go any further into the Badakhshan province and turn back. The village of Tangi was a beautiful place but I had political work to do in Pakistan and in the West. It was a bitter sweet decision but I knew that it was the right time to turn back. God willing, I will be back one day, and hopefully, we will be closer to peace.

Let me tell you about one thing that is funny about our journey to this village called Aiyhood. On the way, our mule gave us a lot of problems as he became so obstinate that sometimes he did not even want to move. What could we do with a stubborn mule? He stands, looks at you, and does nothing but rapidly moves his tails from side to side. You have to stop but for how long, you do not know. Sometimes we shout at him, later we beg him, finally we talk nicely to him to get him to move; and he does, but not more than three steps. All of a sudden, he stops again for maybe another ten minutes. You do not know whether to sit and wait or keep on shouting at him until he moves again.

People all over Afghanistan believe that the most foolish animal in the world is the mule. I do not know. At least on this trip, he fooled us and did what he wanted to do.

Most of the people have left the villages for the nearby mountains. Maybe there is a possibility of bombardment. May God be merciful!

* * *

An interesting thing happened yesterday after reaching this village. I met a man named Gheyasuddin Zara. He knew my father well.

We were sitting and talking about the problems in the Wakhan area when I told my men to go and arrange for a horse for me.

All a sudden with no reason, he became angry and, in an unexpectedly high pitch, said, "Why would your people need to arrange for a horse when I am here and have a horse to give you for such things?"

I was surprised at his anger.

Before I said anything, in an even louder voice, "when I am here, how dare you ask anyone else for help?" I instantly remembered my own uncle who had the same type of generous character. I thanked him again and repeatedly said no to his offer.

As I was trying to decline his offer, Zara Sahib pointed to a beautiful horse and sternly said, "This is my horse and now it is yours. You cannot reject it and, if you do so, I will kill the horse."

With these words, I was left with no other choice but to accept his offer; I saved the life of the innocent horse in the process. If the horse understood our conversation, he would have asked Zara Sahib, "Why would you kill me and not him for declining your offer?"

I then told Zara Sahib that I would accept his offer only after he has heard a story that came to mind. He accepted.

I told him, "One of our kings known for his cruelty named Abdul Rahman wanted Afghanistan to have its first dentist. He called a French dentist and ordered him to teach a man named Sufi *dandan-saaz*, or tooth-maker, how to be a dentist in six months. The French dentist was shocked and said that it was not possible to do such a thing even in three years. The King then told the Frenchman that if the tooth-maker was not a trained dentist in that time, he would have the tooth-maker beheaded. The Frenchman, together with his wife, spent every waking moment teaching the tooth-maker how to be a dentist so he would not be the one responsible for his beheading.

Zara Sahib laughed and understood the point of my story.

I immediately said, "His was necessity and yours is generosity. Your offer is greater than his order."

The next morning he had already arranged to be with saddle-bags, whip, saddle, and a plentiful supply of food for the road.

My dear, listen to what happened when I reached the next village after leaving Zara Sahib. I went to a small shop, made of mud, to buy a cup of tea or some tea-leaves, but the store owner rudely told me that he did not have any. I asked again but he angrily rejected me. I told him that maybe the village was named *Aiyhood*, or Jew, because the people here were as miserly as some of the stories about the Jewish people.

I said, "If you are not generous enough to give a guest a cup of tea, at least do not reject him so rudely."

He did not say anything. I believe he wanted me to leave.

This interesting exchange had not yet finished when an old white-bearded man entered the scene and, pointing to me, asked my horseman, "Who is this man?" Immediately, Mohammad the horseman, without my permission introduced me.

All of a sudden, the rude shopkeeper jumped from behind his little make-shift stall, grabbed the reins of my horse, and touched my stirrups.

With his head down toward the earth, he said with great humility, "Please forgive my ignorance. Everything I have in my life is yours. I did not know who you are."

I touched his head, kissed his face and asked his name.

He answered,

"My name is Naseer and I am one of the grandsons of Yaar Mohammad Khan. The land, the house, the horses, and the guest-houses that we have now were all gifts from your grandfather to my grandfather. You must be my guest and, if you can, maybe stay for a few days."

Despite my attempts at declining his offer, he pulled my horse toward his home. I agreed.

His house was only a few minutes' walk. In no time, he brought for me eggs, tea, delicious bread, and fruit. Naseer remained standing and, despite my repeated requests, he did not sit. This is also a traditional way of showing respect to someone. I asked, "Who else is living in this house?"

He replied, "My family and my old, white-haired grandmother who is about 90 years old. Actually, Khalili Sahib, she met your grandfather long ago."

Within 10 minutes, the old grandmother appeared. What a graceful woman she was! Her half-blind eyes and the absence of eyebrows and eyelashes lent her an even more graceful appearance. Her body was as thin as an old cane. Her clothes were a dark gray color, elegantly matching her silver hair. She wore a very old silver ring with an emerald inset. She had a thin shawl draped around her shoulder. The minute she saw me, she started weeping. I stood up, greeted her, and helped her to sit down on a mattress.

She did not allow me to kiss her hand. She talked in an accent typical of the upper parts of the Panjshir valley.

I said, "Thank you for the excellent bread. I heard you met my grandfather. Is this true?"

She said, "Yes, I have seen him, son." At least four times she repeated the phrase 'yes, I have' in quick succession.

She continued, "Everything in the past was like a beautiful paradise and now God has turned everything into an ugly hell. Look at you, traveling through all these places with so many difficulties. You are the grandson of a graceful man."

I interjected before she could go on and said, "Tell me something and give me your precious advice on life and what I should do with it. I am sure your advice will be like the raining of jewels on a poor man."

She shook her head and said, "What can I tell you? People these days do not listen to us old people."

I persuaded her to go on. She kept quiet for at least five minutes as though she had forgotten my question. Her pause gave me a chance to take in all the details in her face. Each wrinkle might have its own story to tell. I wish I knew which wrinkle of her aged face is telling the story of my grandfather and the story of her own pain, peace, love, hatred, and happiness or sadness. Each line was written by the cruel passage of time.

Here, Naseer the shopkeeper asked her and reminded her very loudly, "Khalili Sahib wants you to give him some advice."

She looked at her grandson in a bewildered kind of way and said, "I will pray for him. What else I can do?" She then looked at me as though a thought came to her and said, "Be as generous and kind as your grandfather."

She then looked at the ceiling as though she was looking up at the heavens and with a deep sigh she said, "Your grandfather was hung in such a cruel way." She looked at her grandson and asked, "What was the name of the king who hung him?"

I interjected and said, "King Amanullah."

Again, after four or five minutes' silence, she twice murmured, "Yes, it was king Amanullah. O yes, it was king Amanullah."

She immediately asked, "Where is the grave of your grandfather?"

I replied loudly so she could hear, "He does not have a grave because the king did not give his body back to the family."

Again after a very deep sigh she said, "Your grandfather had everything: gardens, houses, horses, servants, power, money, friends, gold, diamonds, and even a car when the only other man who had one was the king, and now he doesn't have even a tomb? Is it not in itself an insightful piece of advice for you and everyone else? Even if he had a tomb, what could he take with him but his good actions? My last advice to you is, do not be a bad man, even if you cannot be a good one." Her words started to fade as she said, "Is your father alive?" I said, "Yes, he is alive."

Again, she drifted off into her own world and ignored me totally. I deliberately stayed for another ten minutes. I watched her.

Her words were echoing in my mind, like the last beats of a dying heart, "Your grandfather doesn't even have a tomb."

Her grandson brought me back to reality by asking, "Khalili Sahib, do you want another cup of tea?"

Without answering, I stood up and left the room to get my tea.

On the way, there were many little shops. The weather is very good.

Village of Yalangee

2:40 PM

My dear, we left the last village at 10:45 AM and reached this place about an hour ago. It took us more than three hours to reach here. This village is called Yalangee. On the way, we also passed through a few other smaller villages.

Let me tell you another thing that happened on the way. While calmly riding toward the next village, with the words of the old woman still ringing in my mind, all of a sudden, my horse stopped in its tracks in fear, and almost threw me off my saddle. I looked around, calmed my horse, and dismounted. I could sense the putrid smell of death in the air. I still could not see where the smell was coming from or what had spooked my horse. I suddenly noticed nearby the dead body of a man with a thick noose around his neck hanging from a tree.

The face of the hung man looked very black and burnt like a rusted copper plate. His hands were dangling loose. His legs, longer than the upper part of his body, were swaying in the air. He had no hat on his head and no shoes on his feet. Around his neck, nothing could be seen but the dirty brown and blood-stained rope. He wore nothing but a torn, thin, and long shirt covering the upper part of his body.

The old tree was a type of mulberry. The whole area around stood eerily silent with an air of menace. As I started reciting some prayers, by chance a man called Mullah Malang appeared who recognized me and perceived I was puzzled and wished to know the reason behind the hanging of the man dangling from the tree.

First, he did not want to say anything but when I insisted, he said, "What is the use of talking about someone who is no longer in our world? Let him dangle from the tree until his body dries to dust. Rope looks good around the neck of a rapist."

I insisted that if he knows the story he should tell me something about it.

He reluctantly started, "Three weeks ago, this Godless man sexually abused a nine-year-old girl and, out of fear of being caught, he killed that sinless, innocent girl. While he was trying to dump the body of the poor girl in the river, a local man saw him. In fear, the murderer left the girl on the bank of the river and ran away from the scene. The people of the village followed him, caught him, and brought him back. Instantly, the local Village Council was called. Some wise men, elders, and religious people, who assembled a kind of traditional people's court, put him on trial. The verdict was guilty and he was sentenced to be hung. What you see now, tied by the rope of justice, is that murderer and rapist

"Every morning since, the mother of the murdered girl comes to see the hanging murderer. Surprisingly, the parents of the murderer also show up to see their son dangling in the air."

I asked, "Why did they not take down the body from the *daar*, or noose?"

"It is a tradition here that for such a merciless crime and sin, we keep the body up there for some days to serve as a lesson to the other villagers."

My dear, this was village justice for a rapist and justice was done. We must travel for another hour and a half until we reach the bottom of *Kotali Zard,* or Yellow Pass. I hope that tomorrow we will cross it.

* * *

I forgot to tell you that two young men asked me if they could join me on my trip too. Before agreeing, I said, "You are most welcome but why are you going to Pakistan and what are your names?"

One of them replied, "My name is Ismael and my friend's name is Dur Mohammad. I am going to Pakistan because I am sick and need to see a doctor. I am from Kabul. I graduated from the college of science and immediately joined the resistance."

His friend Dur Mohammad told me, "My glasses were broken in a bombardment and I cannot see. I am now going to Pakistan in order to get myself a pair of new prescription glasses."

Look at this! In all of the provinces where I have traveled, there is no place where a person can buy a pair of prescription glasses. What a miserable life! A man who is in need of prescription glasses must travel by foot through all these passes and mountains to a different country, just to buy a simple pair of glasses.

I asked Ismael, "How blind are you? Can you at least see the path you walk?"

He smiled and replied, "I can see nothing clearly. I am half-blind now. Everything, whether near or far, is blurry to me. This is why I have brought a friend to hold my hand on the dangerous cliffs."

Instead of becoming sad, we all laughed at this. I do not know why. We agreed that they would come back to Pakistan with me and I would help them in whatever way I could. While wondering to myself if anyone can really see clearly in this world, we continued moving forward.

Right now, I am sitting in a corner of the lawn of a small mosque in this small village. A narrow stream with cold water passes through the garden. The mosque looks very modest but pretty. For God, I think, it is more important how many people come to his house, not how big or small it is.

I want to take a short nap, but I do not think the chirping of the birds and the sounds of the small children of shepherds will allow me to do so. My horse is doing well. He knows by now that I am not harsh on him.

As I sat on the lawn, a local man brought me a cup of tea and I asked him if there is anything of interest to see on the way to the next village. He said that once we go a bit further, we would reach the shrine of Khwaja Aziz. Somehow, I felt energized when I heard him say that there is a holy shrine not too far away and enthusiastically asked him, "How do you know that this shrine is a blessed one, and Khwaja Aziz is a friend of God? My question is not out of disrespect but if you can tell me something about him, I will be very glad."

He reluctantly answered, "This much I know: my mother and grandmother used to go to his shrine every Wednesday and ask him to help with whatever wish they had in their hearts. People say that on Wednesday nights, you can see from far lit candles around his grave. When you go closer to his shrine, they disappear but as you go further back, they can be seen clearly again. I do not go now because I was a regular gambler. People say a person who gambles will not be blessed. "

Hearing this, I remembered the beautiful verse of a Sufi poet and recited it for him.

I went to the gambling house,
Everyone was playing fair.
I went to the temple,
Everyone was cheating.

My horse is in a good mood now. The air carries sweet scents. Do not ask me about the blue color of the sky which is like a blue roof hanging on the green garden of paradise. Do not ask me about the crystal clear and cold waters, the beautiful gentle streams, the sweet-scented breeze and the chirping of small birds. It is as if God has instructed all the elements of nature to serve my body and soul.

You must have realized so far that the respect shown by the people and their help to me is not only because of my family line, but is symbolic of the cooperation and love of the people toward the resistance. If I were not a freedom fighter, I may not have received this much hospitality from them. Without the people's cooperation, one cannot move an inch in these kinds of rough areas, among these kinds of tough people.

19

Exorcism, Sufis, and a Royal Hunt

Wednesday, September 3
5:30 PM

I am now in Yas Pogh village. It took an hour and 45 minutes to reach here. The way was flat. I rode my horse, who was happy and content, for an hour. Then we stopped for a cup of tea in the village of Wighnaan, before passing through the last village in Worsaj district, which is called Miyaan Shahr. From there, we came directly here. There are 30 homes and a mosque in Yas Pogh.

The village's old white-bearded elder is named Mohammad Dost and the village leader is Mullah Islamuddin.

It is located in such a beautiful place that when I look outward through its small window, it is as if I can see the whole universe. The weather is as good as in the other valleys I encountered on my way here. The difference between this village and the previous village Wighnaan is that Yas Pogh has certain fragrances which I do not recognize. It has a slightly sweetish scent, which refreshes my mood and reduces my exhaustion.

On the way, something extraordinary happened. A boy of about 12 years rushed out and stopped my horse. He was worried. He was very much out of breath. I knew that something had occurred and he needed my help.

I asked him, "What is going on, boy? What is wrong with you?"

"My elder sister has been stung by a scorpion or bitten by a snake. I do not know which, but she is in a lot of pain and she has swollen up badly."

I asked, "Which one was it, a snake or a scorpion?"

"I saw something that resembled the imprint of a snake on the ground but I do not know. Please help my sister. Do you have the spiritual power of healing or do you know of any anti-poison prayers that could help?"

I replied, "Remain calm, son. I do not have those powers of healing but we will find your sister some help.

While I was talking to him, someone else rushed over and said that they had already found someone with this power, whose name was Khwaja, and he would arrive in 10 to 15 minutes. The moment the boy heard the name of this healer, his appearance totally changed and he loudly thanked God for sending this healer. I accompanied him to see what would happen.

It was a five-minute walk. Khwaja the healer was already there. The snake-bitten girl was in pain. She was about fourteen. Her body looked as thin as the branch of a sapling in early spring and her face was as pale as the color of a late winter sunset. Her beautiful eyes were full of tears, like the eyes of a deer in pain, or like a black tulip filled with rain. She was in shock.

While holding her brother's hands, she begged the healer, "Please recite your prayers loudly. Please read the prayers that are most effective. A long, strong gray snake tried to bite my sheep. While protecting my sheep, I was bitten by that cruel creature. It was not my fault, nor my sheep's. Please help me!"

Thank God, Khwaja had already begun to recite some prayers very loudly. He did not pay any attention to me. He was a middle-aged man, maybe my age, but his beard stretched down almost to his navel. His eyes were half closed. His lips moved very fast as he recited. His voice was trembling up and down.

After five minutes' of recitation, he took some saliva from his mouth with his finger and rubbed it on the bitten area of the poor girl. Khwaja did not stop there. He took a blade from his upper pocket and cut the place, which had been bitten by the snake. It was right below her knee. She was swollen from her knee up to her slim waist. He put his mouth over the cut he had just made, sucked for a few seconds, and spit out a mouthful of blueish blood. Then, finally, he put a little clean dust on the cut.

She was healed. A smile appeared on her face like a strand of silk on a yellow leaf. Her brother instantly gave her a cup of water. I thanked God and Khwaja. I gave her some raisins and her eyes seemed to me like those of a wounded bird and her lips looked like those of a hunted deer. Her pain had gone, thank God. Now she seemed fine.

As far as spiritual healers are concerned, very few are the people born with this kind of power or who have the power transferred from another person; and it does not make a difference if he is a religious or ordinary man. Khwaja told me that his uncle had the power and transferred it to him.

Our neighbor in Kabul had the same healing power but his was to heal scorpion bites and bee stings, not snake venom.

I remembered, once a long time ago, I was playing on the roof and I disturbed a beehive by mistake. Hundreds of bees attacked me at once. This neighbor heard my cries of pain and fright. When he saw I was being attacked, he told me to jump down to the lawn. In no time, he was by my side. The pain was so extreme that I could do nothing but shout. He quickly mumbled a prayer, licked his finger, and rubbed it on the places where I had been stung. In a matter of seconds, my pain had disappeared. He was a dentist and a judge in the judicial system of Afghanistan.

Now since I have a little time as I wait for a cup tea to caress my thirsty throat, I can write to you more leisurely than in the past. This is another true story about spiritual healing. It concerns one of my second uncles who, besides being an important man among his people, was also a *margeer*, or snake catcher, whose power lay not only in catching snakes, but also in healing the people who were bitten by them.

I was about ten or twelve years old. One day in the summer time, my uncle was sitting in his melon fields when he heard a loud cry from a distance. A seven-year-old shepherd boy was crying out for help. The weather was very hot. It was the season of grapes, melons, snakes, and scorpions.

The shepherd boy kept shouting, "There is a long snake here about to bite my goat and my little sister. Come and help me. Come and save us. The snake is slithering toward us."

The old man could not run and had to walk to help because he had problems with his leg. The boy kept shouting for help.

The old man had never charmed a snake from a long distance but he knew he had to do something.

While he started to murmur his special prayers, he shouted, "Don't be scared son. Catch the snake by its neck. My prayers will help. Do not be scared."

The old man instantly thought that he had no other choice but to transfer his power to the boy from a distance. The old man was praying deeply, while the boy was shouting again that the snake had almost reached him.

The old man shouted louder to encourage the boy, "Catch the snake. It cannot harm you. I am praying for you. I am transferring my power to you. I am reaching you. Do not be scared. You are stronger than the snake. You are not alone. God is with you. Be brave. God is with you. God is great, God is great. Grab the snake. I have transferred my power to you."

While it was the first time in his life that he had attempted transferring his power to someone from a distance, the old man gave one last loud roar that echoed in the air, "In the name of God, catch the snake!"

The boy bravely pounced on the snake before the snake could bite his baby sister or goat. The boy had caught the snake around its neck and instantly started to run toward the old man. The snake was twisting around the arm and neck of the boy as he ran.

The old man, while feeling the most severe pain in his leg, used all his strength to hasten toward the boy. All three, including the snake, were trying their best to either harm or help each other.

Before reaching the boy, the old man hears him scream, "I have the snake but now it has wrapped itself around my hand and neck. It is going to kill me."

Both were still running toward each other.

All of a sudden, the old man saw that the boy was in front of him, while the large snake was still twisting around the boy's neck. Seeing the terrified eyes of the boy and the wrathful look of the snake, the old man kept praying loudly. The boy jumped into the lap of the old man. The old man uncurled the snake from the boy's neck. The boy was finally freed. The old man was in tears because, for the first time in his life, he had successfully transferred his power. The boy thanked him for saving his sister and his goat.

* * *

Right now, it is hard for me to write as there is no lantern and it is getting dark. The smell and smoke of the *sargeen,* or dried combustible dung, have filled the air, heralding the fall of night. In these areas of Afghanistan, the local people use dried dung instead of wood to make fires for cooking and for heating their homes.

Abdul Raoof is the Mullah Imam, or chief of the mosque, in this small village.

When I discovered that he believes in the supernatural, I asked him, "Tell me something about these elements in your village."

He replied, "They mainly manifest in the wintertime, when the nights are long, cold, and dark. Actually, this place can be quite frightening and oppressive. Besides us, other invisible things, created by God, are alive here too. You cannot see them but they can see you. You cannot harm them but they can harm you, if they choose."

Most Afghans very much believe in the supernatural and in the existence of good and evil spirits. The evil ones want to possess children and adults that bother them or step on them by mistake. A possessed person is usually taken to a field and beaten with a stick or something similar while a mullah chants verses of the Quran to exorcise the evil spirit.

I am not sure if I believe in evil spirits in my age but I do know one thing, I cannot disprove their existence.

Finally, the men brought dinner. It was a great village dinner, mixed with even greater conversations. From each house, the poor villagers sent a plate of food for me. While I was eating, I felt like a guest of the whole village. There were at least six different kinds of food. Every plate of food was clean and delicious. Each one had its own sweet smell. One was a delicious pumpkin and the other was a tasty roasted eggplant. The mushrooms and the cornbread were very tasty; the kebab, not so much. Some older people from the village also joined me. After all, I was the guest of their village leader, Mullah Islamuddin.

It was a wonderful assembly of the older generations. In the light of the smoky lantern and in the shadows of the muddy walls, these men with their black and white beards, green and brown eyes, unnecessary loud coughs and wrinkled necks, looked very interesting to me. The minute one started the story of a Sufi, the eyes of the other old men would flicker with a special divine joy like a boy playing with his fragile toy. Despite looking young to these men, I also started talking slowly and cautiously about the views of some of the mystic poets. A short story from Sa'di came to my mind.

A king went to a Sufi and asked him, "Do you ever remember me?"

The Sufi replied, "Yes, I do."

The king became happy and arrogant, looking at his minister, he said, "Look, what a great king I am. This is why even a great Sufi like him remembers me."

The minister calmly asked the Sufi, "May I please know when do you remember our king?"

"Son, whenever I forget God, I remember the king."

I should not forget to tell you that in all of the valleys on my way, the elders knew one story about my father more than any other and I do not know if this is a true story or a false one. Actually, a long time ago, when I asked my father about this story, whether it was true or false, he kept quiet. I shall tell it to you.

King Zahir, along with my father, went to visit an influentially rich and spiritually powerful man in the North. This man's name was Sayeed-i-Kayaan. He was the respected leader of the Ismaili Shias of Afghanistan. When the king approached the powerful man's garden, he found a strange note written in a beautiful calligraphy on the wall, which said, "This is my territory around which even Gabriel cannot fly."

The king was surprised at reading this note and asked my father, "What is the meaning of this note and why has he written it on my arrival?"

My father took a pen from his pocket, silently walked toward the wall and wrote under the written claim, "If you think you are a Pharaoh, wait for the waves of the Nile."

Almost 90 percent of the people of those areas that I have traveled through know of this story. I see that the common people really love the content and the way my father responded to the one who claimed to be the most powerful.

Tomorrow, we have a long walk to Yellow Pass, which will not be at all easy. It will probably take about six or seven hours. It will be a long journey to the base of the pass and I know it will not be an easy walk or ride. I hope I can manage it and my horse feels strong enough to help me.

20

Yellow Pass: A Lonely Climber

Thursday, September 4
11:20 AM

We are now at the foot of Kotali Zard, or Yellow Pass. It was a very long journey to reach here and took us six hours and ten minutes. It was a relatively easy track with fewer rocks but with many ups and downs. Today, for most of the day, I rode my horse. Now, I am writing to you from next to a natural dam, which has crystal-clear, emerald green water, through which you can easily see to the bottom. It is surrounded by snow-capped mountains.

The dam looks like a huge, graystone jar, brimming with a green divine wine and guarded by the mountains to prevent any natural disasters from shattering it. It is as if the sun, the moon, and the stars are its regular customers, savoring the celestial wine from this majestic gray jar. The hands of nature have combined all these wonderful scenes in such a beautiful tapestry that I do not know which one I should praise first: the deep dam, the emerald water, the snow-clad mountains, the divine wine in its gray stone jar, or the blue sky. I cannot figure out which gives color to which, the water to the sky or the sky to the water. The world before me stands at an elevation of about 4,500 meters.

Listen to what happened early in the morning when I was about to depart from my previous stop. It was about 3:15 AM when I was readying myself for the trail. I looked around and found that my horse was half-asleep, my bag was not prepared, and the new horseman whom I had arranged to take me to the next part of my journey was not there. I shouted at full volume to see where he was because he had not mentioned anything to me about not coming.

I could not do anything and did not have any other choice but to wake up poor Mullah Islamuddin at three-thirty in the morning and ask him, "Where is my man? Why has he not come yet?"

He simply replied, "I do not know."

I told him that I cannot wait and we have to find someone else to go with me.

Still half asleep, he went and woke up a young man by the name of Mullah Daad right from the side of his poor wife and brought him to me. I could not believe that in the middle of the night, someone would agree to go somewhere with someone whom he does not know and has never heard of. Mullah Islamuddin told me that he is a very trustworthy young man who will accompany me just up to the pass and not beyond.

Instantly, I accepted. Islamuddin advised me to give him some money after reaching the pass and then I should then arrange for someone else to take his place. I agreed and told him that I give would give him 500 Afghanis.

While thanking Islamuddin and appreciating all he had done for me, Mullah Daad, my horse, and I started our journey. Mullah Daad has a small and thin beard like the tail of a spring bird. At least so far, he has been kind to the horse and very much wanted to keep me happy too.

I looked at young Daad and asked him, "Do you not want to go and say goodbye to your wife or inform her that you are going with me?"

He said he has already done that. He is 24 years old and has got married just eight months ago. He has no parents and just one brother.

He avoided telling me the story of his parents by saying, "It has too much pain and too much sadness."

As we were slowly moving forward, I asked him, "Will you come to Pakistan with me?"

He said that he would do whatever I ask of him.

I was thinking he might do well out of this current situation and help me at the same time, and said, "If you accompany me to Pakistan, I will give you this horse as a gift."

A light sparkled in his eyes and he instantly agreed, "Yes, sir, that is great if you will be kind enough to do it. This journey has started off well for me."

While his happiness encouraged me, I told him, "Fine, it is agreed. You will accompany me to Pakistan. There, I will tell my people to rent what shall then be your horse to carry ammunitions or other supplies for the holy war and you will make at least about forty-thousand Afghanis, [$282] on your return trip."

I imagined Daad returning with his new horse, money, and God willing starting a new life. Forty thousand Afghanis will buy him about ten to fifteen goats and his beautiful pearl of a wife will be happily occupied in taking care of them. I smiled to myself when another thought crossed my mind that, in the end, the generous Zara Sahib had given this horse as a gift to Mullah Daad, and not, in fact, to me. This is how destiny works.

Village of Korpay Taw: House of Tooran

It is now 7:20 PM. We have crossed the difficult and exhausting Kotali Zard or Yellow Pass and reached here about an hour ago. I am in the village of Korpay Taw, in the house of someone called Tooran. Do not ask me how I feel. I am so tired and exhausted that I cannot even put my sour feelings into words.

After walking for more than thirteen hours, of which I rode my horse for only five, we arrived here at 6:30 PM. The last section of the pass took me an hour and a half to climb and cross. It was not that difficult but since there was little oxygen and the air was very thin, I ran out of breath. It took us about 5 hours from the top to descend to the bottom.

On the way, before reaching the first summer pasture, we ran into a group of internal refugees who were heading toward the Panjshir valley. There were men, women, elders, and children. Those misfortunate people seemed miserable but greeted Daad and me as we passed. I noticed that the children were running up and down beside their mothers and grandmothers, playing with whatever stones or pieces of wood they could find.

The weather was freezing cold. I could see that the children did not have clothes warm enough to stave off the bitter cold and realized that their playing was probably more to keep themselves warm than for enjoyment. Maybe it was both.

A young man asked, "Sir, do you have any medicine to give? I have a few people who are very sick."

I did not have any medicine but in order to give him some hope, I told him that I would go to see them myself. We walked for five minutes until I saw a very old woman, a child, and a young man lying under a large boulder. Even from a distance, you could see they were sick. Perhaps they were related.

When the old woman with long white hair saw me, she pointed toward the child and the young man and said, "Please give them some medicine. They really need it." When I moved the blanket from on top of the young man and little girl, I saw that the one's leg and the other's arm were injured. Thank God, their injuries were not so serious. I could do nothing more for them but give them the few painkillers that I found.

When I gave them to the young man, he immediately handed them to the old woman and said, "She is very sick and has a high temperature. She needs it more." I searched in my pocket and gave the only pieces of candy I had to the little girl and left.

We passed the refugees and I decided to sit on a small boulder to rest a little. Just as we had gotten comfortable, two helicopters circled around above us and disappeared. As we searched the skies, we saw that they were circling back around.

Looking at the refugees, I prayed to myself that they were not the targets because there were so many that it would be hard for all of them to find refuge. At this moment, I ordered Daad to quickly run and tell the refugees to take shelter just in case the helicopters decided to attack the convoy. Anything was possible with the Soviets.

Before Daad had time to get back to me, four attack helicopters appeared on the horizon. They swooped down in formation like dragons waiting to unleash their fiery breath. The noise from the four helicopters as they flew closer rose to a deafening and terrifying magnitude.

They were camouflaged but were flying so low that I could easily see the pilots inside the cockpits. These awe-inspiring dragons of destruction, circled the area around us as if they were marking their territory and getting ready to let loose their sinister arsenal.

I took my rucksack from my horse and headed toward the closest boulder I could find. I had not quite reached it, when the first of the rockets hit, making the ground tremble and roar. Since I had gone ahead and run further up the track in order to take refuge, I unfortunately had a perfect view of the refugee convoy further down. Another helicopter fired a few more rockets in our direction.

Out of four, only two of these dragons commenced their attack. It was already too much. One rocket hit the ground not more than 50 meters from where I had taken shelter. As I looked up, waiting for more rockets, the dragons started to circle again. They seemed even more sinister now than they did when they first appeared on the horizon.

All of a sudden, they spun their tails away from us and disappeared, probably heading toward Bagram airbase. I stayed in my place for another fifteen minutes just in case they returned. I could see nothing but plumes of smoke and fire. The gut-wrenching noise of screams and cries coming from those innocent refugees had replaced the thunderous sounds of the Soviet killing dragons. I could not take it anymore and rushed toward the smoke and screams.

When I reached the scene, my body stopped of its own accord, faced with the carnage in front of me. I do not have words for the hell that the world had become. An old man was covered in blood and a young girl's injuries were so severe that I dare not describe them to you. A boy of about ten years was crying and bleeding profusely. Four or five other women were sobbing, weeping, and grabbing handfuls of earth and throwing it on their faces in an act of heart-wrenching sorrow.

They were screaming, "Why, O God? Why has this happened to us? We leave our homes to find shelter from war, and the devils bring war upon us! Why has this happened?"

The little children who were playing before were now crying loudly from their meager sanctuaries behind small and large boulders. Some sheep and goats were lying dead. A horse was neighing intolerably in excruciating pain from his injuries. The earth all around us was black and burnt. Some pillows and mattresses the refugees had been carrying before were still burning.

I was in a sort of shock as I walked along the path, looking at horrors that I could only imagine could be fashioned in hell. I could not even think of anything else, my mind and body were numb from what I saw. The dirty smell of burned earth and flesh disturbed my senses even more.

I had to act and called out to the men to form a group in front of me so that we could see what we could do, when at that moment, Daad appeared. I was happy to see that he was still alive but what could any of us do? There were no roads, no hospitals, and no forms of transportation or communication in the immediate area. I thought, as I looked around that the whole universe was bleeding and that the screams and tears of these innocent people could be heard throughout the world. For me, this scene was the real face of war.

I did not see any way of helping these people when, suddenly and fortuitously, a group of young freedom fighters appeared. They all knew me and I knew them.

Their commander came to me and as we shook hands, I told him, "It is good to see you. Please do what you can for these poor people of ours."

He simply replied, "This is why we are here, Khalili Sahib. It is good that you are alive and not injured. We will do what we can for them."

At this moment, I remembered the sick old woman, the young man, and the little girl. I decided to go see if they were still alive. Thankfully, they were still lying beneath that same boulder, alive and free from further injury. I looked at the little girl. She was in a real state of shock. She stared with her big eyes at me and as I patted her on the head, I noticed that she was still clutching tightly one of the candies I had given her. I smiled, rummaged through my pockets, and thankfully found one more piece of candy to give to her.

I left them once again and moved on. I told Daad to try to find my horse and get ready to continue our journey. I walked slowly toward the next village. In about five minutes, Daad had found my horse, and was once again at my side. The screams and bloody images of children and innocent civilians were still fresh in my mind.

It took about half an hour to reach the village where I am now. I was thinking to myself as I walked, what is the meaning of life, when a verse of my father's came to mind: "That moment which you call life is nothing but frustration, sadness, burning, pain, and suffering." This verse kept ringing in my mind but I concluded that despite all of these realities, one should still have hope.

Now listen to what happened as I was entering a sweetly bucolic summer pasture. A little boy of about six years, who was sweeter than a sugar cube, was playing with his goat. The women were working in and around their pasture.

I called out to the small boy, "Where is your father, boy? Whose son are you?"

He stopped playing, looked innocently up at me and said nothing.

I asked again, "What is the name of your father? Where is he? Call him please to come and help us to find something to eat."

Again, he innocently looked up at me but kept quiet. I felt that maybe the little boy is mute or deaf and again I asked louder, "Tell me son, where's your father? Go and call him."

I could see that tears had now filled his beautiful eyes. It then seemed as though he was about to say something. Almost in a whisper, he said, "He has been martyred. I have no father but I am a good boy. Do not harm me. I am a good boy. Do not harm me please."

My dear, you cannot imagine what a burning pain gripped my soul. I thought entire mountain had dropped on my heart, telling me to cry, and I did.

I went closer to him, took him in my arms, and warmly kissed his cheeks and small hands. At that moment, his friendly-looking grandmother appeared and in beautiful Paryani Farsi asked, "Would you like some tea?"

Without waiting for a response from me, she kindly brought a cup of tea. In my rucksack, I had some homemade biscuits, which I shared with the little boy.

I asked the grandmother what happened to the boy's father.

She said, "The communists came one day, attacked our home, pulled his father outside, and after some shouting back and forth, they shot him dead in front of this poor son of his. One minute, he was playing with his father; and, the next, his little hands were covered in his father's blood. Since then, he has been afraid of any men who are unknown to him."

I patted the boy on the head as he sat next to me listening to our conversation. Thank God, somehow he has started talking to me a little. The boy's name was Mutalib and his martyred father was Abdul Qadir. He loved his father. I talked a bit with the little boy.

He told me, "Thank God, my mother now has three goats that my martyred father always wanted to buy for her. She is working day and night to make me happy. She wants me to go to school, if possible."

I filled his pockets with the all the raisins I had. I also gave him a little money. He ran to his mother.

His mother called from afar, "Why did you give him the money? A poor traveler should not do that. Whatever we have belongs to the freedom fighters of this land."

Not even a few minutes had passed when Mutalib, the little boy, ran back to me and brought two big pieces of quroot, dry yoghurt balls.

As I departed, I repeated twice under my breath what he wanted me to believe of him; "I am good boy, I am a good boy."

*   *   *

As far as the pass, our path rose high through beauty and boulders. Today, the boulders looked like gigantic warriors clasping a great array of weapons, riding colossal horses, and awaiting their orders to move on. Each one had its own character, very different from the others. They were each attired in distinct shades of granite hues, in grays, blacks, whites, and even yellows. Some had sharp edges and some had smooth corners.

I climbed the mountain slowly, mainly because I could not breathe properly. My whole body had become like a heavy airless sack, heaving itself up and down. I could hear the sound of my own breath, much louder than ever. My vision became blurred too. It looked as if even the rocks were moving with me, at my own plodding pace.

Anyway, maybe it was because of the long walk, the horrid bombardment, the little boy's story, or the thin air that gave me a very bad headache. I decided then and there not to continue to the fighters base this evening. I had neither the patience nor the willingness to talk or listen to anyone.

My dear, this sometimes happen in war. Your mood is totally off but it passes.

Friendly Lice

Village of Korpay Tow, Paryan
Friday, September 5
5:00 AM

What a beautiful September morning! I am still in the small village of Korpay Taw, which is in the area of Paryan. Last night, after prayer, I was hoping to fall into a deep sleep so that I might have energy for today's long journey. Even though the weather was cold, I had a thick blanket and did not take off my combat jacket, so I felt warm. In no time, I was asleep. After about an hour, I sensed that there was something crawling up and down my body. In the middle of the night, the itching became so intolerable that I woke up, took out my flashlight, and undressed to see what was creating such discomfort.

Do not tell my boys, but in each and every hem and fold of my shirt, I found two or three lice in various guises: white, black, small, big, individual, conjoined, and even on top of each other. I probably looked like a monkey picking lice out of his dirty body and then going to sleep again. I was still uncomfortable as I lay there trying to fall asleep again until, finally, I lost my patience, took my shirt off, threw it outside the window of the guesthouse in which I am staying, and put on another one.

At this moment, another person in the guesthouse, woke up and said, "What are you doing over there?"

I said, "The lice woke me up."

He impatiently said, "Leave the lice alone, turn off your light, and do not disturb us."

I laughed and said to him, "I would leave them alone but I do not think they will leave me alone."

The weather right now is extremely cold. The snow-clad peaks in between the silver fingers of the clouds, delightfully dancing with the golden rays of the sun, look stunning.

When I was coming down from Kotali Zard, I saw the beautiful majestic peak of Mir Samir. It looked like a conqueror with his gold and silver crown, sitting higher and more graceful than the others, on his snow throne.

Today we have a long path to travel.

21

Back to Nooristan and Unacceptable Love

It is eight in the evening of the sixth of September. From where should I start? Once again, we are in Nooristan at the Pushal crossroads, which is called Du Raahi.

Yesterday, at two o'clock in the afternoon, we left in the direction of the caves, which lie at the bottom of the Chimmar Pass. We had not traveled half an hour when, all of a sudden, heavy rain started to pour down. What a rain it was, as if the god of rain had decided to carve large holes in the clouds to mercilessly pour rain down upon us. Since we did not find any shelter on the way, we traveled for about three hours under the cold whip of the rain to find at least some kind of a foxhole to give us shelter.

From head to toe, we were drenched to the bone. No doubt, rain is a mercy of God, but not when your horse is heavily laden, a strong wind is blowing with an icy chill, you lack warm clothes, your stomach is empty, and you happen to be walking through one of the highest ranges of the Hindu Kush. Everything, from clothes to sleeping bags to rucksacks, was soaked through. It became so cold that each one of us, including the poor horse, began to shiver like scared goats. The repeated peels of thunder and lightning flashes made our horse wilder and more frightened. From every side of the valley, muddy floods were rushing toward us.

Finally, we reached the caves, which were unfortunately already full of travelers, horsemen, freedom fighters, lapis sellers, and refugees. In fact, there was no room left to squeeze us in. While we looked for another place to take shelter, the rain kept whipping the backs of the mountains, the trunks of the trees, the faces of the hills, the hips of the horses, and the tops of our heads even more heavily than before. The cold wind slapped our faces, necks, heads, and shoulders, as hard and as fast as possible. The sky had grown dark. The caves had no owners but first come, first served was the rule in these parts.

A man named Abdul Qudoos kindly asked me to stay in his cave but I declined, as I did not think there was enough space for even one more person. Then I proceeded to check a few of the other caves and found that each one was full to capacity with miserable, exhausted travelers. In the last cave, there was a man by the name of Rozi Mohammad who luckily also recognized me and offered me his cave. The size of his whole cave was about one and a half meters squared. I entered.

I did not care about other things but just wanted to take refuge from the rain. Rozi was kind enough to fit me in and he himself went somewhere else. This cave-motel was so small that we could not build a fire, even though my clothes were frozen and wet. I took off my shirt and gave it to Daad to dry somewhere but I had no clue where he might succeed in this task. Rain, wind, freezing cold, hunger, exhaustion, and lack of shelter—all obstacles to comfort had joined hands together to complete my near demise. I sat there shirtless and shivering under my soaking wet combat jacket. I was next to frozen. I had no idea how, but after about an hour, Daad brought my shirt, dried and even half-warm. Thank God, after a few minutes, they also brought me a hot cup of tea. When I took the first sip, I breathed a sigh of relief. I saw Dur Mohammad searching in his pockets and he produced a little handkerchief with some dried mulberries, which he happily gave to me.

After having my cup of tea and some mulberries, despite being in possibly the smallest and dampest cave in the world, I thought that whole world was mine. At that very moment, Rozi Mohammad said, "Khalili Sahib, if you permit me, I must go and help two injured people who are in another cave."

Despite being exhausted myself, I joined him as well.

In the freezing cold, with the rain still coming down hard and the wind slapping our faces, we walked up the mountain for about ten difficult and dark minutes until we saw the entrance to the cave of the injured. It was much smaller than I thought. As I entered, I could smell a horrible stench coming from within. It was so dark that I could not see anything. I turned on my flashlight. Inside, I found a woman about 40 years old lying on some rags, with a girl about 15 years old lying down next to her. There was also a man about 50 years old. They were a family. The mother's arm was injured and the girl had suffered a serious shrapnel wound on her back. She was unconscious. She was dying. The mother looked up at me and said, "Please brother, pray for my daughter Najeeba. Pray that God takes my life and not hers." I talked to the husband. He was unsure if he should take his wife and daughter all the way to Pakistan.

What could I say to this man? His wife could make it but his daughter, with such serious injuries would need a miracle to survive such a long and difficult journey over the mountains of Nooristan.

The mother interjected in a very weak voice and asked, "Please tell me, brother, how long do you think it would take to reach Pakistan?"

To make her feel a bit better and raise her spirits, I said, "Sister, do not worry. It is not too far. By tomorrow, the weather will be much better. You and your daughter will be fine. Do not worry. The only thing we can do is to pray and ask the Almighty to help us."

She simply replied, "Yes, brother, what else do we have? Since my daughter and I were injured, it is the only thing I do, day and night."

The husband then, without being asked, started to tell me how his family's destiny had brought them to this place.

He said, "It was not our fault at all. We are from Khan Abad, in Kunduz province. We were all out working in our fields. It was a day like any other. In total, there might have been 50 people scattered over several little farms when a Soviet helicopter appeared from over the mountains. We thought it would pass and kept working in the fields but it did not. It stayed there hovering and not even a minute had passed when it started to bombard our area. Some of us were killed, some injured, and some were left to pick up the pieces of their loved ones. We have survived until now. I pray that God is kind to me and lets my wife and child live. I have nothing else."

With a deep pain and sorrow in my heart and burning tears in my eyes, I left the cave.

When I reached my own tiny cave, I needed to sleep because the whole experience of going to help those people had drained me, physically and mentally. As soon as I laid my head down, I fell asleep. I had not been asleep for more than half an hour when I felt the crawling of tiny insects along my skin. I awoke with a start. I instantly knew that the lice had come out again, attracted by the slight warmth mustered by my body heat, and had assembled on my body.

Anyway, until about 2 AM, I repeatedly reached my hand underneath my shirt, located one or two lice in the dark, caught them, and threw them away. Who can sleep in such conditions? In the end, I took off my shirt altogether and put on my warm sweater.

I had not slept for an hour when young Daad called out loudly, "It's 3 AM, time to leave. Hurry up and get ready."

I instantly went outside and there was a real storm brewing. The rain had changed into freezing sleet and snow, while the wind was blowing ten times faster than before. I decided not to move in such bad weather. I was so tired and exhausted that I delayed my morning prayers and went back to sleep. I woke again at 6:30 AM.

Ignoring the advice of the men around me, I eventually made the decision to continue our journey. The men were not happy but had no other choice if they wished to join us, and we started out. There was snow everywhere: on the ground, on us, on the horses, on the trees, on the rocks, on the rivers, and on the springs. It was as if a thick white blanket had spread thickly over everything and everybody. Three horses fell at least 3,000 meters down to the valley below. My horse slipped badly many times but, thank God, it found its footing in time and did not fall. Daad was not feeling at all well. To me he looked weaker than ever and I thought that he might not be able to climb another half an hour. It was also not possible to tell him to ride the horse because of the heavy snow and the slippery cliffs.

*   *   *

Now it is 8:20 PM. I am sitting in a dark cave, which the people around me consider a teahouse. It is cold, wet, pitch dark, gloomy, and as small as a foxhole. We started a small fire and, in a few minutes, it became warmer. The rain has stopped. Everything is wet. I lay out all my drenched clothes next to the fire. I first started with my sleeping bag, and then my coat and then my pants. I also took two painkillers and two vitamin B1 tablets to preemptively stop my pain.

By my reckoning, today we walked for ten hours under rain, sleet and snow but faster than a fox running from the galloping hunter.

Listen to one of Mullah Daad stories, which is funny and worth writing to you. On the way here, Daad's Afghan scarf or patoo fell while he was walking along beside his horse and he did not even tell me so that I would not become upset. When we reached here, I had not even sat for more than a minute when I heard the voice of Daad, arguing with someone. I knew that he was in some sort of real trouble; otherwise, he would not be shouting as loud as he was.

I immediately went outside to ask him what was going on. I saw that one end of a patoo was in Daad's hands and the other end was in the hands of an old man. Daad was screaming, pulling, and shouting that it was his patoo.

The old man was also pulling, screaming, and even swearing, "By God and the Holy Quran, this is my patoo. This young man is crazy. He is a thief. He is the enemy of God. He is falsely claiming my patoo. I swear by the grave of my mother and by the dust of the tomb of my father that this is mine."

When I saw the patoo, I recognized it as Daad's. I was surprised that this old man should claim it as his own. I grabbed the patoo from both of them and said, "This must be investigated."

In my mind, I wondered how I was supposed to investigate this. Before I was able to answer my own question, Daad suggested something, which was a good solution and said, "Cover the patoo and whoever can correctly reveal its distinguishing marks, give it to him."

I agreed. First, I asked the old man, "Tell me what makes it yours."

The old man responded, "Why should I tell you? This is my patoo. You test me on my own patoo. You are not a God-fearing person because you trust the enemy of God. You do not believe an old God-fearing man like me and believe a young godless thief like him. Look at his face, he is a liar."

I loudly shouted at him, "Do you know of any marks or any signs on this patoo or not? The question is not who is God-fearing or who is not. Your loud voice or your white beard does not prove that you are right. Tell me if you can reveal any information to prove that this is your patoo, and not his."

The old man was still swearing by every imaginable holy thing but all the while not offering any convincing clue about the nature of the patoo. After ordering the old man to shut up, I instantly asked Daad to mention any signs or marks on the patoo which might confirm his ownership.

He calmly said, "This patoo was burnt in one part and my wife stitched it with black thread. If you look at it properly, there are two other burns on the left side, which she had also stitched but with yellow thread. She also attached a small beautiful piece of metal on the right side as a remembrance."

I immediately spread the patoo out and looked for the clues to know whether Daad was right or wrong and I found that they were all correct. I lost my temper because the old man was still claiming and swearing by God and the Holy Quran that it was his patoo.

I unleashed expletives at the old man and told him, "You are an untrustworthy old liar. May God break your backbone! You are not at all a faithful person. You never feared God. You should be ashamed of your white beard."

The problem was over. When I was giving the patoo back to Daad, I asked, "How did you remember all of these small details?"

"Because we were together when she mended it. I even remember the song she was singing while she was mending. How could I forget it? For the first time, I heard my wife scream out in pain because at that very moment the needle pricked her tiny finger. We are poor people and these things matter in our lives and we live with these small memories close to us."

A few minutes later, as I was talking to the half-blind boy, who was on his quest for prescription glasses, and Daad was enjoying having his patoo back, Haji Fazl Paryani appeared before me. He is a rich and well-known merchant, a lapis lazuli seller, one of the richest men of the north. He looks to be about 55 or more. He is a huge man. He showed immense respect toward me. I was happy to find yet another good fellow traveler. He is also going to Pakistan.

The tea-cave is cold and Daad is busy trying to dry my clothes. Haj Fazl had lots of raisins, goat's cheese, and plenty of deep-fried *khajoor*, or homemade cookies, and kindly offered some to me.

From here until the bottom of the Kantiwa Pass should take other four hours. The Kantiwa Pass is one of the highest passes in Afghanistan. It might be the second highest but I am not sure.

Saturday, September 7
5:30 AM

I am feeling much better. Most of our clothes and my notebooks are now dry. Last night, after drying my clothes, I had two or three cups of tea and went to sleep. I had many nightmares and my screams must have filled the cave. I usually have nightmares on Wednesday nights but I am surprised to be now having them on a Friday night. Either the hardships of Nooristan's mountain caves have changed the essence of my nightmares, or I have confused my nightmares by sleeping in different dark cells within the mountains.

My dear, the toes on my feet are covered with blisters. I am in need of a good shower and a long rest but that will have to wait until I am back home. Soon, God willing, I will be with you and the boys. Tomorrow morning, we will leave from here and reach in early evening the first village on the other side of the Kantiwa Mountain, which is called Chaman. There I know Kaka Musa, who is in a way a relative of yours. He is the uncle of your sister-in-law, Nasrine.

Some minutes ago, Dur Mohammad, the owner of the tea-cave began fighting with a group of fighters who stayed in his tea-cave last night. Why? Two teacups from his tea-cave were missing. He believed that the freedom fighters, or some of the other travelers, had stolen them, so he kept on screaming, "O travelers and holy warriors, you are all godless thieves. O enemies of God, do you not believe in the fires of hell? I am sure with those stolen cups in your hands, you will drink fire in the hottest wells of hell. You should be ashamed of yourselves! You can hide them now but you cannot hide those sinful hands from the eyes of our Holy Prophet in the other world. How can you dare look at him on Judgment Day?"

I called him and tried to calm him down by promising him some money for the cups but he angrily rejected my offer by saying, "Get lost, *laalaa*! Even if you give me the money, where can I buy the cups? This is Nooristan, not *Englistan* (England)."

Then I asked him if by any chance he finds the thief, what he would do to him.

He said, "I will personally break his head and 'rub his nose with dirty dust.' People should see the line of dust on his nose, showing that he is a thief."

* * *

My dear, there is a small child, maybe twelve years old, who looks very much like your brother Suliman. He is the helper of Dur Mohammad, the tea-cave owner. He is wearing eye-catching purple-colored clothes and a purple scarf around his head. From the start of morning until night, this little boy runs around, skillfully serving the traveling guests. He does not know Dari but tries to use some words in the right and wrong manner. If I can, I will take his picture because of the striking color of his clothes.

Haji Fazl, the lapis lazuli seller which I spoke to earlier has appeared. His big smile and loud laughter stretch his bearded face wider than his cheeks. He is about 50 years old. He is tall, well dressed, and graceful. His horse looks even better than mine. He once again kindly offered me some khajoor. His homemade khajoor are deliciously sweet but his way of talking and telling jokes is sweeter.

During our talks, he mentioned that he was in the village of Worsaj some days before. I asked him the reason. While repeatedly filling his big cup with green tea, Haji Fazl told me the story for about an hour, in his very eloquent and stylish way. Let me try to tell you what he said:

"A boy and a girl fall madly in love with each other. The girl is vibrantly young with blueish eyes, black hair, and beautiful wheat-colored skin. Everyone loves her and knows her to be full of smiles and laughter."

"The boy is strong and tall. He has brown eyes, black curly hair, and a thin beard. He is famous for his brave character and hardworking ability. They meet in secret in the fields and behind boulders, whenever they get a chance."

"One day, they decide that their love is too strong. They must do the right thing; and that is to get married. They are so happy at the idea of being husband and wife. The boy is ready to give his life for her and the girl is ready to live with him until the last days of her life. The boy says to the girl, 'Whatever you tell me, I will do for you. What else do I have in this world? In the ocean of my love, you are my only beautiful pearl. You are my river, my sky, my star, my moon, my sun, my spring water, my grape and my apple blossom.' In the back of his mind, the boy knows that there is one problem, which his innocent beloved has not thought of."

"The problem is that they belong to different classes, one rich and one poor, one with a name and the other with none. The girl goes to talk to her mother about her beloved and their plans to marry. The mother says, 'Your father and brothers will never allow this to happen.' The girl with tears in her eye pleads and asks her mother, 'This cannot be possible. They love me and want me to be happy. Why would they deny me my love?'"

"The mother understands the feelings of her young daughter but puts on a strong face and says, 'My sweet innocent daughter, you do not know the strange customs and traditions of our world. The father of your lover is a barber, and even his grandfather was a barber. Your father and grandfather are famous landowners and your uncles are respected religious men. It is not possible for a member of such a respected family to get married to a low class barber. We do not allow our daughters or sisters to get married to someone from the *tabaqa e payaan*, or lower classes, such as barbers, carpenters, tailors, weavers, and even singers.' The girl asks, 'What is wrong with my love, Mother? It is not a sin. My love was born into that family and he did not choose it for himself.'"

"The mother nods sadly and says to her weeping daughter, 'My sweet daughter, this is no one's fault. Our society works this way, we cannot go against it, and what our society tells us is what we should do, whether we love it or hate it.' She fervently asks again, 'Then whose fault is it, mother? What should I do? I cannot live without him. He is good man. He can even read and write. He is not just a barber. He is a very honest and pious person. Please help me.'"

"The mother starts to cry, seeing how much pain her beautiful daughter is suffering from. In her gentle mother's voice, she says, 'I am sorry, *jaan-e-madar* [soul of mother], your father will never allow it to happen. He has lived with grace and honor throughout his life. Do not make your father look bad in the eyes of his brothers and other relatives. I do not know whose fault this is but you are not allowed to marry that man. Forget him and never think of him again. Everybody in your family wants you to marry your second cousin. He is also a good man. He is also a brave and honest person. Your father loves him too.'"

"The daughter lashes back at her mother, 'So what, Mother! I do not want to marry him. I do not love him. I love my barber.' Her mother had no other choice but to repeat her words. She went on, 'My dear, this happens all the time. My young sister was also forced to leave her love and marry a man of our father's choosing. She was not happy then but now has a family and is a good wife to him. You will get used to it, every girl does.'"

"The girl goes out to the garden to be alone. She understands that she will receive no help from her mother and knows now that the marriage she desires will never be accepted. For her, love is above everything else: above name, fame, and riches. She believes that now *shingaree*, or secret elopement, is the only choice she has."

Just imagine, my dear, what a lonely decision this poor girl had to make as she sat in her garden. What a brave decision to go against the old traditions by choosing love over the rules of society.

Her decision is like putting a mountain on the shoulders of a small sparrow. She has no one in the world but God and her beloved.

Haji Fazl took a drink from his cup and then continued his story: "So, this girl goes and tells her beloved what she plans to do."

"The boy insists that she should rethink her decision, saying, 'You will have problems in the future living with me if you choose shingaree and escape to my house.'"

"The girl replies, 'For me, the problem is living without you, not with you. I am ready to take any risk, even if I am killed.'"

"The boy argues with the girl and implores her, 'Please listen to me, my love. It is okay if they kill me but, if you escape to my house, they will kill you, and I could not stand to be the cause of your death.'"

"She clasps his hands and says, 'If you love me, you will understand that I cannot live without your love. I need you.'"

"The boy puts his face in her soft hands and says, 'Love sometimes may not be enough, my sweet.'"

"She kisses his face and says, 'I have already decided. I cannot go one more day without you. You have to come and take me away. We both need to be strong. This decision is mine to make and I have made it.'"

"In the middle of the night, she leaves her home. Her beloved is waiting for her on his black horse. As he grabs her hand to pull her up behind him atop the horse, while anxious and worried, they smile at one another, knowing that their journey together has just started. The boy rides hard and fast to his own village to make sure no one can catch them. His village is a three-day ride. Day and night, he rode with his beloved at his back. She holds him tightly. She feels free and content. She knows that the boy's family will not reject her, because in the case of shingaree, the family of the boy cannot reject the girl. It would be a great disgrace for them if they do so."

"On the way, they discuss what will happen the minute her family finds out and how they will do whatever they can to bring her back. This is when the problems for the boy's family will start. They are poor barbers and have no power or influence, while the girl's family has every resource to their disposal. If they are able to bring the girl back, they will shave her hair and beat every inch of her body; and if they get their hands on the boy, they will kill him and call it an honor killing."

"The boy and the girl finally reached the boy's home safely. His family had already been informed that the girl's family had left their village and were on their way to take her back. The boy's father knows that they are powerless. There is only one way to avoid a tragic outcome and that is to find a mediator with influence."

Here, Haji Fazl smiled, for this is where Haji Fazl himself comes into the story. You see, my dear, the boy's family goes and pleads with Haji Fazl for help. After talking to the boy and girl, Haji Fazl understands that this is true love and agrees to be their mediator. When the family of the girl finally arrives, Haji Fazl greets them to talk about the future of these two lovers.

Both families, the two lovers, some elders, and Haji Fazl sit and try to come to an understanding and reconcile the two sides. It is not an easy task. The girl's family has their honor to defend. But finally, after two days of talking, listening, and arguing, a decision is made that the marriage of the boy and girl will be allowed. Haji Fazl has convinced the girl's family of the love between the boy and girl and gave his word that she would be treated with the utmost care.

When Haji Fazl had finished telling me his wonderful story, I congratulated him sincerely and told him, "May God bless you. You brought peace between the two families and serenity in the hearts of two young people, who committed no other sin but to love each other."

My dear, as you know, these kinds of stories can be found all over Afghanistan. Hundreds of girls and boys, who love each other, cannot be together. Thousands of hearts are on fire because of some wretched tradition or another which comes in between them. It is understandable now, but let us pray that education helps love to live in its proper home.

Over the last two days, I have been worrying about our son Mahmud's school and wondering whether you have enrolled him or not. I hope that he will not be left with nothing to do. I know that he himself is happy not to go to school.

22

Back to Kantiwa

It is three-thirty in the afternoon of September 8. We are once again at the foot of the Kantiwa Pass. This part of the mountain is also called Pushal. When we were leaving the tea-cave of Dur Mohammad, he still had not been able to find his stolen cups and looked annoyed when I said good-bye to him. On the way, besides the blistering mood of the tea-cave owner, the painful blisters on my feet were still bothering me. I put my feet in cold water for about ten minutes but it did not help.

Despite my painful blisters, I am enjoying the beautiful weather we are having today. I should not forget to tell you that, some minutes ago, I was listening to the Voice of America, to a strange piece of news about a Pakistani plane, arriving from New York, which was hijacked by terrorists in Karachi airport and later blown up by the Pakistani police. Fifteen people were killed and about a hundred were wounded. I hope it is not the beginning of something very bad. I do not know who these hijackers are and although we do not believe in this kind of tactic in our war, I hope that there is no Afghan involved in this episode.

5:30 PM

It is five-thirty in the late afternoon. It has now become very cold and is snowing on the top of the mountain. I had a few cups of hot tea, went next to the fire that the men had made to heat my hands a little, and then decided to find a nice flat boulder to sit on and relax for a few minutes.

In the mountains at this time of day shadows and shade from the trees and rocks prevail because the sun sets early behind the high crests, and it is with such grace and beauty, as if the colors have been chosen directly by the Creator. If you were here to see the colorful arrow-like rays of the sunset, you would be in awe. The sun itself looks like a painter with fine golden hair, who gently goes to sleep behind her own beautiful and colorful canvas. The high mountains sit like silver-haired spectators, silently watching the painter and the painting. The beauty lies in the combination of the three, the painter, the painting, and the spectator.

Yesterday, due to heavy snow, some of the poor horses carrying supplies and ammunition fell to their deaths, deep into the valley, and since some of the other horses could not move due to sheer exhaustion, they stayed behind. Four of the horses carrying lapis stones were severely injured and could not move even a single step further. In the end, their owners had to kill them. When I asked Sher Agha, one of the horse owners, why he had killed his horse, he told me, "I killed my poor wounded horse so that he may die without pain; otherwise, the wolves would eat him in the night. It was a mercy killing, not murder."

By now, my dear, you should know how hard it is to provide logistics for the war in Afghanistan. It is hard for horses, mules, donkeys, and camels, but even harder for the people who take care of them. These animals look beautiful on the mountain peaks but, at the same time, it is painful and tragic to see them suffer so much. Horses and donkeys carry 80 percent of the transportation of our war supplies. Providing supplies is the backbone of every war.

This year alone, just to meet the needs of the fighters in only a few northern provinces, there are at least twenty thousand horses and donkeys being used in order to maintain our supply line between Afghanistan and Pakistan.

Four Walnuts, Kantiwa Village

September 9
3:00 PM

My dear, I am now again in your grandfather's old *qala*. It is 3 o'clock in the afternoon. At nine in the morning, we started from Chaman and reached this beautiful emerald-like district of Kantiwa. Geographically speaking, I am standing in the center of Nooristan.

I have been in this delightful place many times and have stayed here many nights. Your grandfather's fort is located on a beautiful hill. It is made of hard rocks and a special white clay. The rooms are very small and the windows are unusually small because of the severe cold weather in the wintertime. This valley has at least six months of winter. Some nights the weather drops down to even minus 25 centigrade.

Compared to other valleys, this has the largest area of flat land. Your grandfather's fort sits exactly on the crossroads of three important valleys. The mountains surrounding the valley of Kantiwa are very high and the many clay huts look like small flies sticking to a big boulder. The greenery here seems like an emerald gem, mounted on a silver ring. Here, the water is indeed very clear and tasty. We take water from the river or from the clear mountain streams.

In addition, they have a hot water spring. Which direction the warm spring water comes from, I do not know and maybe no one knows. This water spring is very warm in the winter and cold in the summer. People say it is good for the skin. I wish we had a system to take warm water from the hot water spring and channel it into individual houses. There is a mosque here, which is a little bigger than other mosques. Your father constructed a part of it many years before the communists killed him.

Some women are busy working in the fields. They mostly wear black dresses, which cover their whole bodies. The poor Nooristani women work very hard in their daily lives. They have no doctors, nurses, medicine, or hospitals, but one thing they have always had is their immense faith.

Here, I cannot stop myself from writing to you about what happened on the way to this village, to illustrate how faithful these poor women are.

I was coming down with my traveling companions from the side of a very deep and dangerous cliff. A Nooristani woman was standing next to the path wearing old clothes and looking at our group with distant eyes. She had her hands extended with her palms upward. It was strange to me to see a woman begging in Nooristan. It was very unusual. They are poor but not beggars. I moved past quickly.

At that moment, one of the men said loudly, "Khalili Sahib, she has something for you." As I turned back, I saw that the woman instantly covered her face with her old black headscarf and kept one hand extended toward me. I took a few steps in her direction and saw that in her outstretched hand, there were four walnuts. She said something in her own Nooristani accent, which I could not understand.

A young Nooristani who was with me immediately translated her words, "This is a donation for the sake of God. Please take it. I have nothing else to give."

Instantly, my body became numb, struck by this extreme act of generosity, which sprang from strong a faith, from a poor woman who had nothing else but the old patched clothes on her back and those four walnuts in her palm. My numbness left me without words. I took the walnuts, thanked her sincerely, and said to my own heart that if God ever wanted to create the mother of Jesus again, this generous woman might be the one.

I was told that Whitney has arrived safely in Pakistan. I have given him a letter to give to you. I am sure you will receive it soon, my dear. I do not think that I will be able to write to you anymore today. I will probably stay for one night here and tomorrow, I will start again.

Moving on

Chatraas Village, Nooristan
September 10, 1986
12:30 PM

I have left Kantiwa, your grandfather's land, and I am now in a village, called Chatraas. This morning, we walked for six hard hours to reach this village. Your cousin, Jalal, kindly agreed to accompany me to the end of my journey. He has been singing Nooristani songs along the way; it is impossible for me to decipher their meaning and even more difficult to like them.

As I have changed my route to get home via Kunar and Chitral of Pakistan, I gave my horse to my horseman, Daad, as I had promised him before. While feeling both sad and happy, I listened as he told me, "Thank you for the horse and thank you for everything else! I wish I were going further with you."

I said, "You are welcome, but the road I am taking now is very tough and demanding and, at the end of it, you will not have the opportunity to make some money by bringing back supplies. I want you to go to Chitral, return home safely, and whenever you reach your home, to see your wife again, and make sure that you have a smile on your face."

He looked very happy at this, and as he was leaving, I shouted back to him, "Mullah Daad, by the way, learn how to feed your horse and do not misplace your patoo again." He laughed.

*   *   *

My dear, it is 8:30 in the evening. I am currently in the house of Haji Sultan. When I was in the mosque, talking war and peace with some local Nooristanis, Haji Sultan recognized me and invited Jalal and me to his home.

I accepted his invitation and now we are in his home, which is located in a beautiful part of the village. He is a happy and kind man. It is a two-room mud house. When darkness fell on the village, it was interesting to see that everyone held a wooden torch in their hands and were trying to find their way home.

A line of four black-clad women, also carrying wooden torches could be seen slowly and carefully making their way down from the side of a high cliff. It was a fascinating scene. They looked like four candles walking on a large piece of rock. They use old style wooden torches that they make from the branches of pine trees. They have never seen and even never dreamed of having electricity in their village.

When I told Haji Sultan that I hope and wish that one day the village is illuminated with electricity, he laughed and said, "I wish it as well, but, even if we have electricity, what do we have in our lives to see, other than poverty. It is better to live in the dark."

I instantly told him, "Maybe you are right but, in the light, you can at least see where you are going so that you do not fall. This is a good first step."

Thank God, Haji Sultan does not use a wooden torch but has a genuine lantern, which is the only lantern in the whole village.

While having food, he sadly told me that, "Unfortunately, illiteracy is a part of our lives. Just eight people are semi-literate in the whole village. If there were no mosque or madrasa to teach a few of our children, we would be totally blind."

He also said that there is a lot of cheese in this village and they make the best cheese in Nooristan. He also proudly told me that in the whole village, or perhaps all over Nooristan, only three people including him have beehives. As soon as he mentioned honey, I prayed that he will offer us a little but he did not. I had heard that Nooristani honey has a deep crimson color and is extremely delicious.

I have to go to sleep earlier tonight because tomorrow we have another difficult rocky mountain with another higher pass to climb. It will be interesting for me because it will be my first time on this pass.

23

The Killer Kunar River

September 11, 1986
9:30 AM

We are now on the top of Waigal Pass. It took us about two and a half hours to climb. There is a village named Anutka located near the summit of the mountain.

While entering the village, I saw a tall, brunette woman, with a yellow goatskin on her back, busy making food. Her beautiful little daughter brought me a glass of dough, a refreshing Afghan drink, but I did not try it. I was not feeling well. She then brought me cornbread, but I declined with a smile and thanked her. She did not understand what I said and before she left, I gave her two sugar cubes, which I had stolen from Jalal's home two nights ago. She took them and said something, which I did not understand. Maybe she was thanking me too.

Like other mountain villages in Nooristan, this one is also very beautiful. It is very calm and quiet with a fresh, clear climate. If the people were to allow me, I would call it Roh Bakhsh, or 'Soul Provider.' It has many walnut and oak trees. The mountains are covered with cedar trees too. Most of the women and children are occupied with farming their very small mountain fields. I will take some minutes' rest here and start our journey again.

Village of Gumbal

11:00 AM

I am in a small village called Gumbal. Before reaching here, I met a tall, well-built man called Hazrat Ali. He was about 26 years old. I asked him for some tea and he kindly agreed to bring it to me, but before doing that, he brought a type of Nooristani divan, which looked like a wooden couch. He kindly spread a black goatskin on it. He also brought a Nooristani table, which was made with strips of black and white goatskin. Along with tea, he generously brought us Nooristani cornbread and cheese also.

Another man by the name of Hashim came to see me. Although he had only one eye, it was a beautiful eye with a deep green color. He was tall and slim. He had a second-hand European jacket, which had a few tears on one of the arms. It was made in Austria and seemed like it might have once been a part of an army uniform. It suited him. He had combed blonde hair, with unusually thick eyebrows. He looked very much like a retired British military officer. He was not optimistic at all about the war and about the future of the country. He considered the war a waste of time and believed that no one would be a winner.

Woygal District

1:45 PM

We are in the center of the Woygal district. Come and see the beauty of nature here. A village of such beauty you have probably seldom heard of, much less seen. I think my father was right to compose a poem for the beauty of this valley. I have just now reached here and only a few individuals can be seen here and there. Most people of the village have gone up to their summer pasture.

The district looks quite empty. I hope we will find someone to help us. Wait a minute, I see a tall, goatskin-clad woman, holding a baby. I cannot talk to her because I do not speak her language and Jalal does not want to talk to her because he is either very tired or does not want to speak to a woman.

While hoping for someone to show up, let me describe to you what I see around me. The whole village of Woygal looks yellowish. The mountain in front of me is covered with yellow mud and yellowish rocks. It looks like a Buddhist monk with patches of green, gray, and black on his yellow robe. The rocks and even their homes are also of a yellowish color. Jalaal told me that this color brings good luck to the people. I do not know how. The people have made their muddy homes out of this yellow earth and this is why the small village on the mountain slope looks like a gigantic beehive covered with bees.

Right now, I am very hungry. The thing I crave at this moment is a traditional dish of soft rice with lentils, yoghurt, and meatballs. I know it is just a dream for now. A hungry cat dreams of a big rat! It would be impossible for someone to arrange it here.

This valley divides into three other valleys, one of which we will choose for our path. We will pass through Agook Pass in order to reach the Kunar province, and then cross into Pakistan. Still no one is here to help us. If the sticky flies allow me, I will take a short nap and then see what happens next. God is great.

5:00 PM

At last, a man by the name of Sultan Mohammad showed up. He was a young man from Woygal. He was from the National Front Party, or *Jabha Milli*. Sultan told me that his party has very warm relations with the Jamiat Party.

He said that the Russians have never attacked this area, and there has never been any fighting in Woygal and perhaps there will never be fighting in the future also. Even so, there are probably about 200 armed men, in case something does happen. He also said that they have machine guns and sniper rifles.

Jalal, my fellow traveler, is not familiar with the way from here on. Although he claims he can manage, how can I trust someone who has not been on this road before? Any mistake could lead us directly to an enemy base or we might end up wandering forever in the deep valleys of Kunar. I hope the new freedom fighters we met can find us a guide that knows the way.

The plan is that tomorrow we will depart and head toward Agook Pass. Agook Pass is not that high but it is very strategic because many paths pass through the top.

I am not so ravenously hungry anymore because Sultan and Akhtar organized a light meal for us. They also had tasty tea but, sadly, no sugar. I have to tell you something interesting about Woygal that I have noticed.

Most of the women and girls carry slingshots. They call these slingshots *palakhmaan*. While standing in their fields, they shout very loudly, 'Haay Haay,' and sling rocks over their fields so that the birds do not eat their seeds. It is mainly to scare sparrows. The women and the little girls have long black dresses with white and black headscarfs. They do not stand in a straight line but in a curved one. Most of them carry large wool-lined baskets made of goatskins on their backs. Their sparrow-scaring screams and shouts conjure up a beautiful scene for me, but do not ask the little sparrows how they feel.

People say that Nooristan, the *Land of Light*, is very hard on women because the men make their women do most of the work in their community but, when I asked a Nooristani woman three years ago, she gave me a different answer.

She said, "We like to go to the fields and work. Better to help our husbands whenever they need us or ask us to do so. Nature is very harsh here on all of us and we do not allow our husbands to do everything alone. Moreover, we take our children to the fields along with us. They enjoy it and learn how to be good farmers and shepherds."

There is no way to know the views of all the Nooristani women on this issue but, as I see it, the women in Nooristan work a lot more than other women in other parts of Afghanistan. They suffer silently in their daily lives and have a dark life in the *Land of Light*.

6:00 PM

A line of women is starting to walk down from the mountains, creeping into their muddy homes. Most bear loads of firewood, wild herbs, grass, and thorns on their hunched backs and some even carry their babies. A few of the younger ones are coming down fast and some of the older ones are taking their time and coming down slowly. Their small pretty animals follow them in straight lines. The streams of water, the pine trees, the cornfields, the river, the colorful goats, and cows look beautiful. While spreading the fragrance of wild herbs through the air, the wind seemed to be playing around each and everything. The sunset is marvelous. Some thin lines of smoke from a few muddy huts form beautiful circles over the village, disappearing into the evening breeze.

With all of these sweet smells, I am sure the spirit of the air lives happily and joyfully throughout the days and nights. Unfortunately, the land of Nooristan does not have much fruit. This is due to the climate, or, perhaps, the Nooristanis have been neglectful in not planting more fruit trees.

My dear, while in Nooristan, I always remember you and miss you.

Foot of Agook Pass
Friday, September 12
1:30 PM

We left the previous village at five in the morning, without having any food except a piece of dry cornbread. Now we are at the base of Agook Pass in the province of Kunar. I feel hungry because, for the last two days, we have eaten very little. It is thanks to my stolen sugar cubes that I have survived until now. Although poor Sultan brought me saltless oily cheese, I could not bear to eat it. It was my stomach's own fault.

The weather is very good. Jalaal and I traveled very slowly because we were still fairly tired and hungry, and I had very little strength to walk due to a general lack of energy. From this point, we are leaving the land of Nooristan and entering into the lands of the Gujur people.

Gujur people are a unique ethnic group in Afghanistan. They have their own origin, their own dialect, their own culture, and their own way of life. Their language is called Pashaee, which is spoken only by them. They are Sunni Muslims. Some of them speak Pashto and Dari too. They manage to live in peace and harmony with other ethnic groups. I tried to learn one or two sentences of their language before I reached here. It was hard. Gujurs look like other Afghans, only they have darker skin and darker eyes. Their eyebrows are thicker and their foreheads are wider. I wish I had time to learn more about them. They live mainly in the provinces of Kunar, Kapisa, and Nooristan.

Their shelters in the summer pastures are most striking. The insides are not very clean but, from the outside, they look very beautiful and are made of wood. Men come to these pastures to take care of their animals. Their clothes are different from those of the Nooristani people and the peoples of the northern provinces. Their animals are the same as in other northern provinces, except they do not have king goats and strong horses.

Today, I took a great picture of an old woman, with a kitten in a sling meant for a baby. The kitten clung to the woman in an adorable way. Perhaps the little kitten with its beautiful little eyes was also enjoying the ride and the beauty of nature around her. Despite her heavy load, the woman petted the little kitten in such a tender way, as if she were telling it a story. I wish I could see through the eyes of the little kitten to know what she was thinking.

I also took a photo of the kitten's mother for our son, Mahmud. I hope it comes out well.

Despite all this beauty around me, there were too many mosquitoes and a few annoying men in the pasture. These men were chewing on tobacco and spitting it out so loudly that I could not take a nap. At the same time, an argument broke out between the young men of Kunar and those of the Gujur tribe. The argument did not last very long. Thank God, they did not use their guns. One used his fist, but not so violently. I intervened in their fistfight and brought peace between them. It was not a serious tribal problem and later I found that the reason was that both were boasting of who was the braver fighter against the Russians.

What a people we have! The young freedom fighters sometimes need to expel their energy in one way or the other. Invariably, it turns into some sort of fight. This is life and things like this happen. Glad no one was killed.

3:00 PM

Despite Jalal's insistence that I should not, I left the previous pasture and now I am in a mosque, which is very clean with a beautifully carved wooden altar. They have crafted it from the trunk of a tree. The leaves of the pine and cedar trees cover the ground of the mosque. People do not have carpets here. The owner of the pasture is also the owner of the mosque.

It has started raining very heavily and this mosque has become a good refuge for me, at least for the time being. We started a fire in the middle of the room. The flames were so high and hot that it even warmed up my bones. The pasture owner kindly brought three cups of green tea. In such a state of exhaustion and with such cold weather, even one cup of tea would have given me a divine feeling. I asked Jalal, if he could buy a baby sheep and slaughter it, so that tonight we would all have something to eat. Despite the insistence of the pasture owner that he would arrange for everything, Jalal has already left to get a goat.

Tomorrow, in the morning, God willing, we will depart toward the Kunar River. The plan is then to cross the river in a locally constructed raft. These rafts are of a very particular construction. They consist of several mashks made of rubber or goatskin. They blow these rubber mashks and fill them with water. They connect ten or twenty of them together. Then they attach some planks of wood or flat timber atop them for people to sit on. Usually the sizes vary but the largest is about three by three meters.

The villagers call these rafts *jhaala*. The raft rider then guides his makeshift raft to the other side of the frightening, gray Kunar River which is probably close to two hundred meters across. The Kunar River is a very intense river filled with fast rapids. On these makeshift rafts, the raft rider transports fighters, horses, mules, and whatever else people need transported to the other side.

4:30 PM

It is around four in the afternoon. I was extremely tired and green tea had a wonderfully energizing effect on me. It caressed all of my body and spirit.

In front of me, there is another summer pasture, belonging to the Gujur tribe. The summer pasture looks so beautiful under the rain that I cannot express it in words.

The sunlight, after the rain, looks stunning as its rays fall upon the glistening grassy fields. Among other things, you can also see a few small hills on the sides of the high, green, rock-filled mountains. The dusty hills add something nice to the mountainous scenery. They are grazing lands for the animals and now gazing lands for my eyes to be filled with beauty. Hundreds of cows, goats, and sheep descend from the high mountains to these grazing fields and create a chorus of animal sounds, as if they are having some sort of serious discussion.

Earlier, I went to a nearby hill, and sat down alone to observe the beauty around me and think about my golden past and unknown future. The weather, which imbued the air around me with the finest fragrances, was heaven-sent. The dew-filled rays of the sun brought the most wonderful memories of the far past to my mind.

My reminiscing was suddenly disrupted by loud and constant machine gun fire. I knew that it was not far away. I thought that the Soviets might have attacked or the other opposition resistance parties were fighting each other. I called out to Jalaal to go and see what was going on. After a few minutes, though the gunfire did not stop, Jalaal returned, gasping for air after racing back to me. He told me that there was a child who had been circumcised and, in their own traditional way, the celebrants were shooting in the air with whatever guns they had to mark the boy's entrance into manhood.

8:30 PM

Jalal promised us a feast. Around six-thirty we had it. The goat they prepared was half-cooked and half-burnt. One part looked reddish and the other part blackish. The best thing was to mix the red and the black parts to make it edible. Whatever it was, this kebab tasted good to me. Even the half-cooked part was delicious. Jalal attempted to offer me the better parts of the goat, which were hard to find in such badly prepared meat, but since everyone was hungry, everyone enjoyed the kebab.

The men who were sitting next to the fire paid no attention to anything else but filling their hungry stomachs. Immediately after the meal, the teapot was ready. The tea was tasty. Despite the smell of oak smoke overpowering the taste of the black Indian tea, no one complained. One of the fighters offered me a little *gur*, a sort of rock-like sweet made of sugarcane. It was very hard and old and took me some minutes to chew into. While one or two of the men started to smoke cigarettes, I began to miss my Polish friend Andy and his British pipe. Thank God, even though we find ourselves in such a remote, impoverished area, we have been blessed with a good meal and a cup of tea, quality notwithstanding.

Every part of Afghanistan has its own stories of the holy war: some they are proud of and some they are not. In the Kunar province, which is one of the most important parts of Afghanistan, the fighters boast that they are the first who started fighting against the Soviets. They are right. They did start first. All of them remembered the fall of the first communist government garrison, by the hands of the resistance fighters of Kunar, when some military men from the regime defected to them and the fighters took control of the garrison.

One of the Kunari men announced loudly, "History will not forget the sounds of the first bullets shot by us against the first communist garrison." They claimed that 90 percent of their province is free now. They repeatedly told me that neither the Russians nor the communist regime has had the guts or power to move around freely in their areas. The Kunari men sitting around the fire with me belonged to the Pashtoon tribes. They were of the firm belief that freedom fighters all over Afghanistan should unite for the freedom of our land and for the sake of reaching heaven.

The leaders of the liberation movement had mixed opinions. Surprisingly, most of them who were sitting around me did not have a very negative image of Hekmatyar and his Hezb party, though they did not like him too much either. When I went on to talk to them more about different parties and the personalities of the leaders, I found that since Hekmatyar is a Pashtoon, they do not want to be openly critical of him, especially since he is a person they do not know so well. However, amongst them, one man was very much against Hekmatyar.

I think that is enough for tonight. Tomorrow will be a long road to pass and a 'hard track to beat.' What may be bothersome tonight are the smoke and sleeping in a small summer pasture hut of only four by four meters with nine other people. My sleeping bag is wet and outside is very cold and rainy.

Mareed Valley

September 12
3:30 PM

I am in the Mareed valley, deep inside the Kunar province. It is raining and hailing intensely. I am sure it is good for the dry skin of the earth but not for the thin skin of a traveler like me. The wind is blowing fast but not as fast as the wind I experienced on the mountain peaks of Nooristan.

We left early today, about 5:00 AM. It was still dark and wet but the sweet smell of unknown herbs filled my lungs and gave me energy. The breeze pleasantly mingled with the silver-colored dawn. Have you ever heard of a colorful breeze? If not, come and stay here for a night. Without tea or a piece of bread, we started our journey and walked for almost ten hours.

After two hours' walking, the rain started again. The hail followed. Thank God, we did not have a horse or a donkey because it would have made our lives miserable. Slowly, we entered the heartland of the Gujur tribe. The little Gujuri children were happily tending their animals, despite the slapping of the rain on their faces and the whipping of the hail on their backs. For them, with their thin necks and thinner legs, running in dense forest was just like gambling in a playground. They ran so fast through the trees, like hunters chasing rabbits to their holes. I wish I were one of them.

The Gujur tribe is one of the smallest minority tribes in Afghanistan. They are such a tolerant, tough, and hardworking people.

Let me tell you something that I think you may like. On the way down from the mountain, I reached a beautiful valley with sweet water streams and dense forestry. I drank some water from the crystal-clear stream and asked my co-travelers if they had anything to eat but they had nothing. Some small muddy huts of the poor Gujuri people added to the beauty of the valley. I asked Jalal to let me take some minutes' rest. While trying to grab a quick five-minute nap, I heard some shouting from three different corners of the narrow valley.

They were women's voices crossing back and forth. I paid more attention and found that the female voices seemed to be moving in the air around me. The shouts back and forth were very quick. I paid more attention and realized that the noisy voices were part of a rapid conversation. I knew it was the Gujuri dialect but could not understand it and asked a Gujur boy to tell me what they were saying.

He simply said, "Those voices in the air are of Gujur girls talking to one another about how to get to an upcoming wedding."

It was amazing that in an area of four to five hundred meters, three to four girls were communicating comfortably from different directions through their small windows. It went on for more than five minutes.

I asked another boy, "What is going on in the air?"

He simply said, "They are Gujur girls. They are talking to each other from their homes that are situated in the four corners of the forest."

I asked, "Can they see each other?"

He had a look on his face as if he was thinking hard and said, "I do not know if they can see each other or not but surely they know each other's voices."

I then realized that another two or three voices seemed to have joined in this long distance shouting conversation. These new voices came from different directions and distances throughout the forest. I have heard the howling of the wolves, communicating to one another in the middle of the night, but not the shouting voices of humans communicating in such a unique way. It was an amazing experience for me.

I enjoyed the way the women were talking to one another, and wished that I could shout a comment in their direction too.

I asked another young boy who was chasing his big dog, "Do you understand what they are saying?"

He laughed and said, "I do not really understand when girls talk but they are talking about some kind of wedding."

I truly missed an excellent opportunity to record their voices. Sadly, I did not have a tape recorder.

Well, it was wonderful that their messages and words seemed to be carried on the wings of the wind, back and forth, and, maybe, if the birds would sing in between, one of the girls would shout, "Do not disturb our airwaves, we are talking." To me it felt like a dream. You could not even imagine such a place until you have lived it and seen it with your own eyes.

7:30 PM

Right now, I am still in the heart of the land of the Gujurs. The Gujur hut, in which I am sitting, is also used as a stable. It is the first time that I stay with a family on this journey of mine. Let me tell you how I got here.

The river had burst its banks and transformed into a muddy torrent. We crossed the riverlets instantly formed by the flood with great difficulty. The locals are used to flooding and put the narrowest of long planks across the raging water courses. The Gujur men cross by these planks with no difficulty.

For Jalaal and me, it was harder, because the waters were deep and turbulent and the planks were narrow, slippery, and shaky because of the intense rain. My vertigo and inability to swim did not help my nerves.

Crossing these narrow planks, I kept my eyes almost permanently closed and my legs shook like a criminal's before an angry judge. We crossed over at least twenty narrow planks, which shook up and down like hanging cradles. To me it seemed like *Pul-e-Salaat*, the Doomsday Bridge, which all Muslims should cross on Judgment Day. If anything, these slippery planks looked more dangerous, thinner, and higher than the *Salaat* bridge.

That was the moment Nasrat, Adam Khan's eldest son appeared from nowhere and said, "Salaam, our hut is near, why don't you just come and pass the night with us." I instantly accepted and without even looking at Jalaal, followed the boy. His hut sits on the edge of the mountain with fantastic, divine views.

The mountainside where his hut was located was covered with oak and pine trees. My poor young God-sent host was probably about 12 years old. He grabbed my hand, guided me to his hut, and pulled me inside. What a warm and welcoming hand from a poor unknown host! Our little host sat us down in his warm hut and told us that for the night, we should feel like this was our home. The warmth of the hut and the warmth of this little child welcoming us, made me thank God for this blessing. His father, Adam Khan, was sitting quietly. His younger brother, sister, mother, and his unclean dog were sitting with us as well, since their hut had only one room.

Despite their poverty, it seemed as though they were the richest of families offering us the little corn they had. Maybe it is good that they do not know of the material world that exists beyond them. Here ignorance is bliss. Luckily, Jalaal had kept a piece of meat with him in his rucksack from the barbequed goat from the previous night.

We divided the meat among the Gujur children, and I told Jalal to give the bone to the dog but the big brother of Nasrat had already given some of his own share of meat with him. I then noticed that the mother threw a tiny piece of meat toward the dog as well. To me, it showed their kindness even more. It is 10:00 in the night. We drank some herbal tea. Listen carefully to what we waited for. It was very interesting to see and more interesting to write it to you. Adam Khan, the father of Nasrat, stood up, came toward the fire, and put a brick into it. After a second, he took the brick out of the fire, sat down, and pressed it against the right side of his jaw. He seemed in pain

His wife said, "He has been in severe pain for a month because of his tooth. We brought two spiritual healers who claimed they could help. Since their prayers did not help, we asked the barber to come."

We had not even finished talking when a man entered. I instantly thought that he is probably the barber the mother talked of. He was a very interesting looking man. He was tall, big, and had a long black beard, which reached right to his belly button. Of all the beards I have seen in the world, his seemed very unique to me, like an upside down pyramid. His mustache was thin, on one side and thicker on the other. His salt-and-pepper hair color that could be seen from underneath his white turban, made him look even more stylish. The turban he wore which had a Jewish looking black cap on the top, gave him an even nicer look. He had used *surma* around his big green eyes, which made his eyes look twice as big. He wore an Afghan *payron* and *tombon* or Afghan traditional clothes.

I could also see two oval shaped *taaweez* or talisman pinned to his left shoulder in order to ward away any evil eye toward him. The two, leather covered talisman looked like two forgotten walnuts hanging from the branch of a walnut tree. He also wore a long muffler that came down to his hips. Although his clothes were not clean, they were at least cleaner than what I was wearing. He had traditional Pashtoon sandals on his feet and wore a deep green vest with some golden string sewn on both of his large side pockets. He was carrying an old bag, which seemed dirtier than his sandals. It was so big that I thought he could have carried a baby goat inside.

He shook hands with me and then with Adam Khan. Their dog started barking at the barber and he instantly pulled his long legs back, kicked the dog and shouted, *Eestasha!* or get away.

To me, this was probably the most stylish and unique barber in the world and was definitely different from barbers in the North. He sat cross-legged on one of the mattresses and started to look inside his bag for something. It was clear he knew that he was here to help the poor pain-ridden Adam Khan because he did not ask any questions from anyone.

Without any delay, he ordered one of the boys to bring some water. Nasrat brought it instantly. The barber took it, had a sip, gargled the rest and spat it out. It was funny to me because I thought he would ask the patient to gargle the water but he himself did so.

Very confidently, he ordered Adam Khan to sit in front of him, so that he could look into his mouth. Jalaal, the boys, the mother, and I, including the dog, were all watching every move of this confident barber. When he finally started looking into Adam Khan's mouth, I told myself that now the barber has taken on the role of a dentist, having graduated from the school of his own experience, run in his family line.

Well, the operation on Adam Khan, the patient, started. The dentist/barber took out a very old rusted tool of sorts, tapped one of the teeth of Adam Khan with it and asked, "Is it this God-damned tooth?"

Before the dentist/barber could even finish his question, Adam Khan shuttered in pain and it was obvious that the dentist/barber had touched the right one.

The dentist/barber laughed aloud and said, "Don't cry like a goat."

I laughed too after hearing this and told him, "Subhaan Allah, God is merciful. You found the exact infected tooth in a second without any technology. I am very impressed."

He looked at me and said, "Brother, you do not know me. I am called Jamaal Khan and everyone knows me in this area. There are seven elite barber families in the whole world and my family is one of them. I cut the hair, shave the beards, trim the mustaches, circumcise the kids, give massages, fix broken bones, and of course take out these evil teeth."

I said louder than he had replied to me, "Yes, I can see. It definitely looks like it."

While Jamaal Khan, the barber/dentist, was busy working with his hands in Adam Khan's mouth, he told me, "Maybe you do not know of people like me. You have dentists in Kabul. They are worthless. They charge a lot of money and even then, the patients still have pain in their teeth. My grandfather took care of twenty five patients a day, without any delay and he was not a doctor."

Here I could not hold my laughter and admiration and said, "Jamaal Khan, as a matter of fact, a barber like you had taken out one of my teeth as well about three years ago in the Panjshir valley."

He looked away from Adams Khans mouth and asked, "Do you know Commander Masood?"

Without waiting for an answer, he turned back to Adam Khan, the patient, and murmured, "He is a brave man and you must also be a good fighter."

Once again, it looked like he made sure that he had found the right tooth because he again tapped the dirty tool on it. He nodded his head and looked ready to take it out but reached back into his bag and brought out a very dirty handkerchief, which seemed even dirtier than the tool itself and started to clean it. I did not think it was possible but I am sure that in his mind, the dirty handkerchief did a great job of cleaning his tool.

At this moment, he looked around, saw Jalaal and shouted at him, "Where are you from? Do not sit idle. Come and sit on the shoulders of Adam Khan so he does not move."

While Jalaal was sitting on the shoulders of the pain-ridden Adam Khan, the mother was murmuring prayers, the astonished children and their confused dog were watching, the barber loudly said, "In the name of God and the Holy Prophet."

As soon as he said this, he pulled back on the dirty tool that was attached to Adam Khan's tooth and with one smooth and strong motion, the tooth was out. Jamaal the dentist had a smile on his face. All of us were relieved to see the bloody tooth of Adam Khan sitting nicely on top of the tooth-pulling tool of the barber.

Paying no attention to what had just happened to poor Adam Khan, the winds were blowing, the stars were hanging, the rivers were flowing, the moon was shining, and the dogs were barking. Life went on. Amazingly, Adam Khan seemed to be feeling much better. The little daughter was the first to ask, "How are you, *plara* [father]?"

After all the shouting and painful procedure, Adam Khan smiled and told his daughter, "Thank you my dear, I am fine."

The mother smiled, the little sons laughed, the little dog barked, Jalaal relaxed, and I whole-heartedly said to the barber, "God bless you, our dear barber-dentist-surgeon. Now, I even like your dirty handkerchief."

Saying Goodbye

Village of Sukee
September 13, 1986
7:00 AM

Last night, since the fire had lost its brightness and warmth, I stopped writing. I was not able to sleep because the dog was barking for no reason or he had a reason that I could not understand. I went out of the room at least three times to order the dog to allow me to sleep, but he kept barking. Maybe, he was angry because he did not like the way the barber dealt with his owner, Adam Khan.

I called Jalal to help me but he was sleeping like a baby goat. I called him again but he just suggested that I should close my eyes, think about nothing, and simply go to sleep. When I called him for the third time, he simply said, "Khalili Sahib, you may have a problem with your stomach, rub it hard for five minutes, and then go to sleep." I did and it worked to some extent, although I had no problem with my stomach."

I performed my early morning prayers and then wanted to take a nap for a few more minutes when the roaring voice of Adam Khan woke me up.

His face looked like that of an inexperienced boxer who has been punched a hundred times on his face. It was so swollen that his jaw looked almost as big as his head. I tried to hide my laughter, but it was not easy. The first thing I asked him was about his tooth.

He replied, "After a whole month of toothache, last night I slept like a sheep in the warm cave of a kind shepherd. I am sorry that it was not an appropriate time for the barber to come. We bothered you. Since he has lot of work to do, he does not give us an exact time for his arrival. He comes whenever he can."

I told him, "Adam Khan, this was a great experience for me. I am happy that you feel good and even happier to know that you slept like a sheep. Thank you for the kind hospitality."

Whatever little money I tried to offer him, he declined. When leaving him, I looked at him and his poor Gujuri family and told myself that generosity does not belong to the higher or lower classes, big or small people, with full or empty pockets, but to the big hearts.

At about five-thirty in the early morning, we left the area of Brollo. The dog of the Gujur family chased us for some minutes. On our way, we stopped for a short break in the village of Mareed. It was a small village and we quickly passed through it. Once again, we had to jump from one rock to another like wounded monkeys. Once again, we had to use those snake-like planks for crossing the river, like fearful circus boys walking on the tight rope. God saved me, because, walking over these planks with closed eyes, I did not fall down into the muddy river. Of course, I slipped many times but did not fall.

I am writing to you from the village of Sukee. From here, it will take another four hours to reach the last river of our journey, the Kunar River. God willing, once we cross that river, our problems will be over. From the river onward, we will still have another four hours to go until we reach the border of Pakistan, which will be the end of my journey.

I am currently in a small room that they call a hotel. It has nothing: no food, no bread, and no tea, but still it is called a hotel. Some minutes ago, the owner of this hotel showed up. I asked him why he calls it a hotel when he has nothing to offer. He exclaimed with pride, "Are you blind? At least, it has four walls and two windows."

We were very hungry and there was no one around to help us find some food. Jalaal tried to give some flour to a household so that they might cook it for us but, sadly, no one accepted. Then I had to take the risk and introduce myself to a man from the Khaalis Party. He was very happy to see me. He happily accepted to do whatever he could to help me and promised that he would also inform someone from my party about my arrival. He instantly went and brought a young man from the Jamiat Party and both of them arranged some food for us. A man from the Mahammadi group also joined us and invited me to be his guest in his home. Since it was far away, I did not accept.

Anyway, thanks to the hunger, which forced me to introduce myself, I found no shortage of people to talk with. Luckily, the Khaalis Party members were even more welcoming to me than others were. They asked me to convey their regards to their leader if I see him in Peshawar. I know their leader. Khaalis is around 65–70 years old and, just recently, got married to a relatively young girl. He visits my father often. He is also a good friend of Ustad Rabbani, the leader of the Jamiat Party. His main commander is Abdul Haq from Nangarhar. Khaalis is a Sufi type of Mullah and knows lot of Sufi poetry.

While talking to these men, another group of young commanders was informed that I was here, and they joined us too. In no time, they kindly offered me their services. Thanks once again to hunger which forced me to introduce myself; otherwise, I would have passed this area without talking to these nice people. They were all from the Pashtoon tribes of the east. All were very brave, determined, traditional, and even knew about how the war was going in other parts of the country.

When I was talking and used the word freedom, more than the word *Jihad*, one of them asked me, "What do you mean by freedom?"

I replied, "Freedom is freedom. We no longer have the Russians occupying our country is what I mean by freedom."

He said, "Khalili Sahib, this is just one side of freedom. The other side is to be good and faithful human beings."

I then said, "Let us first take freedom from the hands of the enemy and then we will work on the other side."

Another very graceful looking spiritual elder of about 60–65 years old said, "We have to work on both simultaneously, freedom from the enemy within ourselves and freedom from the enemy without."

I liked it very much and said, "I like the way you articulated your view that we have to work on the enemy, within and without."

One of the commanders who was sitting in a corner, instantly asked, "I can kill the enemy from the outside with a gun but how can I kill the enemy within?"

The elder looked at him and said, "You do not need a gun for this but good deeds. Fighting against your own enemy, within your own self, is a much harder fight than against any enemy in this world."

Zahir Gul, who had recited a poem earlier asked, "What is the easiest way to win the war inside ourselves?"

The elder calmly told him, "Be good to your family and take care of your poor people."

What a marvelous discussion we had! I enjoyed it so much that it even took away my tiredness. It was time for me to depart again. I had spent about an hour in this village. I thanked them for their tea, hospitality, and wonderful conversation. They all decided that I should not go alone and they insisted on providing security for me. Both the Jamiat and Khaalis men assigned their armed fighters to accompany me. Despite my objection, five men from each party accompanied me to take care of my security until I cross the Kunar River.

Flying Dragon, Nile and Noah

It is now eight in the evening. We crossed the river and reached here, a village named Kayee Dera, about an hour ago. This is our last stop in Afghanistan.

My dearest, thank you for patiently traveling with me until here, and now listen to the last episode. We walked for more than eleven and a half hours to reach here. It was indeed a long walk. Despite all the problems and anxieties of the road and the difficulties of the tracks, the valleys and the mountains we crossed were extremely beautiful. Unfortunately, we did not enjoy the scenery fully because the paths were so narrow and dangerous that we had to keep our eyes always on the path.

Close to the river, the Soviets and their puppets had destroyed most of the houses. The trees had dried up and the water channels were ruined. We walked very fast from Sukee to the river, which took us about two hours instead of the predicted three and half. The closer we got to the river, the hotter the weather became. I had wounds on my shoulders and knees due to our fast trekking, the heat, and the weight of my backpack. I did not give my bag to any of the men traveling with me in the last hours. It was the wrong decision, but I stuck to that decision up to the end. It means I have real Afghan blood; I am stubborn.

On the way, the Saw valley was exceptionally beautiful. We are currently sitting in a small restaurant that has all that we need: tea, candy, biscuits, food, and fruit. Since the border city of Pakistan called Banshee is just five hours walk, they get their foodstuffs easier. The name of the restaurant owner is Ashraf Khan.

In our hearts and minds, we feared crossing the killer Kunar River but no one wanted to talk about it. Even though I had crossed that river two times before, it was from safer crossing points. From what I remember about the last time I crossed it, we only had to worry about the danger of landmines, not enemy ambushes or bombardments.

This is why the commander of the group of freedom fighters there for my security, approached me and calmly said: "We have to make ourselves ready for the last part of the journey, which will be the most dangerous part. It is not just the river or landmines, which pose us the greatest danger, but government or Russian forces, who may create problems here, by bombarding or ambushing us."

He advised me that I should listen to him carefully. Although it was not new to me, I accepted and told him that he is totally in charge of this part of the trip. He also warned me that we would walk for at least seven hours in the minefields, which would be like walking on a naked wire or hidden fire.

We started very carefully. The paths were so rocky, narrow, and slippery that a single second of carelessness could result in one of us falling off a cliff or stepping on an anti-personnel mine. He reminded me that, in the last six years, many children and old people have lost their lives by those killing mines. My bodyguards were warning me every ten minutes to take care of my steps, that I should not touch anything strange looking.

We did not have mine detectors or any other tool to discover where these hidden killers would be waiting for us. Thank God, we passed the first part of the minefields with few problems, except one, which was a real tragedy. We were walking along, concentrating very hard on the path.

We were advancing very slowly when, suddenly, there was an extremely loud explosion some meters ahead of me and, almost instantly, I was covered in sand and dirt.

My ears were ringing from the explosion and my eyes were blinded from the dirt. There were fighters in front and behind me and I did not know what to do. Therefore, we just hunched down in the same spot we had been standing in. The commander shouted, "No one move from their locations!"

He had not even finished saying this when another mine went off. We sat still in our spots for at least ten long, frightening minutes.

When the smoke and dust settled, the first thing I saw was the body of a young man who had stepped on a land mine. He was laying on the bloody ground, very seriously injured. He was about ten yards from me. Another younger boy, who was sitting close to him, had suffered some injuries to his arms and face. He had blood and dirt all over him but, other than slight shock, he seemed fine.

Once again, the commander instructed everyone not to move. He told us that he was going to attempt to try to help the bleeding boy. He slowly inched his way toward him, taking one step at a time. He finally reached the boy who was screaming in pain. The young fighter had lost the foot on one leg and badly injured the other. The commander grabbed him by the arm and shouted at him to keep himself as compact as possible. Slowly and with much care, the commander pulled the boy back toward the path we were taking to cross the minefield. He kept shouting at the young man to be strong and that God is with him.

When he reached a safe spot, the commander stopped, looked around, and when he spotted me, he shouted, "Khalili Sahib, you and the rest of the men move on because there is still a possibility of bombardment. I will stay with two of my men and help this boy through. Do not rush and stay on the path. You will be fine. Keep praying and do not worry."

When we approached the killer Kunar River, we were told to wait while our bodyguards went to check that the way was clear of enemy ambushes and the threat of bombardments. I insisted that I would go and see for myself. At first, none of them agreed, but then they reluctantly accepted. The tracks became narrower, the minefields wider, and the enemy ambush zone closer.

Around noon, three sinister helicopters flew very low above us but did not attack. We stopped to see if they would return. Our fears were justified when they showed up again. Although this time they flew lower than the tree tops, they did not fire immediately on our positions, but withdrew once again. Only on their third sortie, did they finally unleash their rockets. The first barrage fell short of their target but still managed to get within about 50 meters of us.

I cannot describe the loud boom of the exploding rockets all around us, or how the dust, smoke, and flames filled the sky. I felt the reverberation from the impact of the rockets right in my chest and stomach. Some mines, close to us, exploded too. By this stage, we were sure that we were the targets. We could not move much because of the mines. Except for one bodyguard, who received a minor injury, everybody else was safe.

After half an hour of waiting, we started to move on and once again the menacing helicopters showed up and started to attack us. This time, it was dangerously close. I was very scared and could not think of anything but death. Dust, smoke, and fire created hell around us but, miraculously, once again, no one was injured. We waited another half an hour and, thank God, they did not show up again but we knew that more dangers still awaited us. Just a week ago, this river swallowed up three innocent lives from one family in her killing rapids. The river crossing would soon come but, for now, we still had to worry about the mines and the attack helicopters.

As the killer Kunar River roared, those trifold dangers maliciously threatened us: mines, direct attacks, and the river itself. Any minute, we could be the victims of any danger or all three at once. Therefore, we approached these challenges cautiously and gradually. The men around me were indeed experienced enough to give me confidence that we would succeed in crossing the river. When we reached close to the river, the commander told us to walk speedily but cautiously to the riverbank.

Although it was not my first time standing on the bank of this killer Kunar River, it was the most frightening. At first glance, the river looked to me like a gray dragon creeping forward and invisibly changing its position. For me it was a mixture of two fears, the dramatic fear of imminent danger and mundane phobia. Fear of the war because it was a sinister fatal reality and phobia of the rapids because I could not swim.

Strangely, in that very moment, I remembered my Delhi University professor, teaching us about the difference between fear and phobia. It helped me a lot to convince myself that I suffered more from phobia than fear. In order to calm my senses, I kept telling myself that all the dangers around me, whether they were Russian raids or river rapids, were all phobias.

We were moving forward more cautiously. The men repeatedly advised me to be careful of my steps in order not to touch the mines. I already knew from my own experience that the closer we got to the river, the wider and wilder the minefields would become.

On the riverbank, a painful scene awaited. So many children, old women and men, farm animals, including a pair of camels, and several small dogs were waiting to use the smallest and most primitive looking raft I had ever seen to cross one of the most dangerous rivers in the world.

At least a hundred people and their animals were gathered there. A small girl, who had been wounded some hours before by a land mine, was laying on a piece of flat wood. She was bleeding from her face, hand, and head. The poor thing was unconscious, while her mother was screaming and asking everyone for help. Another woman was carrying her sick child in her arms. An old man was helping his elderly and sick wife to avoid triggering the land mines around them. The raftsman was nowhere to be seen.

I asked about him. They said that his brother had been killed in a bombardment and he was busy burying him. There was no one else to run the raft. Before they could finish telling me about the raftsman, I saw a group of liberation fighters rush forward and start working in order to ready the raft. It was not an easy job. None of them had any experience in this regard.

They had to try to fix the raft as quickly as possible if they had any hope of helping the wounded and, even more importantly, avoiding being hit by another bombardment. Everybody was praying for the young fighters to ready the raft more quickly, so that they could all cross the river. The mother of the wounded, unconscious child was praying louder then all of us. Although Pakistan lay far away and the shadow of death was hovering above her child, in very broken Pashto, I said to her, "*Gham makhura khora. Inshallah khuday komak ba wokee.*" (Do not worry, my sister, God will help her).

Listen to what happened next. The men were busy preparing the raft for launch when the sinister sound of two Russian helicopters was heard in the distance. We all looked toward the sky. I looked up and saw the evil helicopters slowly hovering toward us. They looked like two terrifying sky dragons, flying over the ferocious creeping river dragon.

Oh God, a new tragedy was upon us. At the sight of these flying dragons, the mother of the wounded child started screaming loudly, "Allah, Allah, Doomsday is upon us!"

The other men and women began to flee in terror, in every direction. It was a natural reaction.

The dragons' attack started and they mercilessly targeted our location and rained fire down upon us. The sounds of rockets, the burning breath of fire, and the tremors of the earth made every one fall motionless and silent. Even the mother of the wounded child stopped screaming. As all of this was happening around me, all I could do was to pray in my heart for an end to this hell.

Then suddenly, the sound of dragons' wings were gone. They had left. For ten minutes or more, what seemed like a year, we stood confused and shell shocked, amidst the smoke and fire. I felt like all the dust and smoke around us entered into my body, stomach, mouth, ears, eyes, and even under my skin. At this moment, my bodyguards rushed to check if I was injured but I asked them to take care of the little child and his mother first. Thank God, the child was fully unconscious and had no idea what had happened. Her mother had braved the attack without injury. In fact, only one old man had been injured, but not very severely. The rest were miraculously unharmed.

The men started again to make the raft ready. It was very hard. No one knew how to accomplish this task. They needed some stays to fix the mashks or rubber containers together. We could neither go back, nor could go forward. As our proverb goes, 'the ground is hard, the sky is far.'

We were helpless. We could not even help each other. No one dared cross the river by swimming while its thick waves and gray rapids roared menacingly. I could hear the whispers of poor unarmed people beseeching God for help so that the flying dragons would not show their fiery faces once again.

Everybody thought that if the helicopters appear once more, there would be a massacre. All of a sudden, three men arrived.

Everybody started shouting to them, "May you not be tired. O, brave young men."

You know who they were? They were the real raftsmen. They had heard the sounds of rockets and Russian helicopters and had rushed to help the people waiting to cross. They know what happens when unfortunate travelers become trapped in such a situation. The head raftsman had left halfway through his own brother's burial and rushed to help us.

The mother of the bleeding girl heaved a sigh of relief when she saw the raftsmen. In less than half an hour, these brave young raftsmen made the raft secure.

Who should go first in the raft? It was small and it could not take more than eight to ten people at a time. My bodyguards asked me to go in the first round. I pointed to the wounded child, her screaming mother, the wounded old man, and several old white-haired women. Because the bank was five meters higher than the river, first, the bleeding girl and her mother were carefully helped down. After them, they took the others one by one, and then I went down toward the raft.

Just as I was getting on, a small, unclean dog jumped onto the raft with us. The raftsman kicked the little dog, shouting, "Don't let that dirty dog on board."

At that moment, without even looking at the raftsman, the mother of the bleeding child, very innocently pointed to her daughter and said, "It is my injured daughter's dog."

The raftsman looked at the mother, then at the wounded girl for a long second, and allowed the dog to stay.

The bleeding girl was in a deep coma. She did not know the raftsman's unforgettable generosity but God was not unconscious and was a witness to what he did.

Before departure, the raftsman looked up to the sky and prayed loudly to God for help in conquering the killer Kunar River and safely crossing to its far bank. He unfastened the rope holding the raft to the bank and, suddenly, the raft started to drift out and onto the rapids.

The creeping dragon river rolled. The raftsman looked like Prophet Noah. Gray waves tossed and turned like cruel enemies. The raft moved forward. The rapids became faster. The Soviet helicopters, which might return at any minute to kill, were never far from our thoughts. The old wounded man was still in pain. The girl was still bleeding. The mother was weeping. I was in tears. The dog did not know what on earth was going on.

But in the end, we all safely crossed the killer Kunar River.

Disembarking from the raft on the far bank, I said to my own soul, "War is not a phobia, it is fear and terror! May God banish it from our beautiful planet forever! Amen."

A Separate Note for the Last Page

September 13, 1986

My dear, right now, I am still writing to you, immersed in the warm, wonderful weather which today blesses our homeland. Tomorrow, God willing, I will be with you, in the lap of my own loved ones, but in the land of others.

On this journey, I have written to you of many things, which might be interesting and prove useful in the future. These are my personal experiences of this journey and are meant for you and my boys. I have written extensively in other notebooks observations and plans of a military and political nature, which may be for the good of others.

However, with these softer words, which I have written specially for you, do two things: first, read them all by yourself and then to our boys. Second, when the Soviet invaders are kicked out, their communist stooges are defeated, Afghanistan is free, the glorious flag of my beloved land flutters freely on its high mountains, in its deep valleys, and its poor cities, try to publish them all. If I am alive, we will do it together; and if not, do whatever you want. You are always in my heart and in my prayers.

September 13, 1986, Afghanistan

Epilogue

Believe it or not, reading the notes I wrote 35 years ago to my beloved wife, I can still hear and feel the heartbreaking cry of the boy, "Oh, do not kill me, please. I am a good boy. Last year some gunmen killed my dear father. Do not kill me, I am a good boy." Or the sound of the old woman who was lamenting in her dark closet, requesting her grandson, "I do not want to leave my home. I do not want to become a refugee. I love my home. I want to die here in my old closet".

And I can also still hear and see in my dreams or nightmares the roars of the jets, the sound of the exploding bombs, the burning of the houses, and the dead bodies of the innocent people killed by the invading Soviet army and its Afghan puppets.

The unfortunate part of the situation is that despite so many things have happened since then and so many new ones happening now, sadly, the tears of the poor people never dried, the pain of the innocent fathers and mothers never disappeared, the suffering of the children never ended, and the hearts of victims never stopped bleeding because the sinister war still continues in different forms and colors.

After almost thirty years of having written these notes you have patiently read, the events pass in front of my eyes as if I am sitting in a cinema hall and watching a classic movie about the destiny of poor human beings with many sour and sweet scenes. Let me invite you to sit beside me and watch some of the events that happened after *Whispers of War.*

First, look at these happy shots set in 1992 in which the Russians and their puppets are defeated and we freedom fighters are victoriously entering Kabul, the capital of Afghanistan. The people are happily welcoming us by burning candles to show us their joyous hearts. The sky is filled with smiles, laughs, hopes, and welcoming greetings. They are happy that the Russian soldiers have left and their land is now free. They congratulate each other for the freedom they have gained by making so many sacrifices. They are hopeful that their land will no longer look like a killing field or a burnt garden. They are proud to be the conquerors of the Cold War.

But wait for the sad scenes too. In no time, the situation is changing into a new war and a new misery because the people who won the war, lost peace. Look at the hundreds of rockets raining over the poor people of Kabul. Ah, I remember what a young widow told me: "We waited for so long, thinking that you may bring back our happy life but you freedom fighters shattered our hopes and killed our dreams."

A kind of civil war began mainly because the Afghan Mujahideen or freedom fighters were not at all prepared for what would happen when they would win the war and gain their freedom. Intelligence agencies of the neighboring countries, especially those of Pakistan, Iran, and Uzbekistan, started interfering in our internal affairs. Finally, our friends who helped us in our liberation war against the Russians totally abandoned us. For them, the 'heroes' of yesterday became the 'zeroes' of today.

Hence, Kabul and other major cities were again being burnt and destroyed by rockets used by the internal enemies, helped from outside. This continued for five years until the Taliban captured power in Kabul and created an even worse hell throughout the country. Hundreds died, injured, maimed, and left their beloved homes. Schools burnt; hospitals closed down; and radio, TV, and newspapers shut down. The freedom that people gained through so many sacrifices was shattered by the fanatic ideas of the Taliban.

In no time, Al Qaida, a super fanatic and terrorist organization was encouraged, trained, armed, and given shelter by the Taliban in Afghanistan. Thousands of Al Qaida members, led by their leader Osama bin Laden and helped by the intelligence services of Pakistan, started to prepare themselves to reach central Asia and, if possible, the rest of the world.

Life was not easy. Every day, we were losing our people and dear friends. When I now read *Whispers of War*, I see that many of my friends and most of the other people mentioned in the book are either killed or injured.

Commander Massoud repeatedly warned the world, especially the United States, that one day Al Qaida will reach their shores. No one believed him, or maybe, they did not want to believe him.

The tragedy continued and turned into a more painful story. It was September 9, 2001. I was sitting beside my friend Commander Massoud, the hero of Afghanistan, the conqueror of the Cold War, when two suicide bombers, pretending to be journalists, sent by

Osama bin Laden detonated their bombs that killed him and seriously injured me. I survived while losing one eye and carrying hundreds of small shrapnel pieces in my body. What a loss! Afghanistan lost a beloved hero and I lost a heroic friend.

The story does not end there but turns into an even more tragic one. Just two days after the killing of Commander Massoud, on September 11, Al Qaida attacked the World Trade Center towers in New York and the Pentagon. Thousands were killed or injured and a new phase began in the world. The superpower finally woke up, instantly mobilized the world, and attacked the Taliban and Al Qaida in Afghanistan.

A new war started, at least this time, to help us. The poor masses who suffered under the Taliban's fanatic heels welcomed the NATO forces, supported by the UN and led by the US army.

The Taliban and Al Qaida were temporarily defeated and people luckily got a chance to move on. The hopes for a better future replaced the fears from the past. Women were becoming much freer to express themselves. The light of the dawn closed the door on the dark night. The ghosts of the Taliban were no longer overshadowing people's poor huts and homes. Girls and boys began to go to schools, participating in all social and political activities as well. Kids started to fly kites again. A new and hopeful generation was freely and fearlessly walking on social pavements to build their future. Reconstruction of the country started. Schools, universities, hospitals, roads, political institutions, constitution, free media, army, and police force were built or rebuilt. Presidential and parliamentary elections were held. People started to see that their hopes were gradually being fulfilled and their dreams of a developing and peaceful Afghanistan were coming true. Millions of girls and boys were given the chance to go to schools all over the country. Freedom of movement, expression, and media opened a window, if not a door, for my freedom-thirsty people.

This is not a comparison with the past, but if you want a simple comparison, try to remember the story of the pencil in *Whispers of War* when there were just two pencils for the whole class and the story of the cave–operation room that looked like a butcher shop.

Wait, the war movie has not ended yet! After all, we are human beings, not donkeys. Have you ever heard about or seen a donkey killing and burning the house of another donkey? But bad human beings do this. The warmongers and fanatics are still preparing themselves in Pakistan to write a new scenario of war.

After six years of progress and hope, the Taliban and Al Qaida, though weaker, reappeared. Terrorism entered the scene clearer than before. Suicide attacks started and international terrorists joined the battle. Burning, injuring, killing, kidnapping, crying, and weeping slowly started to show their ugly faces in the life of my people again. Fear started to replace hope.

As I write this epilogue, sitting beside my wife for whom I wrote *Whispers of War*, we still hear every day the cry of the hundreds of victims of the war launched by a different form of the Taliban and their international fanatic friends. We watch on media channels the tearful eyes of mothers whose kids sank in the oceans while fleeing their beloved homes to take refuge in the calmer countries of Europe. Three days ago, at least 150 innocents were killed or injured by the Taliban in Kabul. In the last seven years, hundreds of schools have either been closed or burnt. Every day, mothers' hearts are full of fear about whether their kids would come back home alive from schools. Every day, dozens of young boys and girls in uniform give their lives to protect their land from terror attacks. In the last two years, thousands have left the country because of insecurity and extreme poverty.

At this point, I cannot stop myself from remembering my friends as well as thousands and thousands of young freedom fighters who have been killed over the years in the war against the Soviets in the 1980s, the civil war in the early 1990s, and the war against the Taliban in the late 1990s. From President Burhanuddin Rabbani to other patriotic friends, people have died defending their country from our enemies or trying to bring peace. Not only have Afghans died for our freedom but after September 11, 2001, thousands of young men and women from militaries around the world have died to bring freedom to this poor, war-torn country. All of them—Afghans and foreign fighters—died heroes.

You might ask, "What are the reasons for the situation remaining the same and the poor people of Afghanistan not seeing peace in their war-torn country"? Let me try and make it easy for you.

The corrupt Afghan government's lack of honesty; absence of trusted leader(s); insufficient rule of law; political instability; open interference of neighbors, especially Pakistan, by sheltering, encouraging, training, financing, and arming terrorists; Afghanistan being the poorest economy in Asia; global terrorism; and the gradual weakening and even relative withering away of international interests for Afghanistan are sadly the causes pushing the situation for the country to look even scarier and more brutal.

But is it the end? No, it is not the end. Despite the cowardly, brutal, and inhuman acts of the enemy, we march on. People have not given up. The Taliban can burn schools but not the will for learning. The army and police, women and men give their lives to protect the people. Our free media is talking unabashedly against terrorists and also against the corrupt elements in the government. The new generation of girls and boys have tasted freedom and liberty in the last fourteen years and does not want to go back but always to move forward. We are helped to some extent by the global community. We still have hope and we march on. If you have the line of hope in the palm of your hands, you will always be stronger than your enemy, because no enemy can defeat a country and people who have hope.

Index

About the Author and Translator

Author

The son of a renowned Afghan poet, Khalilullah Khalili, **Masood Khalili** is the current ambassador of Afghanistan to Spain and former ambassador to many other countries. He is respected both in his country and internationally as an honest, patriotic, and elder statesman, as well as a political leader.

Translator

Mahmud Khalili, the eldest son of Ambassador Masood Khalili, was born in the United States. He has a bachelor's degree in International and Comparative Politics, a master's degree in International Relations. He is currently a PhD candidate in Peace Studies and Military Strategy. He is also the author of *Afghanistan Decoded: Perspectives on Domestic and Foreign Affairs*.

Printed in the United States
By Bookmasters